USER-INTERFACE DESIGN

USER-INTERFACE DESIGN
Second Edition

Kevin Cox • David Walker
City Polytechnic of Hong Kong   *Ainslie, Australia*

PRENTICE HALL
New York   London   Toronto   Sydney   Tokyo   Singapore

First Published 1993 by
Prentice Hall
Simon & Schuster Asia Pte Ltd
Alexandra Distripark
Block 4 #04-31
Pasir Panjang Road
Singapore 0511

Printed in Singapore

3   4   5   97   96   95   94   93

ISBN 0-13-952888-1

Cover design by Viscom Design Associates

The first edition of this book was published
by Advanced Education Software, July 1990.

Prentice-Hall International (UK) Limited, *London*
Prentice-Hall of Australia Pty. Limited, *Sydney*
Prentice-Hall Canada Inc., *Toronto*
Prentice-Hall Hispanoamericana, S.A., *Mexico*
Prentice-Hall of India Private Limited, *New Delhi*
Prentice-Hall of Japan, Inc., *Tokyo*
Editora Prentice-Hall do Brasil, Ltda., *Rio de Janeiro*
Prentice-Hall, Inc., *Englewood Cliffs, New Jersey*

Table of Contents

Preface

We decided to write this book because we became tired of waiting for someone else to do it. Many of us who design and construct computer systems and those of us who try to teach others how to do it are unhappy with the standard text books on system design. They have good information on techniques to help us understand and control our computing system development, but they are of little help in designing good computer systems. We know that there is more to making a computer system than investigating things, drawing some data flow diagrams, data modelling, writing and testing programs, and implementing the finished system. We know that making good computer systems is like all interesting human activities: it is a creative, stimulating, difficult task punctuated with flashes of insight, recognition of patterns, and emotional satisfaction of a job well done. We know that it is a very human experience spiced with marvellous technical gadgetry, randomness, variety and uncertainty.

You cannot create a computer system by applying a formula. There is no magic button to press and a machine will produce a final product. There is a prevailing myth that a technological solution exists that will allow us to create great computer systems at the press of a button, or by the application of a rigorous proven recipe. We search for the ultimate CASE tool to solve the backlogs of design and construction. These attempts are doomed to failure as there is no prescription. The attempts may help us make better systems but they do not help us design, because design is not prescriptive. Even the Chinese language helps preserve the myth as the word for computer can be translated as electric brain.

Other professions know that making human artefacts takes leaps of imagination. They know that we think visually as well as analytically. They know that the person is more important than the machine. Computing professionals know this as well, but the nature of the discipline and the nature of the technology has made us think that there has to be a computer program that will design computer systems. After all we try to make computer programs to design in other professional areas, why not our own. As a profession we have been afraid to recognise, acknowledge, accept and use our humanness. We have wanted to become mechanical in our design. We have wanted our techniques to reflect the artefacts with which we work.

In this book we start from a different paradigm for the design of computer systems. We think of the design of computer systems as designing something with which we will communicate with other humans. When we make a new computer system we have made another way to express ourselves and our ideas to another person. All computing systems are built for human purposes, all computing systems fit into a world of human needs. We do not create computing systems to talk to other computer systems. Even if they do communicate with one another they do so because we want them to for our own purposes. Users of computer systems communicate by proxy with designers and programmers. When you write a computer program you do not write it to communicate with a machine; you write it to communicate with a person.

When we take this view of our job as designers we can see that the focus of most of our traditional computing training is misdirected. If you look at many curricula for computing professionals you see it weighted with such things as mathematics, computer programming, data modelling and hardware constructs. You occasionally see a little on human psychology or writing skills but you never see an orientation towards human communication. You see courses on computer systems design which only mention users in passing. Students spend all their time communicating with machines using mechanistic principles. No wonder we get *unfriendly* computer systems. They were designed for other computers, not for us.

We have attempted to redress the balance and to put people back into the centre of design. We propose to design for humans as humans. We are not electric brains, we do not want to be electric brains, and we refuse to act as though we are. In this book you will find much more on sketching than you will on mathematical proofs. You will find a chapter on testing with people and a passing reference to testing programs. You will find a lot on writing manuals and a little on program structure. You will see how to design artefacts that people can understand and you will find little on program structure design.

Writing computer systems is a fun activity. It is fun because of the human component. The education industry is rapidly destroying the fun and replacing it with sterility. We would hope that this book might reverse the trend of people viewing computing professionals as boring, mechanical, electric brains. We hope that more artists, communicators, psychologists and humanists will be attracted to the profession and realise the potential of this most marvellous of human artefacts. We hope that students in the profession will rise above the weight of electrons and communicate with us via their programs.

The book starts with our view of what makes a good computer system. Naturally we believe a good computer system is one that works for and with people. We then discuss the nature of design and how we can design around people. We discuss the way people use computing products and how they think about them. The next chapter describes how we can test our theories and models and show that our products are usable. The rest of the book elaborates on these themes and discusses the object/action paradigm for design, the use of documentation as an explanation tool, and how we can organise and control developments when we design this way.

We constructed a small computer system (Crossword Designer) to accompany the book. You do not need the program to understand the ideas in the book as we describe the important parts of the program interface within the text. However, using it will make some things clearer. The compromises and mistakes of a real artefact are exposed. The package with all its faults gives a human dimension to the text and you can see how the ideas we espouse are realised. You can obtain a copy of Crossword Designer by contacting the authors of this book at the Computer Department of the City Polytechnic of Hong Kong.

The book was designed to support courses with such titles as *Human-Computer Interface Design* or *Design and Construction of Computer Systems*. The approach is more engineering than psychological and more practical than theoretical. We have found that students want and need guidance in how to approach the design task and want to know what they should do when designing. The text has been used as the basis for semester courses for second-year undergraduate students at both the University of Canberra and the City Polytechnic of Hong Kong and for various industrial short courses. The courses were all supported by practical projects. Usability projects involved testing commonly available software. Design projects have come from areas of topical interest to students and we select new subjects each time we run a course. For illustration and exercises we use any commonly available computer system. Our main usability criterion for software and computer systems has been student ease of access. We have applied the ideas in the book to the design of many interactive computer applications and implemented them on mainframes, mini-computers and personal computers.

During the preparation of this book we have received ideas and help from many people. The University of Canberra supported one of us with leave from teaching. Our colleagues, family and friends have encouraged us. Our many tutors in courses over the years have contributed much and we would like to thank all the students who have patiently tried out the ideas and given us valuable feedback. At the risk of offending everyone we mention no-one in particular.

Most of the ideas in the book can be found in the bibliography. We have referenced material where we know the original source of the idea or we have used similar material to the reference. Our purpose has been to integrate and present ideas in an easily understood and easily applied manner.

Kevin Cox - Hong Kong (CSCOXK@CPHKVX.BITNET)
David Walker - Canberra
March 1992

Chapter 1

What Makes a Good Computer System?

A characteristic feature of human beings is that they are users of tools. We build things using hammers, chisels and saws, we transport ourselves between two places in cars, trains and aeroplanes, we cook our meals on a stove. A computer is a tool. We use computers to do things such as:

- Control a microwave oven.
- Send the electricity bill for the house with that oven.
- Make models of the atmosphere which predict the changes in world climate caused by the use of that (and many other) ovens.

Use of a tool involves co-operation between a person (the *user*) and the tool. We do not say "The hammer banged in the nail", we say "I banged in the nail using the hammer". The user is in charge. The hammer does not say which nail to put in, or beep at you when you use a large nail rather than a small one. Similarly, the computer does not decide to perform a task, although it is capable of obeying a complex series of instructions. A person must set and switch on the microwave oven, decide that electricity bills have to be sent, and build the atmospheric model.

Because of this requirement for co-operation, the way in which the person has

Figure 1.1 A tool.

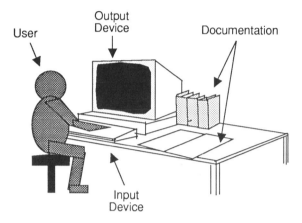

(a) The User-Interface at the Hardware Level

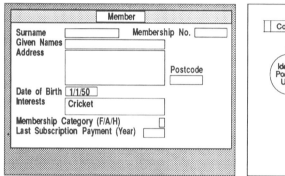

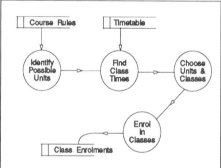

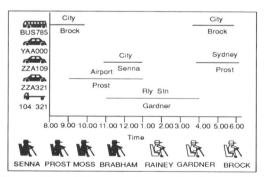

(b) Three Different User-Interfaces at the Software Level

Figure 1.2 The user-interface.

to interact with the tool determines whether or not the tool is usable.

The handle of a hammer must be of an appropriate size, shape and texture for a human hand to grip firmly and must be placed appropriately in relation to the head to provide the correct leverage. The hammer as a whole must not be too heavy to lift, but must be heavy enough to drive the nail home. The user must be able to see where the head will strike in relation to the nail, in order to line up a hit. In addition, the user must have some concept of what a hammer is and what it is used for, or they might believe that it is for stirring soup.

These features constitute the *user-interface* of the hammer. It is easy to imagine a hammer with a poor user-interface: a short, fat, greasy handle, and a ball-shaped head with a cowl around it, all weighing a few hundred kilos. The reason that we do not find hammers like this is that people prefer hammers that they can use, so the design of the hammer has evolved over time to provide a good user-interface. This evolution is still continuing: within the last twenty years, metal handles with rubber grips have appeared to compete with wooden handles.

A computer is a strange type of tool in that the same box (or set of boxes) can be made to perform a wide variety of tasks. Although food processors also possess this property to some degree, they do not have the same versatility. At a distance [Figure 1.2(a)], the interface is seen as being the hardware. On a personal computer, this may consist of a screen on which text or pictures can be displayed, a keyboard and a mouse which the user can use to input data and commands. It also consists of any documentation used to describe and support the system.

Although the keyboard, mouse and screen are the most common ways of interacting with computers, there are other ways. In particular, sound, both in the form of voice input and of audible responses from the machine, is likely to become increasingly important.

Closer up [Figure 1.2(b)], the displays for different systems look different, require different inputs and do different things. One of the systems is used to maintain club membership records, one is used to draw diagrams, and the third is used to schedule vehicles from a vehicle pool. The user conducts a *dialogue* with the computer, in which their input produces some sort of response (e.g. the appearance of text or a change to a drawing) on the screen. The precise nature of the dialogue depends on the task to be performed.

The user-interface constitutes peoples' perception of the tool. The user does not need to know about nor is he interested in the metallurgy of the head of the hammer. If something about the crystal structure results in a hammer that is soft or bends, then it is a bad hammer. If a computer system does not do what it is expected to do, on the basis of what the user knows about it from the user-interface, then it is a bad computer system.

Tools are learned. Learning to use a tool involves two distinct processes:

- Learning *about* the tool, i.e. *what* tasks it can be used to do.
- Learning to *operate* it, i.e. *how* to perform those tasks.

This involves building up a *conceptual model* of the tool, which tells us what it is and how it behaves, and learning the actual skills to use it. In this way we learn that a hammer is for banging in nails and not for stirring soup, and we learn, largely through practice, how to hit a nail so that it goes in straight.

With a tool such as a hammer, the form of the tool is a significant help, since the form gives strong cues as to its function: there is a handle for holding, there is a flat area for hitting the nail with (so our aim does not have to be too accurate), and the claw at the back is for pulling out bent nails, so we pick it up and hold it the correct way without having to think "which way up does it go?"

User Control
Transparency
Flexibility
Learnability

Figure 1.3 Characteristics of a good tool.

With a computer system, the same thing should be true: the form of the presentation of the system to the user should tell them what it can do, and give clear indications of how.

An essential feature of a tool is that it *disappears*. When we are using it, we concentrate on the problem, and not on the use of the tool. When we are banging in a nail, we do not watch the hammer, we watch the nail. We have learned (after a few bruised fingers) how long the hammer is and how to manage the swing, and now do it instinctively. Similarly, if we are using a word processor, we want to concentrate on the document that we are writing, not on which key to press. We refer to this property as *transparency*.

Tools must also be *flexible*. Different people will want to use tools in different ways. Some of us are even left-handed. Thus a hammer can be used for banging in short nails as well as long nails, prising open cupboards, and even for stirring soup. A spreadsheet can be used to produce a balance sheet, predict stock-market trends, or for typing and printing a document if nothing better is available. If we can use a tool for unintended purposes (even if it does not do it as well as a different tool that we do not have) we regard that as a plus.

Unfortunately, many computer systems are not good tools. Dialogues are often clumsy and hard to learn, dictate to the user, and inhibit rather than assist the user's work by hiding information. The documentation describes in gruesome detail how to perform highly specific operations, but nowhere explains what the system can be used for nor relates the user's tasks to the keystrokes that are described. The result is frustration, irritation, and a tendency to use other, easier-to-use tools, such as pens and calculators.

The reason for this is historical (Figure 1.4). In the 1960s and 70s, computer systems performed well defined sets of operations, mainly routine transactions and massive scientific computations, and the interaction was handled by specially trained personnel

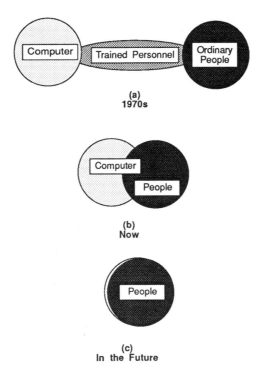

(a)
1970s

(b)
Now

(c)
In the Future

Figure 1.4 People and computers.

for whom their use was the main activity in their job: programmers, operators, data-entry personnel, trained word processing operators, trained clerical staff, research scientists. Most people had no contact with computers, and even those that had did not use them for more than a few specific tasks; a research scientist might use a computer for complex mathematical modelling, but would still have their papers typed up on a manual type-writer. Since the machines were expensive, the major emphasis was on making efficient use of the machine, and not of the people's time, so that the user-interfaces were geared to whatever made the machine work most efficiently. Home computers had been thought of, but had failed miserably in the market place because they were too hard to use.

Thus, although computers were being used as tools, a better analogy would be with a crane or a bulldozer, and not with a hammer. The problem here is that what a crane driver regards as a good user-interface and what an amateur carpenter regards as a good user-interface are two different things. The crane driver has pride in being skilled at a difficult task and would probably resent any innovations that made it possible for every-body to drive cranes.

This is exactly what has happened with computing. The use of computers is now widespread. The number of people who do not use them in some way or another as part of their work is becoming quite small, and they are using them in a different way. They are not using them because their use is the main activity in their job, but to support other activities, and a given individual will use them in a wide variety of ways, e.g. word processing, calculations, information retrieval, "what if" modelling, as well as routine transactions.

However, many of the user-interfaces are hangovers from past times. Worse, many of the ideas about what is a "satisfactory" user-interface are also hangovers, with many computer professionals seeing no need for change. One result is that the operating system currently supplied with the bulk of personal computers sold has an archaic command-driven interface that is hard to learn and stops many potential users at first base. That there is a demand for better interfaces is demonstrated by the success of the Apple Macintosh, a machine whose main selling-point is its user-interface.

The major impact of poor user-interfaces is economic. Computer hardware and software is cheap, but salaries are expensive. A marginal gain in efficiency through a better word processor, easier-to-use information retrieval, reporting or analysis software can

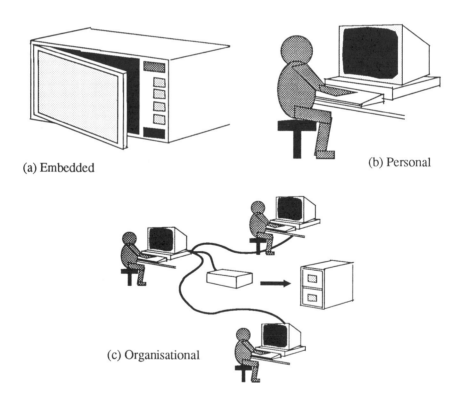

(a) Embedded   (b) Personal

(c) Organisational

Figure 1.5 Uses of computers.

rapidly mount up to thousands of dollars for an individual and hundreds of thousands or millions over a large organisation, for expenditures of a fraction of this amount.

For this reason, the design of better user-interfaces for computer systems has become an area of major interest. Research into user-interfaces covers a vast area, from cognitive psychology and ergonomics on one hand, to graphics and speech recognition. A major benefit already appearing from this research is the current generation of graphical user-interfaces, which started with the Xerox Star in the late 1970s, and which are currently incorporated into such products as the Apple Macintosh and the Microsoft Windows software. This book is concerned with the application of the ideas from this research and development work to the design of computer systems.

In the following sections we will expand on the idea of a computer as a tool by talking about what we do with computers, and about who uses them. We will then develop the idea of a conceptual model, and discuss in more detail the way in which the usability criteria can be applied to computer systems.

1.1 The Role of Computers

1.1.1 Uses of Computers

In order to design tools we must first consider what we use them for. There are three main uses for computers (Figure 1.5):

- As *embedded* systems in electrical devices such as microwave ovens and video recorders. These perform a small range of functions specific to the device into which they are built, e.g. in a microwave oven, the computer operates as a clock, a controller for the power level, can accept and remember commands affecting the cooking time and power level, and controls the alarm that is sounded at the end of the set cooking time.
- As *personal* systems, used for creating and editing documents, drawings, animation and music for personal use or subsequent distribution or publication, and for doing calculations.
- As part of *information* systems within an organisation or a society.

There can, of course, be overlap: an embedded system that operates traffic lights may feed data into a larger information system that monitors traffic flows, while one that is part of a synthesiser may be used to compose music; and documents created on a personal system may be sent to other people within an organisation, and so be part of that organisation's information system.

Within information systems, there are three main types of tasks:

- Transaction processing.
- Decision-making.
- Information retrieval.

A *transaction* is a routine task performed frequently and repetitively. It takes its name from financial transactions: the exchange of goods for money, as in a shop. Typical transactions handled by information systems include making a deposit at a bank, booking an air ticket, paying a bill.

Most large-scale computer systems are oriented towards transaction processing. The transactions are normally presented to the user as a well defined series of steps from which little or no deviation is permitted. Typical of this approach is the withdrawal of money from an automatic teller machine:

- Insert card.
- Type in Personal Identification (PIN) Number.
- Select transaction type (Withdrawal).
- Select account.
- Enter amount to be withdrawn.
- Remove card.
- Collect cash.
- Collect transaction slip.

These steps are always performed in order. If a mistake is made, it is usually possible to repeat the last step, or to cancel the transaction entirely and start again. If the machine detects an error it can force repetition of the step or terminate the transaction. It may also retain the card.

Decision-making requires a number of steps (Figure 1.6):

- The gathering of information on which to base the decision.
- The determination of possible actions.
- Modelling of the consequences of each of the courses of action.
- Choosing the action to take.

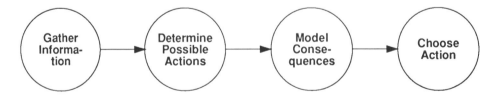

Figure 1.6 Decision-making.

The role of a computer system in decision-making processes is as an aid. It is used to retrieve relevant data from one or more sources, to organise it in a manner relevant to the decision at hand, and to make quantitative assessments of the effects of some possible actions. Its use is normally relevant only to some aspects of the decision. The decision itself is made by the person. Computer systems performing this role are often referred to as *decision-support* systems.

Booking an airline ticket involves a decision: firstly, one must find out what flights are available; one then formulates a series of alternative actions (i.e. taking one of the available flights, going by train or bus, or staying home), weighs up these alternatives in the light of various criteria (e.g. whether the flight gets you there on time for your appointment, whether it means you have to get up too early in the morning, what the cost is for alternative routes), and selects the "best" alternative. The airline's booking system does not make this decision: it merely supplies you with the times of the available flights, and then records the result of your decision in the form of a booking on the chosen flight (if any). Thus the computer system is acting in a decision-support role. The actual booking is a transaction.

The final type of task is *information retrieval*. This is similar to the queries and reports that are the basis of the information-gathering process in decision-making, but we distinguish information retrieval processes from these in that the use of the information retrieved is of no concern to the system. Typical information retrieval systems are the bibliographic, financial, scientific and legal databases available for public access, and the systems installed in museums to give information on exhibits.

1.1.2 Types of User-Interface

The user-interfaces of different kinds of systems are adapted to their function. Embedded systems can have highly specialised user-interfaces, designed specifically for the task at hand, e.g. with a microwave oven, the user presses buttons or turns knobs to set cooking times and powers before starting the cooking process. The oven beeps when the preset cooking time is elapsed. In theory, these interfaces can be very good, because they do not contain any extraneous elements. In practice, many are very poor, because a few knobs or buttons are forced to perform a multitude of functions, and the user rarely learns all of them. Can you use all the functions on a microwave oven or an office telephone system? Do you even know what they are?

For personal systems, general-purpose hardware and software is used, e.g. a personal computer with keyboard, mouse and screen, running packages such as word processors, spreadsheets, and drawing packages. The user commonly has a great deal of flexibility in what they do and how they do it. With a drawing package, the mouse can be used to draw lines, rectangles and other shapes, to select line types and fill patterns, to move, reshape and resize them, simply by pointing to menu options or parts of the drawing displayed on the screen. A conventional keyboard is used to enter text for captions and labels, but keyboard commands are also available as substitutes for many of the menu options. In some cases, there is specialised hardware, e.g. a synthesiser keyboard, with software to match. More special-purpose software is appearing for personal use. The Crossword Designer described in this book is an example of such a system. Where application-oriented software is used, e.g. an accounting package or transaction processing software, this is often because the system is actually being used as part of the organisation's information system.

Transaction processing systems are like embedded systems in that they are highly specialised and perform a limited range of functions. In a few cases, they have special hardware geared to the transactions available, e.g. an automatic teller machine has a small display (one or two lines) giving instructions, a special set of keys for selecting the transaction type (deposit, withdrawal, transfer or account balance), another set for selecting the account, and a numeric keypad for entering numbers (e.g. the amount to be withdrawn). The different keys are used at specific points in the transaction. More usually they use conventional computer terminals (e.g. keyboard and screen devices) running software that displays preformatted screens or which otherwise limits the activities that the user can perform. A common problem with transaction processing systems is that they are often too restricted, so that the users cannot easily correct errors. Automatic tellers provide an extreme example of this: any problems have to be fixed up through person – person interaction inside the bank during normal trading hours.

Decision-making processes usually require flexible access to a wide range of data, plus the ability to analyse the data. This is done through provision of printed reports, through query facilities on databases and often through personal enquiry. Common analysis tools are spreadsheets and statistical packages. These can also be used to model the effects of possible actions, by changing relevant figures and seeing what happens.

Information retrieval systems need to be as simple as possible to use, because most users do not use them very frequently. Museum systems often use *touch screens* so that users can point to an item that they want to find out about, while *videotex* systems use sets of menus. The use of more complex access methods, e.g. the command languages required to access bibliographic databases, places a barrier in the way of ordinary users, forcing them to use trained intermediaries (in this case librarians) to access the data.

The dialogue does not constitute the sum total of the user-interface. The user-interface also includes explanations (*documentation*) about how the interface works, e.g. most video recorders and microwave ovens are impossible to operate without an instruction manual. This manual is part of the user-interface.

1.1.3   Who Are the Users?

Given that we have a large number and wide variety of users, it is useful to be able to isolate characteristics of the user population that might influence the types of interfaces that we provide. There are a number of possible classifications:

- *Frequency of Use.* On this basis, users can be classed into novices, i.e. people with little or no previous experience; casual users, i.e. people who use the system occasionally; and regular users, i.e. people who use the system often enough to become skilled in its use.
- *Application Knowledge.* The distinction here is between experts in the application area, who are familiar with the underlying models and assumptions built into the system, and operators, who know how to perform routine transactions with the system, but who do not necessarily understand why it works.
- *Tasks to be Performed.* Any given user will often only use part of a system, e.g. some users may be concerned with routine transactions, others will be making decisions based on the data from those transactions. Yet another type of user will be concerned with maintenance of the system, e.g. installing new software or modifying software.
- *Assumed Skills.* Performance of particular tasks within a system often requires that the user possesses certain skills or training acquired independently of the particular application, e.g. use of a legal information retrieval system requires some knowledge of legal terminology, use of statistical analysis software requires some knowledge of statistics, creating formulae on a spreadsheet requires the user to be comfortable with high school algebra and many tasks require various levels of typing skills.
- *Attitudes.* Different users have different attitudes towards computer systems, and this often governs the way in which they want to interact and the types of task that they are prepared to perform. Some people regard a new piece of software as a challenge, and try to push it to its limits, while others are very conservative in their usage patterns and will only attempt obvious things, and things that they have already been taught. Some people have preferred modes of interaction (e.g. they are proud that they "have never used a mouse"). In many places, an organisational culture will develop incorporating a particular set of attitudes.

Most systems will be used by people from all parts of this spectrum, e.g. casual users cannot be expected to remember commands or special keys, yet frequent users may want to perform tasks as rapidly as possible, or an application expert may want to be able to vary underlying assumptions made in doing a task, while an operator may just want to do things "the usual way".

A particular class of user to which a lot of attention has been paid is the *power user*. This is a person who is skilled in the use of a particular system, but who stretches its applicability to the limits, exploring situations for which the system was not specifically designed to work, but to which it can be applied. Power users also represent a significant source of expertise within an organisation, in terms of what can be done and how with a given software.

1.2   Conceptual Models

1.2.1   What is a Conceptual Model?

A conceptual model is an idea in our mind of what a system does and how it does it. Part of learning about a system involves the development of a conceptual model. Our model of a microwave oven, for example, is built on our ideas of conventional ovens: it heats things, and the amount of heating is governed by the time that you leave things in the oven, and by the power setting (which is somehow analogous to the temperature setting for an oven, but isn't because the whole oven isn't heated, just the food). Big things take longer to heat than small things. Special containers have to be used (e.g. plastics) which are different from those used in conventional ovens. Because the heating mechanism is somehow "electrical", metal containers cannot be used.

This basic model can then be developed through use of the oven. One soon discovers that a microwave oven's idea of "big things" is different from a conventional oven's. A conventional oven regards scones as "small": there might be a tray of 100 of them, but each is small, so there is no difference between cooking ten and cooking a hundred, provided that the oven has been preheated. In a microwave, on the other hand, what matters is the total amount of food to be cooked, whatever the size of the individual items. This could be adapted into the analogy by seeing a microwave as always starting from "cold", but most people just remember the difference. Other ideas can be obtained from cookbooks describing microwave techniques, to introduce, e.g. the judicious use of aluminium foil to "shield" parts of the food that one wants to cook more slowly. This idea of shielding is like using an umbrella against rain, or sunblock on the nose. It is not an idea that relates to conventional ovens.

What happens to the food is also different. Reheating last night's Chinese takeaway does not dry it out in the same way as a conventional oven, so that the microwave is maybe "better" for this job; but the roast meat does not brown, so it is not as good for this job.

Thus we build our conceptual model by starting with a familiar analogy and then learn about the new device by identifying differences from that original model.

Systems are difficult to learn unless there is both a good starting point for thinking about them, and some relatively easy way to progress from it.

The conceptual model is important for two reasons:

- It is an aid to *learning* a system.
- It is a guide to *predicting* the behaviour of the system.

The prediction process is a crucial part of learning, since we often learn by experimentation, e.g. with the microwave oven, one can predict that choosing a higher power setting will result in faster cooking, and we can test it out to see if it works. We may be wrong:

the result may be something which is overcooked on the outside and still frozen on the inside, but even so, we now know something about the way time and the power settings interact.

Learning new systems is often a problem, not because the conceptual model is different, but because the actual mechanisms for interaction are different, e.g. different brands of microwave ovens have different sets of keys, and different operating systems have different commands which do the same thing.

Conceptual models for computer systems are often based on analogies with the physical environment or manual systems, because these are seen as better known, e.g. filing packages use an analogy with card files, spreadsheets with ruled-up sheets of paper, and the operating environment on machines such as the Xerox Star and the Apple Macintosh with a desktop. As with the microwave oven, these analogies help to establish the essential features of the system, e.g. the picture of a spreadsheet as a grid of cells into which a user can enter numbers or write captions. Numbers are restricted to a single cell, but captions can span more than one cell. Numbers are usually aligned in rows or columns which are totalled, or have other operations performed on them.

These analogies are, by definition, incomplete. On a paper worksheet, one adds up the columns by hand or with a calculator, and writes the answer in the appropriate cell. On a computer spreadsheet, one can do this, but the normal practice is to put a formula

Figure 1.7 Mathematical and visual
representations.

into the cell in which the answer is to appear. This has the advantage that, if one of the figures is changed, the answer can be automatically recalculated. It also creates problems: it means that a simple arithmetic operation is replaced by the use of algebra; and it is possible to get the formula wrong, either initially (e.g. by leaving out a row or column) or later (e.g. by introducing a new row or column and not changing the formula). Part of the learning process is to identify these differences and to assimilate them into the model.

Many authors refer to these analogies as *metaphors*, i.e. statements that the system is the analogous object, e.g. that the Xerox or Macintosh Desktop is an actual desktop. This creates problems, because it isn't true. For example, when the power fails, a piece of paper does not suddenly go blank, losing the last hour's work, but because that is exactly what happens with a Macintosh, the user must develop an additional concept: that of saving their work, even if it is not finished. Some authors get around this by talking about partial metaphors, but this is exactly what an analogy is. This is the reason why we do not use the term metaphor.

Another valuable source of conceptual models comes from visual representations of data. The reason for this is that visual representations of data are far more immediate than mathematical or verbal descriptions (Figure 1.7). Information can be represented in

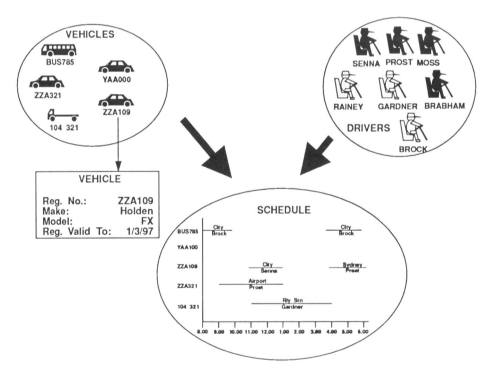

Figure 1.8 A vehicle pool.

a more compact way visually, in particular relationships between different objects, which can be represented by spatial relationships. It is also easier for a person to manipulate, because they can point to something, or move it, rather than having to describe it and describe what to do with it.

Scheduling systems commonly make use of Gantt Charts, PERT Charts or grids (e.g. a timetable grid). These represent activities to be or currently scheduled, and their relationships with each other. Spreadsheets also represent a visual (tabular) organisation of data, while a relational database pictures data as being held in a set of tables.

Figure 1.8 illustrates the sort of representation that we are talking about. The system concerns the management of a vehicle pool. There are a number of vehicles of different types, and there are a number of drivers with different classes of licence. When a request is made for a vehicle, an appropriate vehicle and a driver are allocated, and the allocation recorded on a chart. The visual representation of the vehicles and drivers is in the form of icons, which are small pictures identifying the objects. The icons for the vehicles are of different shapes, depending on the vehicle type, and are more-or-less self-explanatory. The shading of the driver icons is intended to indicate licence type, but is not as good because the user must know what the shadings mean. Additional detail about a driver or a vehicle can be obtained (e.g. as with ZZA109 on the diagram). The representation of the schedule is a Gantt Chart, with different vehicles occupying different lines. Additions and changes to the schedule are made by making the appropriate changes to the chart.

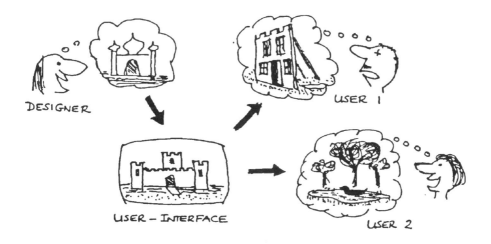

Figure 1.9 The problem of different
conceptual models for the same system.

Besides being a visual model, this model has another feature. If consists of a series of *objects* (the vehicles, the drivers and the schedule itself) on which we perform *actions*. This is a fairly characteristic model for the use of a tool: we swing a hammer, we set a microwave oven and then turn it on, we start, stop, drive, garage, refuel, lock and unlock a car. As we shall see in the next section, this object/action picture provides a very powerful way of structuring our conceptual models.

One problem that we encounter is that there are always many conceptual models for the same system (Figure 1.9): the designer's, the model actually enshrined in the user-interface, and one for each user. The amount of divergence is a good measure of the quality of the designer's original model: a good, conceptually "clean" model should translate effectively to the user-interface, and should be readily comprehensible by the users, so that there should be a large degree of agreement on the model being used; while with a poor model, there is likely to be significant confusion.

1.2.2   The Structure of Conceptual Models

There are five common ways in which conceptual models are structured (Figure 1.10).

In a *black box* model, the user has no idea of the internal workings of the system, and merely knows that certain specified inputs are converted to an equally well defined set of outputs. Systems of this type are very common, and are the source of the belief that computers perform "magic". The user is forced to take the results on trust, and has no basis on which to assess their validity. An obvious result of this is the tendency to blame errors on "a computer error" and to make no attempt to rectify them.

Scheduling systems that use optimising algorithms are good examples of black box systems: they supply a final schedule or timetable which the user cannot modify in any way. Although the user can supply criteria (in the form of constraints) as input, they do not know which are critical and which have even been used.

A more complicated variation on the black box is the *partitioned black box* model. Most operating systems fall into this category. The user has a well defined set of commands which, when supplied with appropriate input parameters, can be used to generate outputs. The various commands seem to bear no relation to each other, and viewed in isolation work as black boxes.

In the *functional hierarchy* model, the functions performed by the system are grouped into a hierarchy (usually represented at the user-interface by a series of menus). Most mainframe application systems are structured in this way. At the bottom level of the hierarchy are a series of transactions, which are the routine tasks performed by the system. Each transaction consists of a series of steps which are spelled out by the system. They require specified inputs in a set format and their outcome is well defined. Typical transactions include making a deposit at a bank, booking an air ticket, paying a bill. The system then groups the functions into a hierarchy, e.g. in a banking system, one group would consist of all transactions on individual accounts (e.g. deposits, withdrawals, trans-

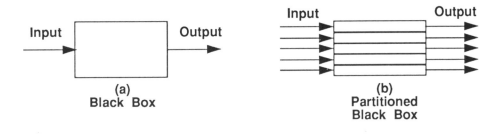

(a)
Black Box

(b)
**Partitioned
Black Box**

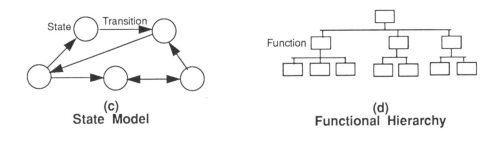

(c)
State Model

(d)
Functional Hierarchy

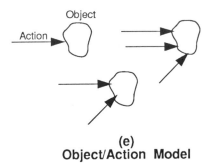

(e)
Object/Action Model

Figure 1.10 Structures for conceptual models.

fers and requests for balances or other information), a different group would cover the opening and closing of such accounts, a different group again the production of statements. At a higher level again, "workface" operations such as those described above would be separated from centralised administrative functions (setting of interest rates, creation of new branches) and management reporting functions. Note that while individuals may only have access to some of these functions, the parts of the system that they do know about will represent sub-hierarchies.

State models regard the system as consisting of a well defined set of *states*. Transitions between different states are caused by well defined events, usually the receipt of input. This model is widely used in data communications software, where what a terminal can do depends on what it is expecting to happen, e.g. it may have transmitted some data and is waiting for an acknowledgement of receipt. Once it receives the acknowledgement, it may move into a *Ready to Send* state with the next message, but may not send until it receives a message saying the line is clear. If the acknowledgement indicates that the data was not received correctly, it may move into an *Error* state before attempting to retransmit.

Many of the older style text editors operate in a number of different states or *modes*, e.g. there may be an *Edit* mode where various characters represent commands, and an *Input* mode where the same characters are stored as text.

The steps in a transaction can be represented as a series of states, each taking the form of a screen or message on display, awaiting input. Transitions between states are initiated by user input. A state representation of an automatic teller machine is given in Figure 1.11. The diagram is simplified in that some error responses and a confirmation step have been omitted, and so represents a conceptual model of what is happening rather than the full details of the dialogue. The initial state corresponds to a message asking the user to enter their card. Insertion of the card causes a transition to the next state where an ENTER PIN NUMBER message is displayed. Entry of the PIN number causes a transition to the next state, where the transaction type is requested. The four possible inputs (*Withdraw, Deposit, Transfer* and *Balance*) cause transitions to different states corresponding to the start of the separate parts of each transaction type. Although the messages may look similar, there is now no way of getting to another transaction type without terminating the transaction and starting again.

State diagrams are very useful for representing simple dialogues, or small parts of a dialogue, and will be used for this purpose in this book, but for any complex situation, they become too complex to provide a useful model.

The idea behind the *object/action* model is that we work with *things*: physical or conceptual objects, on which we perform actions, in just the same way that we hammer a nail into a piece of wood. So if we are to build a computer system that we can use as a tool, we should use the same sort of framework, i.e. we should supply the user with a set of *objects* on which they can perform a predefined set of *actions*.

If we apply the model to the automatic teller (Figure 1.12), we obtain a much simpler picture than that incorporated in the state diagram. There are two types of object: a

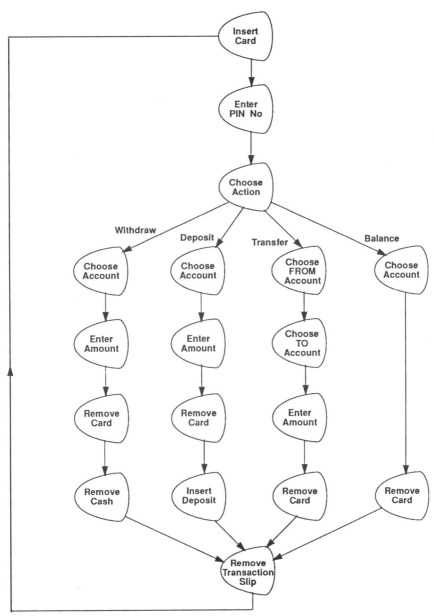

Figure 1.11 State model for an automatic
teller machine.

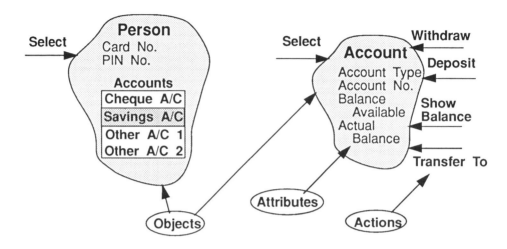

Figure 1.12 Object/action model of an
automatic teller machine.

person, who has a list of authorised *accounts*. Each account is of a particular type (e.g. cheque or savings), has a current balance, and also a balance available for withdrawal (which may be less than the actual balance because of restrictions on withdrawals from automatic tellers). The first action that a user makes is to *select* the person object that refers to them (by putting in their card). This, then gives meaning to keys such as *cheque account*, because it refers to the cheque account listed in that *person* object, not any cheque account. These keys can then be used to select an account. There are four actions available on each account: *deposit, withdraw, transfer from* and *show balance*. They apply to whatever account has been selected. In the case of *transfer from* a second account must then be selected in order to specify where the money is to go, but the action still applies to the first account.

  Our model of the vehicle pool (Figure 1.8) is an object/action model. The objects are the vehicles, the drivers and the schedule. Actions on drivers and vehicles consist of placing them on the schedule, or moving them on the schedule.

  One of the reasons for the simplicity of the object/action model is that it does not attempt to specify how the task is to be performed, but merely gives the scheduler the necessary tools to do so.

  We can look at it another way when we remember that the kinds of data in a given system do not change very much, but the ways in which we want to use the data do. This is the basis of most database design methodologies. However, as will be discussed in detail in Chapter 4, a data model does not necessarily constitute a good conceptual model for a user-interface. Our objects, however, perform the user-interface equivalent. The actions form a set of "primitives" used to manipulate the objects, and can be assembled into an enormous variety of possible courses of action, thus also providing the user with a wide variety of possible functions, and the ability to develop more without changing the structure of the system.

Much of the more recent personal computer software uses an object/action model. A spreadsheet, for example, presents the user with a grid of *cells*. Each cell is a distinct object with distinct *attributes* (e.g. its contents, how it is formatted). The user can move to any cell on the grid (using a mouse or cursor keys) and has a range of operations (*actions*) that they can perform on that cell: entering numbers, text or a formula into the cell, deleting the contents of the cell, formatting the cell (e.g. so that numbers are displayed with two decimal places), protecting it against change. The actions always refer to the *current* cell (i.e. the one with the cursor on it). To make the actions refer to another cell, we move the cursor to that cell. Ranges of cells, entire rows and columns, and the grid itself are also objects with their own distinct set of actions. Some of these are the same for different types of object (e.g. one can format the entire grid, a row or column, or a range) while others are different, e.g. one can insert an entire row or an entire column but one cannot *insert* a cell (only data into a cell) because this would distort the grid.

Thus there are a number of major advantages to the object/action model:

- It lends itself easily to visual representations of the system, which are conceptually attractive, easy to learn and easy to manipulate.
- It leads to relatively simple models of complex systems, which are flexible to use, and easy to enhance or change (e.g. by adding new objects, adding or changing actions).

We will develop this model further in Chapter 4.

1.3   The Form of Interaction

1.3.1   Introduction

At the beginning of this chapter, we gave four characteristics of a good tool:

- *User control,* i.e. the user is in charge at all times, and dictates what the tool is to do, and not vice versa.
- *Transparency,* i.e. the tool becomes an adjunct to the person, so that the user can apply their thoughts to the problem at hand, and not to the manipulation of the tool.
- *Flexibility,* i.e. the tool can be used in a variety of different ways and for a range of purposes, many of which were unintended by the original designer.
- *Learnability,* i.e. it must be relatively easy to perform basic activities with the tool, and it must be such that users can increase their skills through use.

In this section, we want to discuss some key features of the user-interface that will assist in achieving these goals.

1.3.2   User Control

User control means that it is up to the user, not the computer system, to decide how a particular task is to be performed.

Even the processing of the most routine transactions can suddenly become complex. Consider the simple act of withdrawing money from a bank. The teller says "There isn't enough money in your account." You say, "Why not? There should be $500 there. What have you done with it?" A simple withdrawal suddenly becomes a complex chain of investigation, involving transaction histories of this and other accounts, additional transactions (e.g. a reversal of the transaction that credited the money to the wrong account) and eventually the resumption of the original transaction. It may also involve overriding constraints built into the system, e.g. by allowing the account to become overdrawn until the problem is corrected. A good system will let the user perform whatever actions are appropriate; a bad one will make heavy weather of it, or forbid it altogether.

Many technocrats do not understand the idea of user control. To them, users are inherently stupid, and they (and the system) must be protected from their own actions. One of the ironies of this is that the resulting systems are both simple-minded (from the users' point of view, since they will only handle the straightforward cases and not the exceptions that require any level of discretion) and overly complex (from the maintainer's point of view, because they have code built in to handle everything that the user "can do wrong"). It also means that the users are not prepared to take responsibility for data on or output from the computer system, but blame errors on the computer. Although matters are improving, most mainframe systems still have a long way to go. A lot of the elegance of the better personal computer software comes from abandoning this approach and putting the users in charge. This means, of course, that they must have the skills to control what they are doing, e.g. in setting up a spreadsheet, the user must know how to make (or build in) checks to ensure that the formulae are really doing what they were intended to do, but this is a good thing, because it means that the users are genuinely responsible for their results.

Providing user control, then, involves the provision of facilities that allow the user to organise their work in their own way.

The first of these is the use of *windows*. Windows are distinct areas on the screen performing distinct tasks (Figure 1.13), e.g. one window may contain a document currently being edited, another part of the same or a different document, another a drawing. The user can arrange these windows on the screen in any way that they like, by moving and resizing them. They can move from one task to another simply by moving a cursor to the window containing the new task, and resume the old task by moving back to its window. The old task will be in exactly the state it was when they left it. A window not in use can be shrunk to an *icon*, a small graphical image used to represent not only windows, but objects of all sorts (e.g. the vehicles and drivers in Figure 1.8).

Windows give the user the capability both to visually organise their work, in just the same way that one organises books and papers on a desk, and to control the sequence in which they perform various tasks.

The object/action model provides a powerful structure for user control. The user is supplied with a set of objects (e.g. the vehicles, drivers, trips and schedule of the vehicle pool) and a set of actions with which to manipulate them. How they put them together to carry out a task is the user's concern, although the system will provide assistance in the form of appropriate displays. The dialogues used to implement the object/action model are *modeless* (Figure 1.14), i.e. if an object is selected, any of the possible actions on that object can be performed at any time. This allows the user to decide on the appropriate action after seeing the data. This contrasts with the *modal* dialogues which are customary in many mainframe systems, where one first has to select an action (e.g. *add, modify* or *delete*) and then selects the record on which to perform the action. If one is in modify

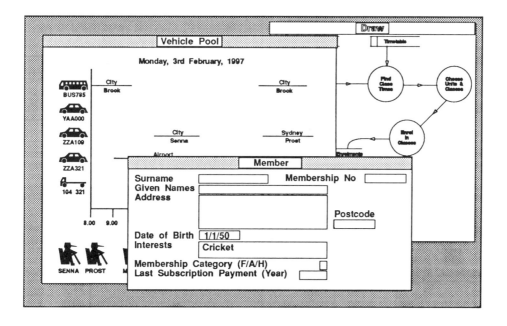

Figure 1.13 Windows.

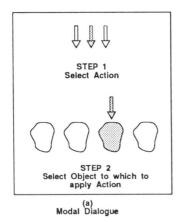

(a)
Modal Dialogue

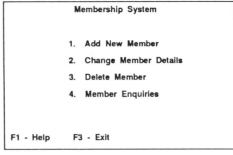

(b)
Modal Dialogue Menu

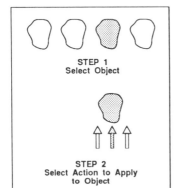

(c)
Modeless Dialogue

(d)
Modeless Dialogue with the Same Actions

Figure 1.14 Modal and modeless dialogues.

mode, one must go out, select a new mode, and select the record again before one can add or delete. This is very inflexible.

The user must also be able to display objects in different ways to suit their needs, i.e. to be able to go from an icon to a detailed view and vice versa, as in Figure 1.8 or from an overview to detail, as in Figure 1.15.

1.3.3   Transparency

The most important aspect of transparency is so obvious that it should not need stating: the user must be able to see the task that they are working on. Unfortunately, most computer systems *hide* crucial information from users: full-screen menus ask the user what they want to do before letting them see what it is to be done to; or they must make decisions on the basis of the one record in front of them without being able to see where it fits into the scheme of things. It is important that the user can see all relevant data, including relationships between different items of data.

The best way of doing this is through the use of pictures. Conceptual models for user-interfaces need to be visually oriented. In order to implement such models, we need to be able to draw pictures. Although character-oriented screens can be used to produce crude pictures, it is only with graphical user-interfaces using high-resolution bit-mapped screens that we are beginning to be able to take full advantage of our visual abilities.

The user must be able to see *overviews* of what is happening, so that they can orient themselves, make comparisons between alternatives, and see the implications of any proposed action. Figure 1.15 shows three possible displays of trip information in the vehicle pool system. The first one shows only a single trip and would be useless for any scheduling purposes, because the user cannot see what other trips have been scheduled and what vehicles are free. The second one shows the trips scheduled, but the user would still have to work out free times and vehicles. The third one is a pictorial representation of the schedule and shows both trips scheduled and available vehicles in a clear, comprehensible way. Details of individual trips [as in (a)] should be able to be summoned up from this picture, but they should never form the basis of a display or the first thing displayed on entry into the system.

The aspect of transparency that most authors emphasise is the instinctive operation of the system, i.e. the user does not need to think about what keys to hit to perform a particular action. A good example of the breakdown of transparency at this level is given by the package *Symphony*, an integrated package built around a spreadsheet. In *Lotus 1-2-3* (from the same makers), a slash brings up the menu, so that the use of commands (once memorised) becomes instinctive. Symphony has two separate sets of menus, invoked using F9 and F10, one handling global operations (e.g. Save) and the other operations specific to the context (e.g. spreadsheet operations). Because both are menus, even a regular user has to stop and think "which menu?". Similarly, the use of the escape key to bring up the menu on the IBM PC versions of Microsoft Word is not transparent: escape not

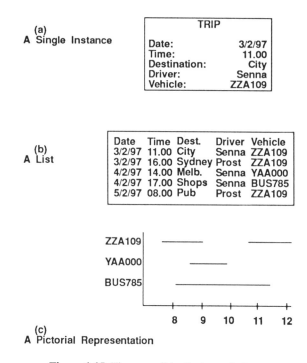

Figure 1.15 Three possible displays of trip
information in the vehicle pool system.

only means something completely different (cancel the last command and go back to
where it was issued), but Word actually uses it for that function as well.

A good way of making the operation of software instinctive is to allow the user to
point to things. It is usually far easier to say "I want that one" than to explain what "that
one" is. This idea underlies a large number of features on the current generation of interface:

- Selection of objects by clicking on an icon or on part of the object itself.
- Selection of actions through pull-down menus, where the required option is
  selected by moving a highlight.
- Selection of attribute values through selection from pick-lists similar to the
  pull-down menus, or clicking on check-boxes or radio buttons corresponding
  to particular values.
- Moving, resizing and reshaping of objects and scrolling of windows by
  dragging them with the mouse.

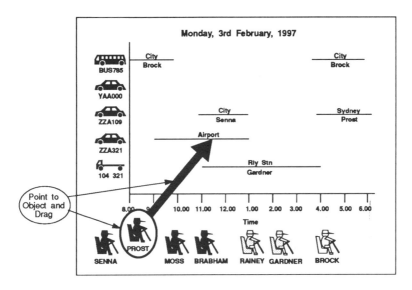

Figure 1.16 Assignment of a driver by
"dragging" with the mouse.

This kind of interaction is referred to as direct manipulation, e.g. in the vehicle pool system, a driver could be allocated to a vehicle on the schedule simply by placing a cursor on the icon for the driver, and dragging it to the correct place on the schedule (Figure 1.16).

1.3.4   Flexibility

Good general-purpose software is highly flexible. For example, the number of applications for spreadsheets is growing all the time, yet most of them are quite straightforward to implement because of the power of the basic idea. Spreadsheets still will not let us do all the things that we want to do in the way that we want to do them, however, e.g. if a student drops out half-way through the semester, we want to leave them on the marks sheet but somehow not add them into the totals and averages *without* having to go through and redefine all the formulae.

One of the most inflexible systems available (but with reason) is an automatic teller: it will do four things (give money, accept a deposit – although not very well, transfer money between accounts or give an account balance) from designated cheque or savings accounts (or a designated other account if you can key in twelve digits correctly), but it has only one response to an unusual situation: it eats your card and leaves you to sort out the problem in person with a person in the morning.

The way of achieving flexibility is through a conceptual model that is sufficiently general to encompass a class of problems rather than a single narrow problem, e.g. the spreadsheet did not restrict itself to handling budgets or balance sheets, but addressed the problem of all calculations involving rows and columns of figures. There is a risk, of course, of becoming too general, in that the tool will no longer perform the functions for which it was originally intended particularly well, but it is usually possible to reach a happy medium.

One approach that is often used to provide "flexibility" is the provision of a *macro* facility. This is essentially a programming language that can be used to "tailor" a general-purpose piece of software to a specific environment. Unfortunately, most people find programming extremely difficult. It requires the ability to spell out a series of steps (many of them hypothetical) in advance, and think of various unlikely contingencies just in case they occur.

It is far easier to work interactively with a system and to cope with real problems when they occur. Thus any "tailoring" of a system must be done by giving the user the ability to change display options interactively. This can be done using two features. A *preferences* menu allows users to change the way in which an object is displayed (often this is only changing colours, but it can involve more, e.g. selecting which attributes of an object are to be displayed). A view menu can allow selection of particular objects, and their display as a list or individually. If the system "remembers" its state between uses, these provide an effective means for tailoring systems.

1.3.5   Learnability

In learning a new system, there are two distinct levels: learning the *semantics* of the problem, and learning the *syntax* (grammar) of interaction.

Since each system should be tackling a different problem, the semantics (i.e. the meanings of things) will always be different. This is where having a good conceptual model is essential.

Typical syntactic problems are:

- Every microwave oven has different sets of keys, which have to be relearned.
- Every operating system has a different, arbitrarily chosen set of commands to perform functions that one already knows how to perform elsewhere and could perform here if the stupid idiots that designed the system hadn't tried to be clever and invent a new set of commands for things that already exist.

The problem with commands is that they must be *memorised*, which places an enormous hurdle in the way of a beginner, and also of a user of more than one system, since the commands will be confused. Push-buttons with cryptic names and which have to be used in combination to achieve the desired result (if you know that it is possible) are not much better. Menu-driven systems remove some of this strain: one merely must know what the options mean, which is a far easier task.

Even so, menu systems can become confusing if different names are used for the same set of commands. For this reason, it is necessary to identify commonly used sets of actions and to give them common names. Various guide-lines (e.g. the IBM Common User Access standard) attempt to do this. The *File* option on Apple Macintosh and Windows systems is a good example. The name is standard across all applications in these environments, and so are the meanings of the various options, e.g. *New, Open, Save, Save As .., Print.* If the user wants to retrieve a file, or print one, they know exactly where to go.

Whatever type of syntax is present, the user must be able to experiment, i.e. to enter commands that they think might be correct, or to push buttons or select menu options to see what happens, without fatal results. Any action that might create a disaster must be warned against or prevented, and ideally, the user must be able to undo the last command.

1.4   Conclusion

In this chapter we have attempted to define the characteristics of a good computer system. The design of such systems is a creative process. In the next chapter we discuss design as a process and show how it can be applied to the design of computer systems.

Summary

A computer is a tool. Use of a tool involves co-operation between a person (the user) and the tool. The user is in charge. Good tools are transparent to the user, so that they can concentrate on the problem at hand and not on how to use the tool. They are flexible, so that different people can use them in ways that best suit them, and for unforeseen tasks. They must be easy to learn. Learning involves two distinct processes: learning about the tool, i.e. what tasks it can be used to do; and learning to operate the tool, i.e. how to perform those tasks. Many computer systems are not good tools because they are clumsy to use and hard to learn, dictate to the user, and inhibit rather than assist the user's work by hiding information.

The point of interaction between the user and the tool is called the user-interface. The user-interface of a computer system consists of the hardware used by the user to interact with the machine (e.g. keyboard, mouse and screen), the software used to display information and accept commands, and the documentation used to describe and support the system. The user conducts a dialogue with the system, in which they issue commands (in an appropriate format) and the machine responds, to complete their tasks.

To design a tool we must know what it is to be used for. The main uses of computers are as embedded systems in electrical devices, as personal systems, and as part of information systems within an organisation or a society. Embedded systems can have highly specialised user-interfaces, designed specifically for the task at hand, using hardware features such as knobs and buttons. Personal systems normally use general-purpose hardware and software, giving the user a great deal of flexibility in what they do and how they do it.

Within information systems, there are three main types of task: transaction processing, decision-making, and information retrieval. Transaction processing systems perform highly specialised routine operations, and either use special hardware or conventional computer terminals running software that limits the activities that the user can perform. On the other hand, decision-making processes usually require flexible access to a wide range of data, plus the ability to analyse the data and to explore the consequences of the decisions made. The computer system is used to support the user's decision-making processes, not to make the decisions. Information retrieval systems share many of the retrieval requirements of decision-support systems, but are directed to a wider audience of infrequent users.

A number of characteristics of the user population influence the type of interface required for a system: frequency of use, application knowledge, tasks to be performed by that user, assumed skills and attitudes. Most systems will be used by people from all parts of this spectrum, and so must exhibit sufficient flexibility to satisfy a range of user types.

A conceptual model is an idea in our mind of what a system does and how it does it. Part of learning about a system involves the development of a conceptual model. This is commonly based on an analogy with something already known, and then refined through subsequent use of the tool. If there is not both a good starting point, and some relatively easy way to progress from it, then the system is difficult to learn.

Conceptual models for computer systems are often based on analogies with the physical environment or manual systems. A valuable source of conceptual models comes from visual representations of data, which are both easily comprehensible and easily manipulable. Commonly used types of conceptual models are: the black box, which converts inputs to outputs but in which the user has no idea of the internal workings of the system; the partitioned black box, where the system is made up of a number of such black boxes; a functional hierarchy; state models; and the object/action model, in which the system is seen as consisting of a set of objects, on which we can perform a predefined set of actions.

There are a number of major advantages of the object/action model: it lends itself easily to visual representations of the system, which are conceptually attractive, easy to learn and easy to manipulate; and it leads to relatively simple models of complex systems, which are flexible to use, and easy to enhance or change.

User control means that it is up to the user, not the computer system, to decide how a particular task is to be performed. Techniques for ensuring user control include: use of windows, modeless dialogues and flexible display facilities (including provision of overviews).

The most important aspect of transparency is that the user must be able to see the task that they are working on. The best way of doing this is through the use of pictures which can be used to display overviews and relationships between data objects as well as individual items of data. The other aspect of transparency is instinctive operation of the system. A good way to achieve this is to allow the user to point to things, e.g. objects on the screen, menu items, values on pick-lists.

The way of achieving flexibility is through a conceptual model that is sufficiently general to encompass a class of problems rather than a single narrow problem. The user can then use menu options (such as *preferences*) to tailor the system.

In learning a new system, there are two distinct levels: learning the semantics of the problem, and learning the syntax (grammar) of interaction. Since each system should be tackling a different problem, the semantics (i.e. the meanings of things) will always be different. This is where having a good conceptual model is essential. Problems arising from different syntactic usages are being addressed by the development of syntactic standards and guide-lines, e.g. the IBM Common User Access guide-lines, which are aimed at providing a standardised syntax for common actions.

Exercises

1. The three lists below contain a number of tools. Within each list, rank each tool according to each of the four criteria of user control, transparency, flexibility and learnability.

   - Escalator, horse, bicycle, motor cycle, car, crane, tank, train, aeroplane.
   - Knife, egg-beater, food processor, mortar and pestle.
   - Automatic teller machine, videotex system, word processor, spreadsheet, database package.

2. Describe what the following tools do and how they do it:

   - Knife.
   - TV.
   - Camel.

   How would you structure your description in terms of the five types of conceptual models?

3. The following pointing devices are used in computer systems:

    •   Touch screen.
    •   Mouse.
    •   Joystick.
    •   Cursor keys.
    •   Trackball.

    How do these rate as tools?

    Can you suggest an alternative pointing device that might overcome problems that you have identified with the existing devices?

4. Try to think of one or more systems in which the primary representation is not visual, but uses some other sense (e.g. sound or smell).

Chapter 2

Systems Development

We pointed out in Chapter 1 that computers are tools which people use to perform tasks. In designing computer systems, this must be uppermost in our minds. However fascinating our programming tricks or our database organisation, if the user of the system feels that it is too difficult to use, gives wrong answers or does not perform the tasks required, then the system is useless. To ensure that this does not happen, we must do two things:

- Base the system design around those areas to which the user directly relates, i.e. the user-interface.
- Make sure that the user is an integral part of the design process and not merely a spectator.

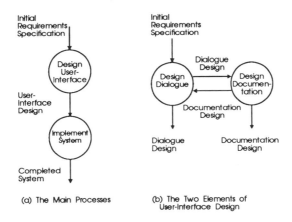

(a) The Main Processes

(b) The Two Elements of User-Interface Design

Figure 2.1 User-interface design.

33

Figure 2.1 gives an idea of this process. The starting point is a *requirements specification* of some sort, which attempts to describe what the user wants the system to do.
This involves both *functional* requirements, i.e. the tasks that the system should perform,
and some idea of the manner in which the system would perform them. The form of this
specification can vary widely: it can contain formal specification components, such as
data flow diagrams, less formal written or verbal specifications, it could be an existing
system, or an already developed prototype, or, more likely, a mixture of all of these. We
will discuss the form of these specifications in more detail and give some examples in a
later section. Different types of specification are appropriate to different systems and to
different organisations.

This specification is *not* static: as the system develops, the users' understanding of
the system and what it can do will also develop, and so their requirements will change.
There is nothing wrong with this: it is perfectly normal, intelligent human behaviour. It
does mean, however, that the designer must be aware of and receptive to this process, or
the system will not meet whatever the eventual requirements of the user turn out to be.

Since it is the user-interface that the user perceives as being the system, this must
be designed first. This runs counter to many current approaches to design, where the program structure is designed, and the user-interface "tacked on" to the front.

There are two components to the user-interface:

- The *dialogue* through which the user interacts with the computer to perform
  the functions of the system.
- The *documentation* which describes what the system is supposed to do and
  explains how to do it.

There is a wide variety of possible documentation, the precise nature and content of
which depends on the particular system. The following is a typical list:

- Advertising material, for potential customers.
- An overview manual, describing the conceptual model for the system.
- Tutorial materials, for people wanting to learn the system.
- Help and advice systems.
- Shorthand ways of describing the system, e.g. keyboard templates.
- Reference manuals.
- A system maintenance manual, for programmers needing to make changes in
  the future.

The dialogue and the documentation must be designed in conjunction with each other, although the first stages of the conceptualisation of the dialogue will normally precede the
start of the documentation design. The user-interface design may include fairly concrete
tasks such as the development and testing of a prototype system, as well as pencil and paper activities.

The designers are often computer professionals, working in close co-operation with the users, in much the same way that an architect designs a building. It is important to realise that the users themselves do not make good designers for two reasons:

- They are often too close to the present problem to be able to generalise easily to produce a solution that is flexible enough to adapt to changing future requirements.
- They usually do not have the level of technical knowledge to know which design solutions are possible and which are difficult to implement, and usually underestimate the capabilities of the available technology.

This does not mean that users with appropriate knowledge and outlook should not be designers, nor is it a charter to ignore users because "they don't know anything about what we're doing". Rather, it means that the user works as a sounding-board for the designer, stating and clarifying requirements, evaluating proposals and making suggestions.

Once the user-interface design is in a reasonably advanced state, the design of other parts of the system, e.g. program and file designs, can take place, followed by the building and implementation of the system. Design problems encountered at this level may impact on the user-interface design, but, provided that any gross limitations of the software environment have been taken into account in the original design, the effect of these should be minor.

In the following sections, we will elaborate on this scenario. We will discuss the limitations of current systems development methodologies, analyse the processes involved in design and describe some techniques used, and then suggest an approach to user-interface design.

2.1   Design Methodologies

A computer system is a highly organised combination of hardware and software that operates in a well-defined and predictable manner. For that reason, many practitioners believe that computer systems can be created in a similar manner.

There are two related aspects to this way of thinking (Figure 2.2):

- The belief that the design process is a well-ordered set of steps which, if followed correctly will yield the "right" answer.
- The belief that these steps, both singly and in combination, can be expressed in the form of an algorithm that, given the "correct" inputs, in the form of a "complete" set of requirements, will provide the "correct" outputs.

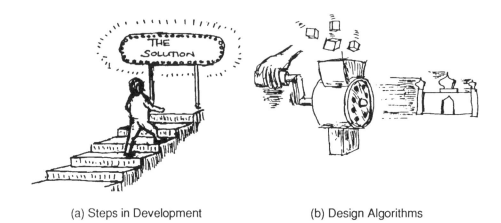

(a) Steps in Development   (b) Design Algorithms

Figure 2.2 Conventional attitudes to design.

The *Structured Analysis* methodology of Yourdon and DeMarco is typical of this approach. It breaks the development process into a series of steps, each of which must be completed before the next is begun:

- Investigate the system.
- Produce a model of the existing system (*current physical model*).
- Abstract to produce a model of the functions of the existing system (*current logical model*).
- Modify this to create a model of the functions of the new system (*new logical model*).
- Produce a physical specification for the new system (*new physical model*).
- Implement the new system.
- Test the new system.

Although the model is widely used, its success is not, in fact, due to these series of steps, but to the incorporation of a very powerful set of modelling tools (*data flow diagrams*) which provide designers with an excellent way of exploring certain aspects of the problem. In particular, data flow diagrams provide a tool to strip features from a current implementation and look at what the system is attempting to achieve, and a way to express the subdivision of a problem into smaller units through functional decomposition. Neither of these is algorithmic – in fact data flow diagrams require considerable expertise and imagination to use well.

     The steps themselves involve a number of weaknesses and fallacies:

- It is assumed that the user can specify their requirements precisely at the beginning, and will not change them as the development process proceeds.
- All knowledge of the implementation of the existing system is (officially) discarded.
- No attention is paid to the mechanisms through which the steps can be carried out, the assumption being that they are logical and obvious. The very name of the methodology, in which the word *analysis* is used instead of *design*, is indicative of this.

In practice, there are always unofficial adaptations of the methodology:

- Users do get to make changes, but they are regarded as wooly-headed and fickle, and there is constant discussion of the "penalties" to be imposed for such changes and of the assignment of "blame" for "misunderstandings" and "misrepresentation". Design "errors" found during testing are rectified if they are "serious" enough, even though this involves going back some steps.
- Information about existing implementations is used in two ways: even the "official" versions of the methodology allow for the specification of a *domain of change* outside of which the implementation remains the same; and designers often incorporate parts of the existing implementation if they know about them and if they think they will be useful.
- Designers incorporate their own methods of doing things. However, they are usually on the defensive in doing so, and are unlikely to be as creative as they would be in a different environment, so that the resulting systems are predictable rather than imaginative.

Approaches of this type appear to work for simple systems that are, at most, minor variations on existing systems, and where the users already have a good understanding of the problem. The end result is never good, but may be usable. The approach is taken to its extreme in some *Computer-Aided Software Engineering (CASE)* tools, which attempt to generate systems automatically from functional specifications or from database file structures. The resulting systems are, at best, crude.

There are various ways in which these methodologies can be made more realistic:

- Rearrange the steps, to allow repetition and reconsideration of aspects of the design. There are numerous variations on this, e.g. *iterative* and *spiral* approaches where some back-tracking is permitted, *prototyping*, in which a throw-away prototype system is constructed for user comment before the final system is built, and *evolutionary* approaches in which the system evolves gradually in consultation between the users and the designers and programmers. Managers often object to these approaches as they are seen as "expensive", because work must constantly be "redone". A good methodology

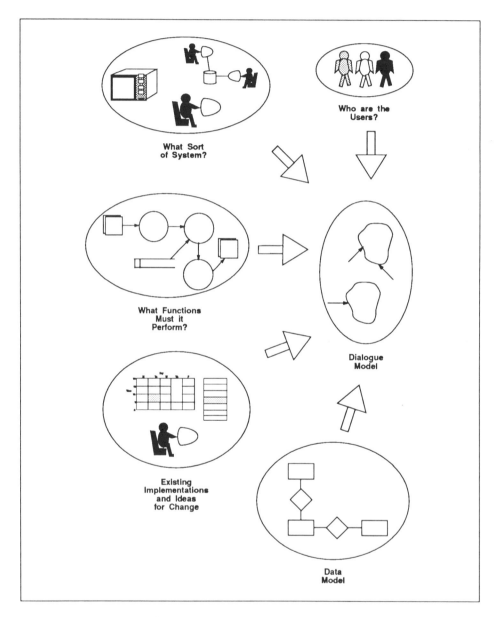

Figure 2.3 Some components of the initial
requirements specification.

should address this issue, not by minimising the amount of repetition, but by making it as painless as possible.

- Incorporate all aspects of knowledge of the system into the design process.
- Pay explicit consideration to the design process.

In the following sections, we will attempt to address these issues. The resulting methodology is, in essence, an evolutionary one. This allows the incorporation of the users' increasing understanding of the problem, through the use of extensive testing of the conceptual models of the system, at a stage where they are easy (and cheap) to change.

2.2   The Initial Requirements Specification

We have already pointed out that the determination of requirements for a system is an ongoing process as the users develop an understanding of the problem and of the tools needed to solve it. There must, however, be some sort of a starting point, where we formulate an initial idea of the system to be developed. This initial idea, which we will refer to as the *Initial Requirements Specification*, is of necessity both relatively general and incomplete, although it may contain quite specific requirements in some areas.

It must address the following issues (Figure 2.3):

- What sort of system are we trying to develop: an *embedded* system, a stand-alone *personal* system, or part of an *organisational* information system?
- Who are the users: e.g. will they be skilled operators using it daily, managers using it occasionally, members of the public using it once only?
- What functions is it to perform?
- What ideas and expectations do people have of it, e.g. if it is to replace an existing system, why and what improvements are expected?
- How is it expected to relate to other systems in the organisation, e.g. to existing corporate databases?

As we discussed in Chapter 1, there are three main uses for computers:

- *Embedded* systems in electrical devices such as microwave ovens and video recorders.
- As *personal* systems, used for creating and editing documents, drawings, animation and music for personal use or subsequent distribution or publication, and for doing calculations.
- As part of *information* systems within an organisation or a society, where it can be performing transaction processing, decision-making or information retrieval processes, or a mixture of these.

The types of user-interface that we develop for these systems vary widely. With embedded systems and certain types of transaction processing system we may build a large part of the dialogue into hardware, through the use of push-buttons or knobs. On the other hand, a decision-support system may require very powerful and flexible retrieval, analysis and formatting tools, accessing data from a wide variety of sources, but which will run on a personal computer on the user's desk.

Most systems are going to be used by a wide variety of users with different skill levels and experience (if only because everybody has to learn), and so must be usable by them all. The types of characteristics that need to be taken into account were listed in Chapter 1. There are situations, however, where there are significant features of the user population that have considerable impact, e.g.

- A system designed for the use of the general public cannot involve a significant learning curve.
- A system designed for the use of research scientists can legitimately incorporate technical terms and mathematical operations which would be inappropriate in another environment.
- A system designed for blind users will not use visual displays.

The specification of the functions to be performed by the system forms a significant part of the initial requirements specification. These commonly take one of two forms:

- Formal specifications, based on diagrammatic representations of the system, with supporting information in a highly structured format.
- More informal specifications, based on English descriptions of the required system.

The first of these is typified by the *structured analysis* documentation of Gane and Sarson and of DeMarco. This consists of a set of *data flow diagrams* accompanied by *process specifications* (expressed using a formalised technique such as *structured English*) and a *data dictionary*. The data flow diagrams are arranged in a conceptual hierarchy, in which the system is broken down into a series of functional subsystems. A major advantage of data flow diagrams is their use as a tool during the exploration phase of the design process (Section 2.3) for abstracting the functions of the system from the implementation detail. Some examples of data flow diagrams are given in the accompanying box. The more informal specifications might list the functions required in point form, or as part of a memorandum, or even be verbal specifications.

It is also possible to mix the two approaches. We commonly use fairly simple data flow diagrams as a visual representation of the main functions of the system, but more detailed description of processes is in plain English.

In terms of the approach that we will use for dialogue design, the form of the functional specification is not important, because the conceptualisation of the user-interface is a separate process rather than the conversion of the functional representation into an implementation. Instead, the functions are used as a guide to the scope of the system and to the actions required, and can then be used to test the dialogue model by checking whether the objects and actions supplied do, in fact, satisfy the stated requirements.

It is rare for any system to be designed from scratch. More usually, it either develops from an existing system that has outlived its usefulness, or it is based on existing systems in operation elsewhere. Ideas about existing systems involve both *what* they do, and *how* they do it.

Often, an existing system within an organisation performs most of the functions needed, but is tedious and difficult to use, and the users have become tired of battling with it and want something better. In most cases, this involves replacing a batch system or a very simplistic on-line system with something more interactive and which gives the users more control. In this case, users may be quite specific about certain aspects of the interface, e.g. our vehicle pool manager may specify that they must be able to see an entire day's schedule and a list of the vehicles available and a list of the drivers available, and that they want the schedule to look like the one on the wall. Provided that the request is not totally unreasonable (in which case extensive negotiation is required before anything at all is done), it provides an excellent starting point for the visualisation of the user-interface.

References to systems running in other organisations are usually even more straightforward, since the initial specification is often "we want one like that". It is usually then qualified, however, by statements of the form: "But this bit will have to be changed to ...".

Very few computer systems operate in isolation. Any new system must fit in with existing systems in an organisation, whether this means that they must communicate with them, or merely that they must refrain from corrupting other applications' data or hogging all the memory. A typical issue encountered with personal computers is that, if one has graphics software and a word processor, it is nice if they would communicate, so that the graphics can be incorporated into documents produced by the word processor.

The major issue in most organisations is that of corporate data. The idea here is that data belongs to the organisation as a whole, and not to individual users or applications. The organisation (conceptually if not actually) has some form of corporate database, on which all data resides. This means that any new application must take into account the definitions and structure of the corporate database. For this reason, a data model is often part of the requirements specification. Some features of data models are outlined in the accompanying box.

There is a wide variety of other formal system specification techniques, each useful as a way of representing different aspects of a system. Yourdon (1989) describes a number of these.

Object-oriented analysis techniques are also presented as an approach to requirements specification. An object-oriented model is used in this book for our formal dialogue model, which we will discuss in Chapter 4. However, much of the literature (see, e.g. Coad and Yourdon, 1991 and Shlaer and Mellor, 1988) treats object-oriented analysis as a form of data modelling with an element of functional analysis, and the consequent model contains only "low-level" objects. We discuss this problem more fully in regard to data models in Chapter 4. In addition, this analysis is presented as part of a linear, rather than an evolutionary, process. Despite this, these books form a valuable source of ideas about the types of objects that can be found in systems.

At the end of the chapter, we give initial requirements specifications for two systems that we will use extensively in this book: the Crossword Designer, and a Personal Timetable System. The specifications are (quite deliberately) in contrasting form. That for the Personal Timetable System makes use of formal specifications in the form of data flow diagrams and a data model, although not in the detail of a full structured analysis specification. That for the Crossword Designer is in plain English.

Data Flow Diagrams

A very popular way of specifying requirements is through the Structured Analysis methods of DeMarco and Gane and Sarson. These are based on the use of *Data Flow Diagrams*, which represent the functions to be performed by the system. Data flow diagrams consist of four components (Figure 2.4):

- *Processes*: These are the functions performed by the system. The name normally consists of a verb followed by a noun.
- *External Entities*: These are people or organisations outside the system which are sources of or receivers of data from the system.
- *Data Stores*: These are long-term repositories of data within the system.
- *Data Flows*: These represent movements of data through the system, e.g. between different processes, or between processes and data stores and processes and external entities.

Figure 2.5 gives examples of data flow diagrams for two small systems. The system in (a) maintains a file of records on people. The data comes from the people themselves (represented by the external entity *Person*). The process *Maintain Personal Records* uses this data to add, change and delete the records held in the file, represented as the data store *Person*. The system in (b) represents the operation of a vehicle pool described in Chapter 1. There are three functions: the scheduling of vehicle trips, based on requests from potential passengers; arranging for maintenance, based on distance travelled since the last service; and arranging for the vehicles to be registered when their registration falls due. There are also three data stores, one containing information about vehicles (including their maintenance history), one about drivers (including, e.g. their licence type) and the last one about scheduled trips. No-

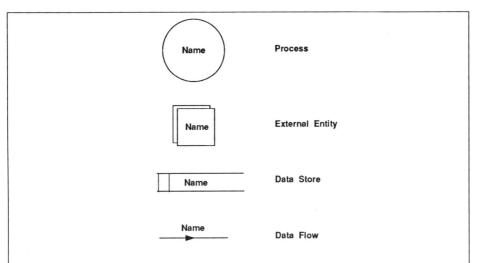

Figure 2.4 Data flow diagram symbols.

tice that, to schedule a trip, all three data stores must be accessed, *Vehicle* to find a suitable vehicle, *Driver* to find a driver who can drive that vehicle and *Trips* to check that it is free. *Passenger* is an external entity because, although they are the reason for the trip, they do not actually participate in the process of scheduling it. Similarly, the *Garage* performs the maintenance, but does not actually arrange it (it is simply asked to do it), while the *Motor Registry* is very distinctly an outside organisation.

In looking at a requirements specification, it is as important to notice what is not there as what is there. The vehicle pool system does not contain provision for the addition of new vehicles nor the removal of old ones, nor for the maintenance of driver records. These would have been omitted for a reason (e.g. the intended users of this system do not have responsibility for these functions) and so must not be included in any implementation.

Data flow diagrams for more complex systems are *levelled*, i.e. there is a hierarchy of diagrams in which each diagram is an expansion of one process at the next level up. This allows the user to be presented with a simple overview of the system, but can then look at selected parts in whatever detail is appropriate.

Data flow diagrams do not contain any information about the *implementation* of the processes, e.g. whether they are manual or automated, or who performs them. The reason for this is that the analysis process leading to the requirements specification is a process of abstraction, in which there is a deliberate attempt to get rid of any presuppositions about how the system might be implemented, leading to a statement of the *functions* to be performed by the system. The data flow diagram is this statement. The reason for doing this is to avoid locking the system designer into past practices that have become irrelevant.

During the design process, it is sometimes useful to include implementation information on the data flow diagram. Gane and Sarson allow the analyst to annotate processes to include information about the implementation. DeMarco has two techniques: he suggests drawing a line on the diagram (the *person-machine* interface) to indicate which processes are manual and which automated, and has a different type of diagram (a *physical data flow* diagram) in which the processes represent structural units in the system rather than functions. In addition, some analysts erroneously in-

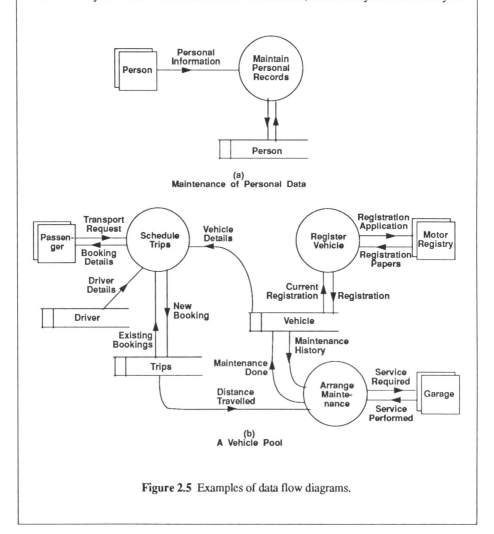

Figure 2.5 Examples of data flow diagrams.

clude all the people using a system as external entities. This is wrong since, if a person performs a process within a system, then they are part of the implementation of that process, and so should not be shown.

In addition to the data flow diagram, a structured analysis specification contains two additional types of information:

- *Process Specifications*: For each process (or in a levelled diagram, each process that has not been expanded as a lower-level diagram), there must be a detailed specification of what it does. Gane and Sarson and DeMarco recommend that these be given in a formal way, e.g. using structured English, which is a formalised version of English using a simplified vocabulary and incorporating certain programming language structures (e.g. if ... then ... else ... and loop structures). Other methodologies use plain English. The examples in this book (e.g. the timetabling system below) are in plain English.
- *Data Dictionary*: This contains definitions of all the names in the system, e.g. for a data store or a data flow it would list all the data items in the store or flow, and would then contain an additional entry for each of those items. The data models discussed below perform some but not all of the functions of the data dictionary, but still need to be supplemented by a data dictionary.

Data Models

Data on a corporate database must be organised in such a way that it can be maintained in a consistent manner, but can be accessed by many different applications. Our current methods of organisation of data (e.g. relational databases) attempt to achieve this through the use of the following three criteria.

The most important feature is the avoidance of *redundancy*. Each fact is stored once and once only, e.g. a person's address will appear once in the system, so that if it is changed, all applications needing that address will immediately have access to that change.

A second feature is the avoidance of structures which favour one form of access over another, e.g. in the Vehicle Pool system, it should be equally easy to ask *What vehicles has driver Fred Bloggs driven?* as to ask *Who has driven Vehicle YAA000?* With current software technology, this means avoiding structures in which,

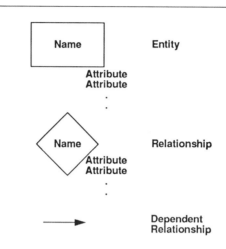

Figure 2.6 Entity-relationship diagram
symbols

e.g. a vehicle record contains a list of all trips made (i.e. a *repeating group*), since this would make the first of the two queries very difficult, while favouring the second. Instead, we create a separate *Trips* file or table that makes the link between *Driver* and *Vehicle* in a way that is accessible in either direction. This results in the data being fragmented into a multiplicity of files or tables. We will discuss the impact of this on the dialogue in Chapter 4.

A third feature is the requirement that files or tables be *homogeneous*, i.e. that each record contains exactly the same data items. Again, this is a convenience at the database level, but is not always convenient in a dialogue.

The data models are conceptual models that assist in the structuring of data in this way. We shall describe one commonly used model, the *Entity-Relationship Model.*

The main components of an Entity-Relationship model are shown in Figure 2.6, and some examples in Figure 2.7.

An *entity* is a type of data object in the system, e.g. a *Person* or a *Vehicle. Instances* of these entities are, e.g. a person *Fred Bloggs* or a vehicle *YAA000*. Relationships between these entities can then be identified, e.g. a *Trip* is a relationship between a *Vehicle* and a *Driver*, e.g. *Fred Bloggs* drove *YAA000* on a trip starting on 13th March, 1997 at 3.00 p.m. Although relationships are often identified by verbs (e.g. we could have used *Drives* instead of *Trip*) it is important to recognise that they are not actions or functions as on a data flow diagram, but merely data representing some sort of link between entities. Entities and relationships have *attributes*, which

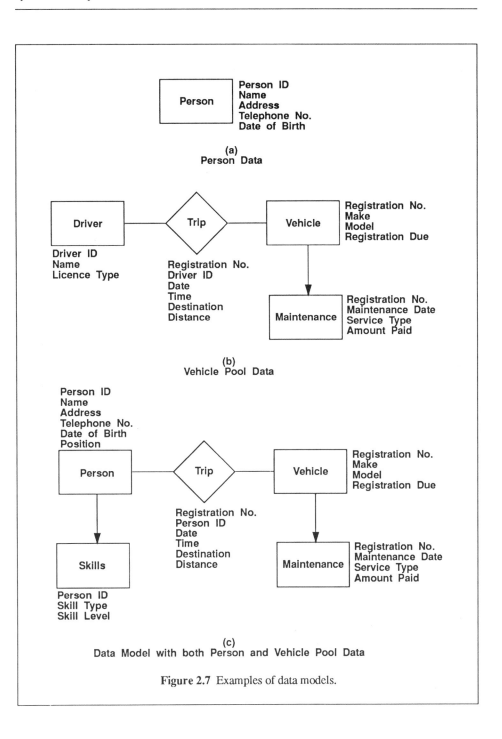

Figure 2.7 Examples of data models.

```
Type:          Data Element
Name:          Person ID
Description:   A unique identifier issued to each person
Domain:        Numeric, 6 characters
               First two characters are last 2 digits of year
                 of issue, remaining four are serial no within
                 year, e.g. 870213.  First year of issue, 1969.
```

Figure 2.8 A data dictionary entry.

are data items describing properties of the entity or relationship, e.g. *Person* has an identification number (*Person Id*), a name, address, telephone number and date of birth, while the relationship *Trip* contains the identification number of the driver, the vehicle registration number, the date and time of the trip, the destination and the distance travelled.

A special class of relationship is a *dependency relationship*. In a relationship of this type, an instance of the entity pointed to by the arrow (known as a *dependent entity*) cannot exist unless there is a corresponding instance of the other entity, e.g. there cannot be any *Maintenance* records for YAA000 unless there is a *Vehicle* record for it (i.e. unless the vehicle exists). The main use of dependent entities is in splitting off repeating groups of records into a separate data object.

Each box (*entity set*) in the diagram is usually implemented as a "flat" file (i.e. a file with fixed length records) or a table in a relational database.

A database often contains data from more than one system. Figure 2.7(c) illustrates the data model that might result if the personal and vehicle pool data was held in the same database. The fact that a person is a driver is now identified by the value of the attribute *Position* being *Driver*, while their licence class (which will determine what types of vehicle they can drive) is the value of the attribute *Skill Level* of the dependent entity *Skill* when the attribute *Skill Type* is *Driver*. This type of arrangement makes a lot of sense when attempting to store information about a diverse range of employees, but makes the data model one step further removed from the dialogue that will be required for the vehicle pool.

The data model is accompanied by a *data dictionary* which gives the meanings of names used in the diagram, and in particular detailed information about attributes. An example of a data dictionary entry is given in Figure 2.8. The information consists of the attribute name, a comment on its meaning, and the *domain* from which its values are drawn, e.g. their data type (character, numeric, date, ...) and allowed range of values.

The data model and data dictionary are of use in the system design in two ways:

- They provide information about the definition of and relationships between data items, and allow the dialogue designer to identify whether data items needed already exist or have to be added to the database (in which case, the mechanisms for their update must be considered).
- They provide the base information that the program designer must use to implement the mappings between the dialogue objects and the database.

As with the rest of the requirements specification, the data model and data dictionary will evolve during the system development process, as additional data requirements are encountered and meanings are refined.

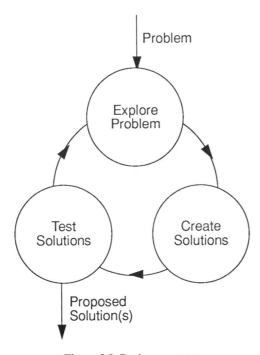

Figure 2.9 Design processes.

2.3   The Design Process

There are at least as many ways of looking at design as there are designers. However, there seem to be three main processes occurring (Figure 2.9):

- The *exploration* of the problem to be solved.
- The *generation* of ideas for possible solutions.
- The *evaluation* of those solutions to see if they will work, and to select one or more of the "best" solutions for further work.

2.3.1   Exploration

The exploration stage (also referred to as *incubation*) is a head-clearing process: trying to determine exactly what the problem is, and trying to develop an appropriate frame of mind for the next step. The designers have a vast jumble of ideas, including knowledge of previous and current systems, theoretical ideas, requirements, and many seemingly extraneous factors, circulating in their heads (Figure 2.10) which they are attempting to organise in order to get a line on possible solutions to the problem.

The techniques used here have two main aims:

- To *organise* and *relate* different aspects of the problem.
- To look at the problem in as many *different* ways as possible.

A good way of organising information is by drawing diagrams. These provide a means both of showing the essential features of the information, and the relationships between different pieces of information. This is the reason for the emphasis in many areas of mathematics (not noted for its visual approach) on drawing diagrams.

In a similar way, attempting to reformulate a qualitative problem quantitatively often helps. Scheduling systems often have a multitude of tasks, all of which could be done, and a multitude of resources to do them, but until most are scheduled it is not easy to see that the last few cannot be. The approach here is to schedule the "hard" tasks first (e.g. those that take a long time or require resources of limited availability), but in order to do this, one must develop a measure of

Figure 2.10 Exploration.

"hardness" by looking at what factors are involved and how they interact. Although this measure of hardness is never perfect, the act of trying to develop it may lead to a greater understanding of the underlying problem.

A good organisational technique is *abstraction*: the isolation of a particular set of features and the examination of the system in terms of those features. We often do this automatically, e.g. when we are drawing we usually only put in the "important" bits, but we can often direct our abstraction in specific ways. The structured analysis techniques discussed in the last section attempt to do this by concentrating on one aspect of the system, the *functions* to be performed, so that the designer is not locked in to ways of thinking that are purely artefacts of existing implementations.

The opposite to abstraction is the process of writing down and working through specific examples, e.g. by attempting to prepare a timetable or build a crossword by hand, in order to understand how the person doing the task thinks about it, and discovering what information they need and when they need it.

Another approach is to identify how the problem differs from a related problem and so identify in what areas a solution must differ, and the nature of those differences. The search for analogies, e.g. the desktop "metaphor" used by the Xerox Star and the Apple Macintosh, is one aspect of this approach.

What we are doing here is "worrying" at the problem, sniffing it, chewing it, turning it upside down, until we feel that we really know what it is. If the process appears tentative and chaotic, it is, because we are trying to learn and understand.

2.3.2 Generation of Possible Solutions

The generation of possible solutions is the creative part of design. It is best thought of as a leap of the imagination (Figure 2.11) in which the disparate ideas that have so far been milling around come together into a coherent whole.

Since the imagination is a fickle beast, it is useful to have techniques to stimulate its operation.

One of the most productive ways of generating ideas is *brainstorming* (Figure 2.12). Although an individual can do a form of brainstorming, it is best done by a group of two or more people. For the sort of problems that we are interested in, a whiteboard is useful. The idea is that people in the group talk around the problem, throwing in ideas about possible solutions. These ideas can be completely crazy (except in that they must have some link to the problem). Other people can throw in their own ideas, or pick up and refine ideas already suggested. The important thing is that there is no analysis: statements such as "but that won't work because ..." are forbidden, because they stop the creative process dead. Statements such as "that would be better if ..." are acceptable, however, because although they incorporate a judgement, they are also offering an idea, and so are a necessary part of the refinement process. Ideas generated in a brainstorming session are either verbal, visual or both. Since a user-interface is visual, the facilities

Figure 2.11 A creative leap.   **Figure 2.12** Brainstorming.

available should assist in generating visual ideas. This is the reason for the whiteboard, to which everybody in the group should have access. There is one obvious criterion for a brainstorming group: it must consist of *peers*, so that members of the group are not constrained by the need to impress or to follow a "party line".

A related approach is the use of *free association*. This involves drawing or looking at patterns and seeing if we can see something. A well-known game is to look at clouds and see what things they represent. We can sometimes do the same by simply starting to draw and see what happens.

Attribute lists are check lists to go through. The most famous and common is the WHO, WHAT, HOW, and WHEN list.

A very powerful technique of wide application is the use of throw-away analogies. Given a problem we think of something else and draw analogies between the two. This helps generate many ideas. The reason that we call them "throw-away" analogies is that we only use them to generate ideas, not believing that they are really the same.

Figure 2.13 illustrates the sort of analogies that we might use if we drew an analogy between cooking dinner and creating crosswords. The analogy gives us ways of starting to think about our real problem. We do not pretend that making a crossword is the same as cooking a dinner. It is just that thinking about one may give us ideas about the other. Often we can use seemingly ridiculous comparisons to see where they might lead. For example we might compare creating crosswords to big-game hunting (Figure 2.14).

Admittedly the suggestions in this case are a little weak but we can try out as many analogies as we like for little cost and they can help us come up with good ideas. Note

When we cook dinner we use recipes. Perhaps we can find recipes (or standard procedures) for creating crosswords.

We need ingredients to make a meal. We need words and clues to make crosswords. Fresh ingredients are often best and perhaps we need ways of finding fresh ingredients for our crosswords. New words, new combinations, different clues.

When we have finished cooking then we give it to someone to eat. When we do this our enjoyment is enhanced if we present it well. Perhaps we should think of ways of presenting our crosswords in an appetizing manner.

Cooking is a skill and we have cooking classes. Perhaps should have crossword classes to help people learn how to make crosswords.

Figure 2.13 Analogies between cooking
and crosswords

When you go hunting you need to prepare yourself well with appropriate equipment. When we create a crossword we need to prepare ourselves with appropriate tools to help us catch our crossword.

When you have completed your mission you need a good way of displaying your trophies. With crosswords we need a good way of showing what we have produced.

Figure 2.14 Analogies between big-game
hunting and crosswords.

that the use of metaphors is a common way of describing user-interfaces. However, the metaphors are no more to be believed than our analogies between big-game hunting and crosswords. They are useful tools for thinking.

Another approach is referred to as the *express-test* cycle. This is actually the design cycle repeated very rapidly many times. The designers make sketches, which they review critically and modify until a satisfactory result is obtained.

There is one approach which we have not included: design from first principles, i.e. application of the basic theoretical principles (e.g. the principles of cognitive psychology, ergonomics and guide-lines for screen layout) to generate a design. This is because designers do not work this way. The reason is simple. We rarely, if ever, have to create something from scratch. There is always somebody who has tried this or something similar before, and we build on that. Early motor cars were called horseless carriages for a very good reason – that was precisely what they were. The current generation of cars is the result of a century of refinement of that original concept. If we attempted to discard the work of previous designers and return to "first principles", it would not merely be fiendishly difficult (there are a very large number of "first principles" and their application is rarely clear), we would make all the mistakes and fall into all the traps that the previous designers did (Figures 2.15, 2.16). This does not mean, of course, that we cannot discard elements of our predecessors' work if we believe that we can improve on it. It does mean that we should be aware of their work, and take account of it.

The place where basic principles have a significant role is in testing. We use them as some of the yardsticks against which we can test our design proposals.

This reliance on past practice has two important implications:

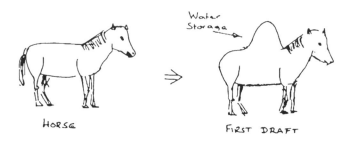

Figure 2.15 Designing by copying.

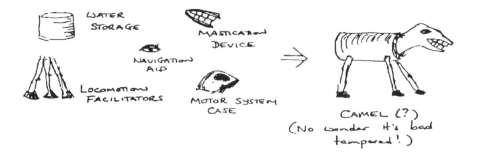

Figure 2.16 Design from first principles.

- The designer *must* have a good knowledge of the subject area.
- There is a constant danger of *rigidity* – of slavishly following past practice when a more innovative approach is needed.

The first point is an argument for computing professionals to do the actual design work for computer systems, since they have been through the design process before, have the technical knowledge, and have seen a wider variety of systems than the average user. The role being performed, however, is that of an architect: a person with a breadth of vision and an aesthetic sense, who can at least attempt to realise the users' dreams of the ideal system. A computer professional who is merely a technical specialist does not have the required knowledge or expertise.

Rigidity can only be tackled by a conscious effort to look for good solutions, not just obvious ones. Some of the exploration methods discussed above are attempts to break a mind set that might ignore any but the most obvious solutions.

The aim at this stage is to generate a number of solutions (Figure 2.17), which can be compared, modified, combined and used to generate still further solutions.

There is no point, of course, of having the solutions in our heads. We must *express* them in some way. In the early design stages, this is often through sketches. These can be a single picture representing, for example, a possible conceptual model, or a set of pictures (a *storyboard*) showing a sequence of action. Later on, we may draw pictures of screen layouts, and we may build a *prototype* of the system which demonstrates the main features of the dialogue.

Figure 2.17 Generation of alternative
solutions.

2.3.3   Testing

At this stage, many people think that they have "got the answer". This is not the case. All we have is some possible solutions to the problem, most of which will probably not work. We must now test the proposals (Figure 2.18) to see if they will meet the users' requirements. There are numerous criteria against which one can test: does it look right, will it perform the required functions, will it be easy to use, is it an elegant solution to the problem (or is it confused and messy)?

It is important to realise that even very preliminary design sketches can be tested by showing them to users and obtaining reactions. Testing does not have to be postponed until the building of a prototype or of the final system. This testing is a major source not only of problems to be fixed but also of new ideas. The testing process makes an apparently imprecise and chaotic process into one that can produce a precise, well-defined finished product. Solutions that are unsatisfactory can be weeded out, or the problems in them can be analysed and further work (another design cycle) done on them. As a result, design becomes a process of constant refinement (Figure 2.19), which is repeated until a satisfactory solution is obtained.

The time-scale for each design cycle varies enormously: the incubation period for a difficult problem may be weeks, months or even years; but during an animated discussion, ideas may be produced, tested, refined and tested again many times in a few minutes.

Figure 2.18 Testing.

Figure 2.19 Refinement.

2.3.4   The Outcome

The outcome of the process is one or more solutions to the problem which, in the opinion of the designer and the users, should work. Different designers will come up with different solutions to the same problem. This creates problems only for people who think that there should be one "right answer". For everybody else, it provides a richness and a diversity which can then be built on in subsequent designs.

One implication of this is that the design (and consequently the completed system) contains numerous assumptions about how best to present information, how best to manipulate it, and about how people will actually think about the system and how they will use it. Some of the assumptions are explicit in our approach (e.g. that it is better to point to something than to try and describe it) while others may be there but not stated (e.g. that a Gantt chart is the best way to display the schedule in Figure 1.8). If we make these assumptions explicit, then they can be used to test whether the design (or the system) works, as described in the next chapter.

Airline Flight Information

To illustrate the design process at work, we will consider the development of some ideas for provision of airline timetable information. The users of the system are potential airline passengers, some of whom are local people but some are tourists who are not necessarily aware either of the geography of the country (except for the names and rough locations of some of the main cities), and are not sure which places are well-served by the airlines or how the airline system works.

As part of the exploration process, we look at one particular scenario: how to get from Darwin (in the far north) to Canberra (an artificial, and hence small, national Capital, in the south-east).

An obvious starting point in our investigation is the existing printed airline timetables. These are structured in one of two ways: one airline issues a timetable organised by *sector* [Figure 2.20(a)], listing direct flights between pairs of cities; the other issues a timetable showing *through* flights between pairs of cities [Figure 2.20(b)]. Since we want information on all flights, we have combined the information from the different airlines. Another standard form of the timetable is the railway timetable [Figure 2.20(c)], where possible stopping places on one or more routes are listed down the page. Each flight has a column to itself, with arrival and departure times listed against the places where the flight stops.

We can test out the proposals to see how they perform:

- The sector timetable is difficult to use, because we have to look at a number of timetables to piece together the full journey. To do this, we need geographical knowledge (e.g. a map of Australia). And since there are different possible routes, we need to look at different sets of timetables.
- The list of through journeys seems to give us what we want, but it hides a lot of information. Which way do the flights go? At what times do they reach intermediate stops?
- The railway timetable gives more information, but is difficult to read, and will contain a lot of data which is not relevant to the problem at hand.

In addition, all of them may be loaded with extraneous information because they contain information about every day of the week, not merely the intended day of travel.

Our testing has given us two ideas already:

- We might like to let the user specify a particular day, and show only the data for that day. (We would also have to let them move from day to day, or show a whole week if they wanted to be able to pick the best day to travel.)
- If we use sector timetables, we need a map. Why not supply a map? Figure 2.21(a) shows what it might look like. The "best" flight is highlighted, but the other possibilities are also shown, and can be selected (e.g. by touching).

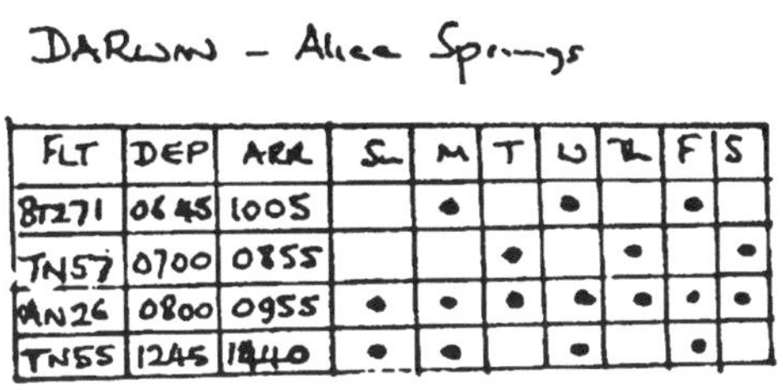

DARWIN – Alice Springs

FLT	DEP	ARR	S	M	T	U	Th	F	S
BT271	0645	1005		•		•		•	
TN57	0700	0855			•		•		•
AN26	0800	0955	•	•	•	•	•	•	•
TN55	1245	1440	•	•		•		•	

(a) Sector Schedule

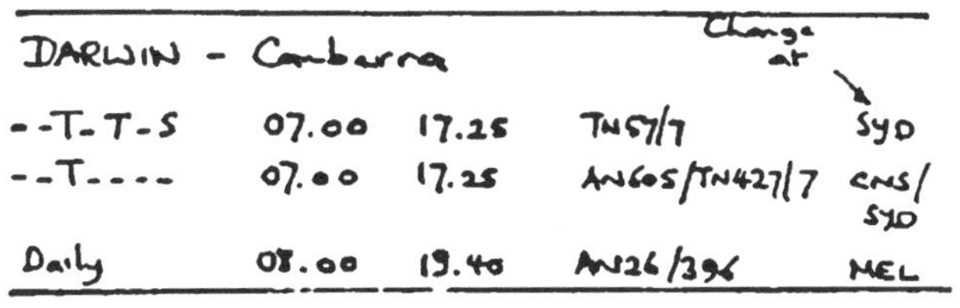

DARWIN – Canberra   Change at ↘

--T-T-S	07.00	17.25	TN57/7	SYD
--T----	07.00	17.25	AN605/TN427/7	CNS/SYD
Daily	08.00	19.40	AN26/396	MEL

(b) List of Through Flights

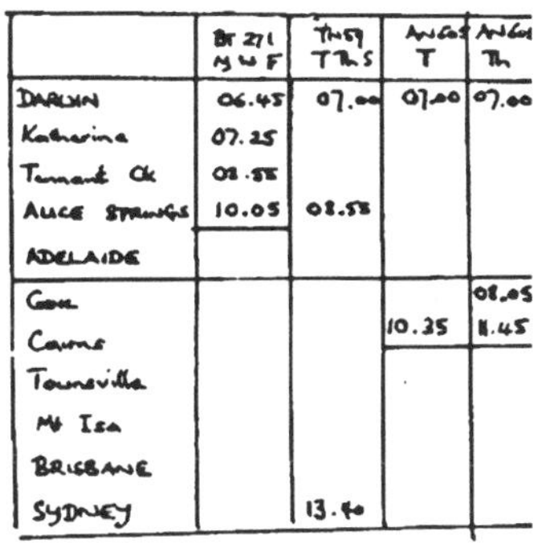

	BT271 MUF	TN57 TRS	AN605 T	AN601 Th
DARWIN	06.45	07.00	07.00	07.00
Katherine	07.25			
Tennant Ck	08.55			
ALICE SPRINGS	10.05	08.55		
ADELAIDE				
Gove				08.05
Cairns			10.35	11.45
Townsville				
Mt Isa				
BRISBANE				
SYDNEY		13.40		

(c) Railway Timetable

Figure 2.20 Ideas for airline timetable.

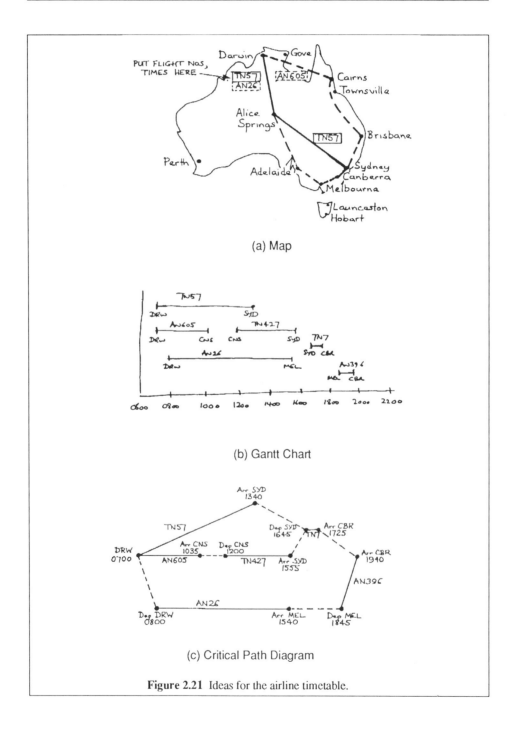

(a) Map

(b) Gantt Chart

(c) Critical Path Diagram

Figure 2.21 Ideas for the airline timetable.

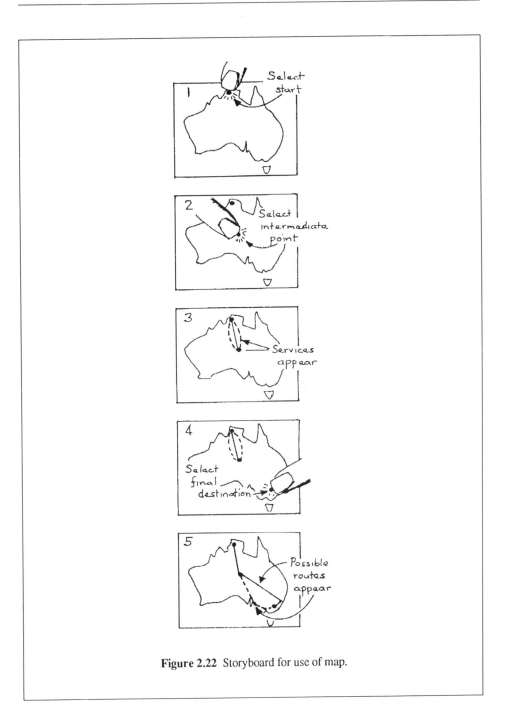

Figure 2.22 Storyboard for use of map.

The storyboard in Figure 2.22 gives some idea of how the map might be used. To select all flights between two places, one selects first the origin (e.g. by touching), then the destination (e.g. one would press Darwin first, then Canberra). To select a route via one or more places, one selects the places on the route in turn, e.g. to go from Darwin to Canberra via Alice Springs, one presses Darwin, then Alice Springs, then Canberra. Note that when one presses Alice Springs, all services between Darwin and Alice Springs will appear, but will vanish again when Canberra is pressed. Pressing on the same city a second time would deselect it.

How else could we do it?

The problem is a type of scheduling problem, so could we use any of the scheduling approaches? Figure 2.21(b) and (c) show two possibilities:

- A *Gantt Chart*, on which the horizontal lines are flights. The end points of the lines are labelled with the start and finish points for the flights, and the horizontal axis gives the time of day.
- A *Critical Path Diagram*, on which the solid lines are flights, the dotted lines waiting time at airports, and the nodes are events such as arrivals and departures.

We now have to test our ideas again. All of the representations could be used to develop a journey, and it would be possible to highlight the "best" flight on any of them. Some have features that others do not. The map gives the geographical information in a way that the other two do not, but does not give information such as waiting times between planes.

In our opinion, the map is by far the best. It has an immediacy and an understandability that the other representations do not have. It gives tourists valuable information about where places are, and the actions required to spell out a route are reasonably obvious. There are three important points to notice about this example:

- We have been around the design cycle at least twice, but we have jumped around a lot. When an idea comes, it gets written down. The cycle is not an algorithm. It is just an idea of what happens.
- We have used a lot of sketches, but they are very rough. There is a good reason for this. We are not going to spend a lot of time on beautifully drafted drawings that we are going to throw away five minutes later. It is better to work quickly and freely.
- Our solution is by no means complete. It gives us an idea of what the system would look like, and how it might work, but nothing more. As we elaborate it, we may encounter problems, but that is not our concern here.

2.3.5 Design of Large Systems

We have suggested that the design process could be represented as a cycle involving exploration of the problem, creation of possible solutions and testing of those solutions. The cycle is repeated many times to refine the proposed solutions. For large and complex systems (and even the "simplest" computer system is complex), there is another dimension. The system as a whole is too complex for all its facets to be treated together during a single design process, so that there has to be some way of breaking the problem into smaller problems. Figure 2.23 illustrates the basic idea.

The difficulty lies in identifying suitable sub-problems. An obvious approach is to *partition* a complex system into subsystems, e.g. in designing a car one looks at the engine, the steering, the transmission, and the body as separate problems, and tackles them separately. Each of these can, in turn, be broken down, so that with the transmission, the gearbox, the drive shaft and the differential can be considered separately.

The danger in this, is that one loses sight of the problem as a whole, so that one finishes up with a thirty tonne truck with the brakes from a small car.

We tackle this by introducing the idea of *conceptual levelling*, in which the level of a problem in a conceptual hierarchy (in this case, our breakdown into sub-problems) dictates the nature (in essence, the amount of detail) of the solution. We do look at the whole problem (e.g. the overall design of the car), and at each of the larger subproblems (e.g. the transmission), but in less detail than the smallest sub-problems. This means that we develop an overall design for the car (how it will look, how we expect it to behave, what features it will have, the engine power), and develop it by doing more detailed design work on each of the subsystems. From time to time, we will have to return to the overall

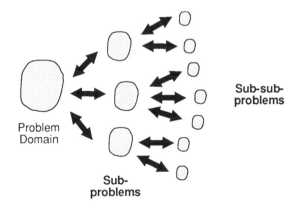

Problem Domain

Sub-problems

Sub-sub-problems

Figure 2.23 Breaking a problem into smaller problems.

design, either because discoveries or decisions made at the lower levels impact on the overall design, or because we want to ensure that everything still fits together.

Conceptual levelling allows us to concentrate on the "important" aspects of the problem first, and leave the detail until later.

Figure 2.24(a) illustrates this approach. Approaches such as *top-down* development adopt this approach, but are much more rigid, as they specify that the higher levels must be completed before the more detailed sub-problems are considered. As we pointed out earlier in the chapter, approaches of this kind are excessively constrained.

The starting point of this design process is a broad-brush solution to the whole problem. Sometimes, this is inappropriate. Figures 2.24(b) and (c) show two other ways in which we might get started.

If we have problems in understanding a problem, we *nibble* at it. We try to look at it from a number of points of view, and eventually we find a sub-problem area that we are confident to tackle, and which we hope will give us a lead on the problem as a whole. We develop solutions in this area, and gradually spread to other areas. At some point, our understanding has reached a stage where we can pull back and see the problem as a whole. This usually involves a total rethink of what we were doing. Other approaches can then take over.

This book was written in this way. We started from the end-product: what sort of systems did we want people to produce. This involved building a framework for user documentation (Chapter 7) and for the dialogue model (Chapters 4 and 6). We then worked backwards by thinking about the sorts of processes needed to design and test the user-interface, and about how we could explain them. At some point in this process, we rethought significant aspects of our approach, because we realised that we had been failing to place sufficient emphasis on key parts of the design process (in particular the visualisation of ideas). Suddenly carefully drawn diagrams using graphics software began to give way to sketches and cartoons, and significant restructuring took place. After this, we dropped into a design-test loop for the book as a whole: we prepared a draft version (a prototype) of the book, and tested it by using it ourselves and getting colleagues to use it in a number of courses, by observing and obtaining feedback about problems, confusions and omissions, and using this information to rethink and rewrite significant parts of the book.

In other problems, certain sub-problems are *critical*. In an aircraft design, solution of an airflow problem around a wingtip may be crucial to any further development of an established design. Hence it makes sense to tackle this problem first, before any work is done on any other part of the project. Once the critical problems are solved, then the remainder of the problem can be broken down in another way. This approach differs from nibbling in that the critical areas are well-defined, and represent difficult areas in what may otherwise be a straightforward problem, rather than being "easy" lines of approach.

Sub-problems are not necessarily subsystems. They can also represent separate processes in the solution of a problem at the same conceptual level. The dialogue design methodology outlined below incorporates this feature. Looking at the system as a whole,

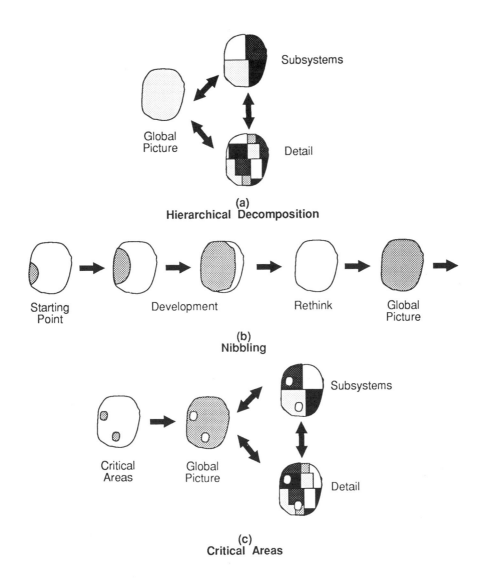

Figure 2.24 Strategies for large systems.

we ask that firstly, the designer *visualises* possible solutions to the problem, and then *abstract* from those pictures of the system a set of objects and actions to constitute a formal dialogue model. The visualisation and the abstraction both constitute sub-problems, and are best separated because they involve different ways of thinking. This does not mean, of course, that all the visualisation must be done before any abstraction begins. More likely, the designer will move to and fro between the two processes many times.

The differences between different strategies reflect the choice of sub-problems and the order in which they are solved. Different problems require different strategies, and it is up to the designer to decide how they want to tackle a particular problem.

2.4   User-Interface Design and Implementation

2.4.1   Dialogue Design Steps

In the last section, we discussed the design process in considerable detail. In dialogue design, the most important aspect is the development of the conceptual model. This consists of three stages:

- *Visualisation*, in which the main features of the model are developed, usually in the form of a series of sketches.
- *Abstraction*, in which the model is expressed in the form of a set of objects and actions.
- *Detailing*, where the form of the presentation of these objects and actions to the user is decided.

A prototype of the system is then built, during which stage the precise syntax of the interaction is decided. Following testing of the prototype and revision of the design, the final system can be built.

These steps are summarised in Figure 2.25. The visualisation step was the basis of our airline timetable example, and will be discussed further in Chapter 6. Testing strategies will be discussed in more detail in Chapter 3. We will discuss the object/action model in more detail in Chapter 4, give guide-lines for dialogue syntax in Chapter 5, and then use these to discuss the abstraction, detailing and prototyping steps in Chapter 6.

The final stage in the software development is the implementation of the software. Under this heading, we include the program design, the coding of the programs, and the design and implementation of the database or file store (if it does not already exist). The program structure is dictated to a significant extent both by the dialogue structure and by the need to map the objects used in the dialogue on to often quite different underlying database structures (e.g. a relational database). These issues are discussed in Chapter 9.

We have pointed out the need for any system development process to take account of the fact that the initial requirements specification is not and cannot be expected to be

Design Stage	Design Outcomes	Tests
Visualisation	Sketches of possible solutions	Do these solutions "look right"? Do they solve the right problem?
Abstraction	A set of objects (with attributes) and actions on those objects.	Is the set of objects complete? Are all the attributes included? Can the actions be used to perform the functions of the system?
Detailing	Detailed representations of the objects and actions	Do these representations look right? Do they contain enough information? Are they usable to perform the functions of the system? Do they conform to guide-lines and standards?
Prototyping	Detailed design and implementation of screens	User interaction with system – screen layouts, usability of actions and dialogue structure
Construction	Program design and implementation	Correctness of results Reliability, performance, reusability Modifiability, maintainability.

Figure 2.25 Dialogue design steps.

static. Although this specification often looks very detailed and precise, it is not. There are always large areas of vagueness and uncertainty. As the system develops, the users' ideas about what is required will become clearer, with consequent changes in requirements.

This methodology is designed to facilitate this evolution of the users' requirements by emphasising the expression and testing of design concepts at the earliest possible stage in the process. It is quick and easy to discuss and change simple sketches, whether of a visualisation of a conceptual model, of a detailed representation of that model, or of actual screens. By the time a prototype is developed, the testing of a range of different concepts has become difficult, but most of the detail of representation and interaction within a given concept can be tested effectively. By taking this approach, the largest possible range of design options can be explored, with the minimum of effort and expense.

2.4.2   Documentation Design

The design and production of the documentation goes hand-in-hand with the design and development of the software. Although at the very beginning of the design process, some idea of the dialogue design is needed before much meaningful work can be done on documentation, it is crucial that it is not left until after the dialogue design is complete.

The reason for this is that, in attempting to explain how a system works, one often has ideas about how to improve its working. These can range from clarification of a conceptual model to a realisation that the use of a particular keystroke is inconsistent with its use elsewhere in the system. The implication of this is that documentation should be kept in step with the dialogue design and implementation, e.g. one should be documenting the conceptual model (e.g. by preparing a draft of the overview manual) as it is being developed, and documenting the detailed operation of the system (i.e. how to drive the system with the mouse and keyboard) while the prototype is being developed. Since written documentation is often far more understandable by the users than much of the more technical documentation (e.g. the class definitions used in Chapter 4), it also provides a far more powerful way of getting user feedback on design proposals, and so assisting in ensuring adequate user participation in the design process.

As with the dialogue design, the design of the documentation goes through a number of stages, starting with the development of a documentation plan which says what documentation is needed, followed by the design of particular documents, e.g. the selection of organisation and subject matter for a user manual (expressed as a Table of Contents), and the development of a series of draft versions of these documents, which can be refined until the final version is complete. These issues are discussed in Chapter 7.

2.4.3   Implementation of the Completed System

The last step is the implementation of the system itself in the workplace. This is preceded by acceptance testing of the system by the users, who look at the system as a whole and decide whether it is satisfactory. The actual implementation involves providing access to the software (e.g. by moving it to a "production" environment on a central machine or by distributing and installing copies on personal computers or networks), distributing manuals, training users, and putting amended working procedures into operation.

Personal Timetable System

One of the applications that we wish to use as an example is the *Personal Timetable* problem. We consider the case of a student in a tertiary educational institution working out their timetable for the current semester (or term or year). The student is doing

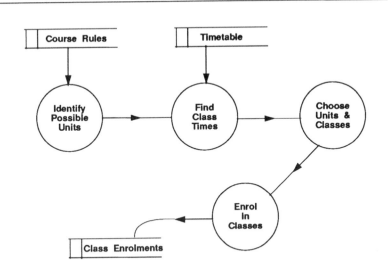

Figure 2.26 Derivation of a personal
timetable.

a specific course, which permits a choice of *units* to be undertaken (subject to various
course rules and prerequisite requirements). Within each unit are a number of
classes. Some, e.g. lectures, are given one for all students attending the unit, but others, e.g. tutorials, are designed for small groups, and there are alternative times available. However, classes such as tutorials also have an enrolment limit. Once the
tutorial is full, it is not available for subsequent enrolments.

The data flow diagram in Figure 2.26 illustrates the processes through which
the student goes.

Identify Possible Units: The student uses the course rules (e.g. from a published Faculty Handbook) to determine the units that they could undertake in the current
semester. The rules usually contain guide-lines like a "normal course progression",
i.e. which units (either specific units or a class of unit) should be done in a given semester. Specific units may also have prerequisites which may or may not have been
done. These can either preclude a unit from being taken, or make doing the prerequisite unit a necessity if the unit is to be taken in a later semester. At this stage, the
student normally has some preferences, e.g. because a unit is compulsory, because it
is part of a major sequence being undertaken, because it is a prerequisite, because it
seems interesting, or because it is known to be easy.

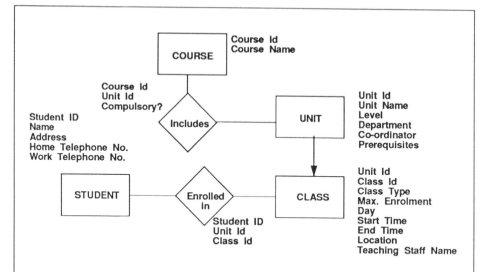

Figure 2.27 Data for personal timetable.

Find Available Class Times: This involves consulting the institution's timetable to find out what classes are available and at what times. Some units may not be offered, and so are immediately eliminated.

Choose Units and Classes: The basic requirement is to choose a set of classes that do not clash (i.e. they are not on at the same times). However, there is more to it than this. Although academics like to believe that students choose units on purely academic grounds, the timetable often plays a major role, e.g. a part-time student may opt for a unit whose lectures are in the evening, and a full-time student avoid it for the same reason. Work, family or recreational considerations (e.g. a part-time job on a particular day, the need to be home to feed the kids, or football training) will make certain times undesirable or impossible. Different people prefer different groupings of classes: some like to "block" their timetable, attempting to create long periods of free time (often whole days), while others prefer an even spread of classes over the week. The location of a class can also be important, e.g. in a multi-campus institution, where the student will probably want to minimise travel time, but will also need to take it into account when considering possible clashes. Finally, a student may like a particular lecturer or tutor, and dislike another, and use this as a factor in selecting a unit or a class.

Enrol in Classes: Having made their decision, the student must enrol in the units and classes of their choice. Typically, this involves making a formal enrolment for the units (or changing an existing provisional enrolment) with the institution's central administration, and putting their name down on tutorial lists held by the departments running the chosen units.

The system that we will design is one in which the student uses a computer to assist them in deciding on their personal timetable. The information to be held on the computer is shown in the data model in Figure 2.27. It consists of the timetable information (i.e. data about courses, units and classes), student information, and data about enrolments in classes. The class enrolments are needed because knowledge of which classes are full is required. Students are assumed to have been assigned a unique identity number (*Student Id*). The other data kept is basic information needed by a lecturer or tutor to contact a student. Courses and Units have unique identifiers (*Course Id, Unit Id*), in the form of a number or mnemonic, and each class has an identifier (*Class Id*) which is unique only within the unit, e.g. L1 might be the first lecture for the week, and T3 is tutorial number 3, so to fully identify a class, the Unit Id and Class Id must be given. Strictly, the *Class Type* field is not needed here, because the Class Id includes the class type.

The significant feature of the data model is the information that it does not hold: the enormous amount of data on individual personal preferences and constraints. Although some gross features of these (e.g. the provision of evening lectures to suit the majority of part-time students) can be taken into account by the institution's timetabler, most are not known and cannot be known to them. Hence any attempt to use the computer to assign students to classes (e.g. based on unit enrolments already made, with simple criteria such as the avoidance of clashes) is bound to be unsatisfactory. Incorporation of more sophisticated criteria is virtually impossible, since each student has their own set of trade-offs which are impossible to quantify. Hence, it is better to let the student build their own timetable, incorporating those factors as they see fit.

The aim of the computer system is to make this task as easy as possible by providing ready access to the timetable data, and by permitting a trial and error process in which the student can try various options until they achieve a satisfactory timetable. Note that there is no attempt to develop a "best" timetable, because we do not know the criteria.

The user is likely to use the system only once or twice a year, so its method of use should be immediately obvious. However, it can be assumed that the user uses a computer for other tasks, and so is familiar with the dialogue style to be used, i.e. the use of menus, dialogue boxes, windows and a mouse.

There is a specific problem with this system: it is very likely to have been specified by people who are not the actual users, e.g. by members of the institution's administrative staff rather than by students. The implication of this is that great care will be needed to discuss the system with typical "real" users at each stage in its progress, otherwise it might turn out to be unusable, either because it really is, or because the users think that it has been foisted on them.

This problem is part of a much larger timetabling problem, encompassing decisions on unit availability, development of the main timetable (i.e. what classes are held when and where and who teaches them), staff allocation, room and equipment bookings, examination timetabling, and a number of other issues.

Crossword Designer Requirements Analysis

In this section we describe the ideas and steps leading to the Crossword Designer program. This description is a narrative of the steps involved. Formal systems specification techniques were seen as inappropriate because there are few data items and processes. The problem is more one of how the user wants to perform the processes. For this reason, we developed a command language as a thinking tool to help us understand the actions. The description here is an example of the way in which the design process is driven by the increased understanding and changing needs of the end user of the package.

A Sample Crossword

To understand this application you have to understand crosswords. Figure 2.28 shows a small crossword. Some of the words and clues relate to the subject matter of this book. The clues are cryptic – which means all is not as it seems. (The solution is on the next page.) When you look at the crossword notice the pattern for the grid. It is symmetric about the diagonal. Notice also that over half the letters occur in more than one word. This style of crossword is the so-called English style as opposed to the American style which has all its letters occurring in two words. See Figure 2.29 for an example of an American pattern.

Figure 2.30 shows a set of crossed words. Note the absence of pattern and the large number of black squares. This crossed words style is un-aesthetic and the few intersections make it difficult to solve. It is hard to classify it as a genuine crossword.

Idea for the Package

Programs, products and systems arise from a perceived need by some person or persons. In this case the "need" came from a frustrated attempt at creating a crossword

Across
1. Doctor throws thousand dice (5)
4. Solid computer output (5)
7. Buried and look towards boundary (9)
8. Backwards scoundrel is black (3)
9. Shows up less load (7)
11. In a tame moving screen (7)
12. Unhappy South Australian daughter (3)
13. Computing career is almost a holiday (9)
16. Let it disguise ownership (5)
17. The power of two pieces of gold (5)

Down
1. New Zealand mother and I (3)
2. Endless bound insect helps solve linear equations (11)
3. Blended or a cell parrot (7)
4. Tasman or Australian Education System goes backward (3)
5. He is trying in chapter three (4,7)
6. Described deed includes French ending (7)
8. Public service runs on this vehicle? (3,4)
10. Green Ad blows up (7)
14. Single digit (3)
15. Backwards hundred miles an hour sounds twisted (3)

Figure 2.28 Sample crossword.

Figure 2.29 American crossword.

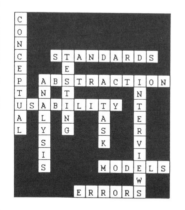

Figure 2.31 Crossed words.

M	E	D	I	C		S	O	U	N	D
A		E		O		E		S		E
I	N	T	E	R	F	A	C	E		F
		E		E				R		I
T	A	R		L	I	G	H	T	E	N
E		M		L		R		E		E
A	N	I	M	A	T	E		S	A	D
C		N				N		T		
A		A	V	O	C	A	T	I	O	N
R		N		N		D		N		O
T	I	T	L	E		E	I	G	H	T

Figure 2.30 Solution to 2.28.

many years ago. One of us spent a long time, as an undergraduate, trying to make a crossword for a magazine. After an inordinate amount of time the crossword was created, but as a set of crossed words, not as a proper newspaper style crossword. As well as this desire to overcome a long felt frustration we felt a tool to help people make up crosswords would be a useful teaching tool. We also believed it would make a good example for our courses.

We floated the idea of making a crossword program with a group of students who decided to attempt the task. They came up with a solution which we used as a prototype for the solution described here.

Other Systems

Before we started we examined existing crossword programs. There were three in the public domain and two commercially available packages. All operated in the same way. They made crossed words by the user typing words into a grid. There was no attempt to help the person find words, although we thought this was the hard part of making a crossword. The underlying model for creating the crossword was the idea of crossed words, in contrast to filling in an existing pattern of word slots. There was also an emphasis on solving existing crosswords on the computer, as opposed to creating a new crossword.

We thought this was an inappropriate medium for presenting crosswords for solution. Putting a crossword on the screen made the task much more complicated and added nothing to the puzzle. Crosswords were designed for a paper medium and it becomes a different game on the computer. We felt that solving crosswords on a computer was boring and incongruous.

Another program we had written gave us some ideas. In that program we searched lists of words for words with particular letters. We discovered that finding these words was fast and relatively easy to do.

What is a Crossword?

Before we started we tried to abstract the idea of a crossword. What exactly makes a crossword and why do 50,000,000 people try to solve one each day? The things that seem to make them interesting are:

- Finding answers to clues. This is also evidenced by the popularity of quiz games and Trivial Pursuit.
- Solving one clue helps you with the next by giving you letters for other words.
- A clear goal for the solver, good indications of how well you are doing, and feedback on success (words fit each other).
- The patterns are pleasing. Compare Figures 2.30 and 2.31 for symmetric and unsymmetric patterns.
- The essential parts of a crossword are the clues, the words, the interconnections of the words, and the pattern formed by the words. These give us good ideas for our objects.

What Should a Crossword Compiler Program Do?

A hard part of making a crossword, by hand, is finding appropriate words that fit together. Finding good clues is also difficult, but in a different way. It requires imagination and has twists and humour. Making patterns is tedious and error prone, and printing is relatively difficult. Computers are good at calculation, sorting, finding things and printing. We can best assist the crossword compiler by concentrating on finding words, creating patterns, and printing. Finding clues requires more human capabilities and is not as good an initial candidate for computer assistance.

Looking at existing programs and analysing for usability showed that they gave little help for "real" crosswords as opposed to a set of crossed words. About the only thing they did was help print, if you had already created a crossword.

We created the program by following the steps outlined in 2.25. A more detailed description of the dialogue and testing is given in later chapters. The objects in the crossword are the grid, a slot, words and clues.

Summary

Computers are tools which people use to perform tasks. If the user of the system feels that it is too difficult to use, gives wrong answers or does not perform the tasks required, then the system is useless. Thus the system design must be based around those areas to which the user directly relates, i.e. the user-interface; and the user must be an integral part of the design process and not merely a spectator. As the system develops, the user's understanding of the system and what it can do will also develop, and so their requirements will change. The design methodology must allow for this. The actual designers are commonly computer professionals, working in close co-operation with the users, in much the same way that an architect designs a building.

Traditional design methodologies (e.g. Structured Analysis) lack the flexibility needed to cope with changing user requirements. Instead, an evolutionary approach is required which allows the incorporation of the users' increasing understanding of the problem, through the use of extensive testing of the conceptual models of the system, at a stage where they are easy (and cheap) to change.

The starting point is an initial requirements specification, which attempts both to describe what the user wants the system to do and give some idea of the manner in which the system would perform them. There are a wide variety of different techniques, some formal, some informal, which can be used for this specification. The specification is not static, but will be refined and changed during the design process.

Any design activity consists of three main processes: the exploration of the problem to be solved; the generation of ideas for possible solutions; and the evaluation of those solutions to see if they will work, and to select one or more of the "best" solutions for further work. These activities are repeated in a cycle of constant refinement until a satisfactory solution is obtained.

Exploration is a mental exercise aimed at coming to grips with the problem. The techniques used have two main aims: to organise and relate different aspects of the problem; and to look at the problem in as many different ways as possible. They include: drawing diagrams, reformulation, abstraction, working through specific examples, looking at related problems.

The generation of possible solutions is the creative part of design. It is best thought of as a leap of the imagination in which a whole lot of disparate ideas come together into a coherent whole. Techniques to stimulate the imagination include brainstorming, free association, attribute lists and analogies. However, design does not take place in a vacuum. Most solutions are refinements of existing solutions, thus allowing us to build on the good ideas already developed and to avoid repeating previous mistakes. However, it also poses the problems of rigidity and of inappropriate use of past solutions. The solutions must then be expressed in an appropriate manner, e.g. through drawings or a prototype, so that they can be tested to see if they will meet the users' requirements. Testing does not have to be postponed until the building of a prototype or of the final system – even very preliminary design sketches can be tested by showing them to users and obtaining reactions. Testing is a major source not only of problems to be fixed but also of new ideas to begin another cycle of design.

For large and complex systems, the problem has to be broken into smaller problems. Techniques of doing this include: the partitioning of a complex system into subsystems; conceptual levelling, in which the level of a problem in a conceptual hierarchy dictates the nature of the solution; nibbling, where we find a sub-problem area that we are confident to tackle, and which we hope will give us a lead on the problem as a whole; and the isolation and solution of critical sub-problems.

Since it is the user-interface that the user perceives as being the system, this must be designed first. There are two components to the user-interface: the dialogue through which the user interacts with the computer to perform the functions of the system; and the documentation which describes what the system is supposed to do and explains how to do it. The dialogue and the documentation must be designed in conjunction with each other.

Dialogue design goes through a number of stages:

- *Visualisation*, in which the main features of the model are developed, usually in the form of a series of sketches.
- *Abstraction*, in which the model is expressed in the form of a set of objects and actions.
- *Detailing*, where the form of the presentation of these objects and actions to the user is decided.
- *Prototyping*, in which a prototype system is built and tested.
- *Implementation*, which involves the design of other parts of the system, e.g. program and file designs, followed by the building and implementation of the system.

These are not a rigid series of steps, where each must be completed before the next is started, but rather a framework describing the types of process required, and a rough order in which they are likely to occur.

The design of the documentation also goes through a number of stages: development of a documentation plan; design of particular documents; the development of draft versions; and their refinement until the final version is complete.

The system must then be implemented in the workplace. This includes acceptance testing, moving the system to a production environment, distributing manuals, training users, and putting amended working procedures into operation.

Exercises

1. The best way to understand what designers do is to talk to some practitioners in the field. Try to locate a graphic designer, an industrial designer, an architect, a stage designer and ask them what they mean by design.

2. Driving around a strange city (or an unfamiliar part of your own city) using the current style of map is very difficult. Conduct a brainstorming session to come up with better ways of helping a motorist to find their way around.

3. Draw analogies between:

- An oil tanker and a spreadsheet.
- An orchard and a word processor.
- A student enrolment system and an ocean liner.

4. Draw the way in which a library borrowing system works (from the borrower's point of view).

5. Select a piece of software with which you are familiar and draw a storyboard showing the operation of a particular function.

6. How would you adapt the interface of a spreadsheet for use in a payroll program?

7. How would you adapt the Crossword Designer's grid creation dialogue to become an icon editor?

8. Many large organisations, such as subways and telephone companies, issue prepaid plastic money cards for use for their services. Think of other ways they could exploit this form of money.

9. The so-called paperless office often seems to generate more paper rather than less. Think of ways to reduce the amount of paper used within organisations.

10. This book gives suggestions on designing user-interfaces. Draw a picture or a diagram that illustrates the process of user-interface design and that summarises the main ideas in the book.

11. Global warming may cause many Pacific Island nations to disappear because of rising water levels. Think of some solutions to this problem.

12. Examine your wallet or handbag and count the number of cards or forms of identification you carry with you. Many of these are used for identification purposes to interface with computer systems. Think of other ways of fulfilling this identification function and examine the advantages and disadvantages of such systems.

Chapter 3

Usability Testing

Usability testing is a cornerstone of user-interface design. Testing drives our design, gives us a way to evaluate it and shows its success or failure. This chapter defines usability testing by discussing what it is and how to do it. It gives some guide-lines for designing usability tests, it outlines the different dimensions to testing and discusses why usability testing is a crucial part of user-interface design. Testing can become the basis for developing and extending design guide-lines and we outline how to build upon testing experience.

Testing	Things to test	*Testing methods*	Task analysis
	Users to test		Questionnaires
	Approaches to take		Interviews
			Against standards
			Against guide-lines
			Aesthetic judgement
When to test	Pre-design Testing		Observations of free
	Testing concepts		use
	Testing task design		
	Testing task definition	*Benchmarks*	Existing system
	Implementation		Competitive systems
			Manual systems
			Absolute scale

Figure 3.1 Overview of usability testing.

Figure 3.2 Same parts arranged differently.

While there is no single definition for usability, our ideas are based on what makes a good tool. A usable tool is one in which the user has control, it becomes transparent to the user, it is flexible and it is easy to learn. In this chapter we apply these ideas more specifically to computer systems. We know, for example, that some artefacts are hard to use while others fit the tasks to be done. Our favourite editor for program development is about the simplest of editors on the market. It has few features, but those it does have work well and it only does the tasks we need. Comparing it with others for functionality and even for simplicity in certain operations it is not the best, yet for our purposes it is the most usable of products. This fact that usability is more than a simple summation of parts and includes the total environment of the user makes it difficult to provide an all encompassing definition. However, there are common strategies and techniques that apply to most usability testing and these form the framework for testing.

Figure 3.1 summarises the points discussed in this chapter. The different sections overlap because usability is a property of the whole artefact. It is a property like beauty. We might say that a person with eyes a certain distance apart is more likely to be handsome, and we can measure other characteristics to indicate whether a person is handsome, but the final judgement is made by a consideration of how all the parts fit together (Figure 3.2).

Notwithstanding the fundamental difficulty of defining usability, we know certain properties enhance usability as certain features increase the likelihood of a person being

Functionality	Can the **user** do the required tasks?
Understanding	Does the **user** understand the system?
Timing	Are the **user** tasks done within a reasonable time?
Environment	Do the tasks fit in with other parts of the **user** environment?
Safety	Will the system harm the **user**, either psychologically or physically?
Errors	Does the **user** make too many errors?
Comparisons	Is the system comparable with other ways the **user** might have of doing the same task?
Standards	Is the system similar to others the **user** might use?

Figure 3.3 Usability considerations.

handsome. In this chapter we expand on these points, give an example set of usability ideas and show how we applied the ideas to the testing of Crossword Designer. The tests used for any particular project will vary depending on the product, the environment and the users, but the principles given here apply to most situations.

3.1   What is Usability?

Shackel (1990) gives a definition of usability in terms of goals and operational criteria which can have numerical values specified and measured. This is a useful approach and where possible try to measure and test performance, but for our purposes it is too restrictive. We define another set of attributes (Figure 3.3) expressed in qualitative terms and which encompasses more factors. This gives a way of classifying and describing features that make for usable products even though it still falls into the reductionist trap of assuming the sum of the parts is the same as the whole. Reducing the problem to smaller parts helps us understand, but it does not tell if the whole is satisfactory.

When we examine usability of any device we find many parts may be imperfect and it is still quite usable, yet if we have one thing, often minor, wrong then the product is unusable. We once rented an excellent apartment with an *ensuite* bathroom with all the latest fittings. The bathroom had all the components required of a bathroom and each worked well and each was usable. Unfortunately when we took a shower the water drained onto the floor and the slope of the floor took the water into the bedroom. This made the shower difficult and messy to use as we had to find ways of stopping the water flooding outside. In this case a small implementation fault, which cost nothing to rectify if it had been addressed in the initial construction, made the whole system almost unusable.

A usable product is one that users find satisfactory for the tasks for which it was designed. However, measuring user satisfaction is difficult as it is a complex function which depends on the users, the tasks and the environment.

This working definition gives a basis for defining usability testing. To test we have to include the user in the testing. We have to observe people doing things with the product and we have to make judgements on how well those tasks are done. We can express this in three principles of usability testing.

- Usability testing requires a user.
- Usability testing is done by observing people doing tasks with the product being tested.
- Usability measures are imprecise and there is no prescription that tells us how usable an artefact is. Interpreting observations always requires judgement and will vary depending on the circumstances.

3.2   Examples of Usability Testing

Usability testing checks to see how well a user can operate the system. This section illustrates how to test the points listed in Figure 3.3.

To test the airline timetable system shown in Chapter 2 for *functionality,* see if a user can find a flight from Darwin to Canberra. If a flight exists, it must be possible to obtain the information in a form the user can understand. We can ask users to do a set of tasks and measure how well they perform those tasks. If they cannot find a flight from Darwin to Canberra, even though it exists, the system has failed its first important usability test. Functionality is the first and most important usability test. If the system does not let the user perform the required tasks then it fails.

The user *understands* a system if they have a conceptual model that explains how it works. Test this by giving users tasks that require an understanding of the conceptual model. If they have an incorrect model they will misinterpret many operations. The timetable system only shows flights that enable a connection to be made on the same day. In the map of Australia in Chapter 2, because we ask for flights to Canberra, only the flights from Darwin that connect to the destination on the same day, are shown leaving Darwin. If we now ask people to find a flight from Darwin to Canberra leaving after midday, and allow a night stopover in Melbourne, many other solutions are possible. The user finds these by treating the flight as two separate flights, the first from Darwin to Melbourne and the second from Melbourne to Canberra. People will do this successfully if they understand how the system is structured. If people have the wrong conceptual model they will not break the flight into two parts.

We test for a reasonable *time* by timing how long people take to do tasks. What is a reasonable time? This depends on the circumstance, but for the airline timetable system, it becomes unusable when the time taken is such that people will prefer to do the task in a different way. In this example a reasonable time will be less than the time to do the same task with a paper timetable.

Figure 3.4 Different words - same function.

Do the tasks fit the user's *environment?* The airline's timetable system is unusable if the user does not have easy and quick access to a computer. If it requires them to walk up two flights of steps and then queue for a machine the system will not be used.

Will the system *harm* the user? Physical harm through repetition strain injury caused by keyboarding is a possibility with some ill-designed systems. If we require people to type for long periods of time, under pressure and without breaks, they may develop physical pain. Psychological harm is more difficult to measure, but some things such as using emotive terms like Abort, Kill, Execute, Terminate or by causing the system to emit loud noises when an error occurs, may well cause psychological damage. They certainly do no good and should be removed. If there are any doubts or concerns discuss these issues with experts in appropriate fields.

We can measure the number of *errors* made when doing given tasks. Sometimes errors are a sign of the user exploring and trying out the limits of the system; this might be a good feature as we wish to encourage exploration and learning through discovery. However, if the errors interfere with user tasks then we need to correct the system. With the timetable system, if the user often selects the wrong city the first time, often presses the wrong key whenever they want to print a timetable, fails to find the cheapest and shortest route, then we should correct the system.

We can *compare* our computerised timetable with other ways of doing the same task. Perhaps the user can call a travel agent and get them to do the booking for no cost. If this is a viable option then the system may fail the usability test, as it may always be easier (or there may be extra side-benefits) to call someone than to do it yourself − no matter how easy it is to use the computer system.

When we have many applications on a computer, where possible, those applications should look the same and be *similar* in operation. Similarity involves using standards and guide-lines common to all applications. Figure 3.4 shows different words to finish a pop-up dialogue. Use the same words for this function throughout all our applications − not choose different words in different applications or within an application. This makes it easier for users to move between applications. If the same operations use the same names and look the same, the user will have little trouble transferring knowledge from one application to the next. This makes all systems with standard style interfaces more usable.

3.3 The Idea of Testing

Usability is only one of the forms of testing done on computer products. When we test we test for different system attributes. A common breakdown of attributes from Yourdon and Constantine (1979) is:

- Reliability.
- Maintainability.
- Modifiability.
- Efficiency.
- Usability.

Building a successful system requires testing for all these characteristics as all affect usability. Reliability tells us that the program will work, as expected, when we want it to, and will give dependable results. Maintainability means that if something goes wrong we can correct it, while modifiability gives confidence that we can adapt the program for changing circumstances. Efficiency tells us the program will not take an excessive amount of resources to operate. Usability, although last in the list, is the first testing to do. It gives assurance that building a reliable, maintainable, easily changed, efficient product is worth doing as our users can and will use the product.

The Pencil

A reliable, easily maintained, flexible, user controlled, cheap and easy to use word processor.

The benchmark against which we measure all word processors.

Figure 3.5 Word processor benchmark.

In this text, we concentrate on usability testing. In most systems development methodologies usability testing tends to be left to the last, and then done in a relatively *adhoc* manner. It should be the first testing done, be a disciplined effort, and continue throughout development. There is little point in other forms of testing if users cannot use the product.

Usability testing is the critical evaluation technique for successful computer products. It has the virtues of concentrating on the reason for having a computer product, namely to do something for a user. Even though it is imprecise and may give ambiguous answers it is always worth doing as the application of the techniques assist the design process and gives us guidance on improving and developing systems.

Some of the most visible failures of the modern age, namely some architectural projects of the twentieth century (Wolfe 1981), such as the high-rise low-cost apartments built in the 1960s, 70s and 80s or the impractical glass office boxes of the same period, arose because designers ignored the wishes of the ultimate users. No definitive history of computing disasters has been written, but when it is, the stories of designers who ignored the end users and failed to carry out appropriate usability testing will figure prominently.

3.4   Approaches to Testing

We can get an idea on how to test computer products by looking at the testing of consumer products. To see how this is done look at a consumer magazine that tests everyday goods – such as *Choice* or *Consumer Reports*. When *Choice* tested dishwashers they

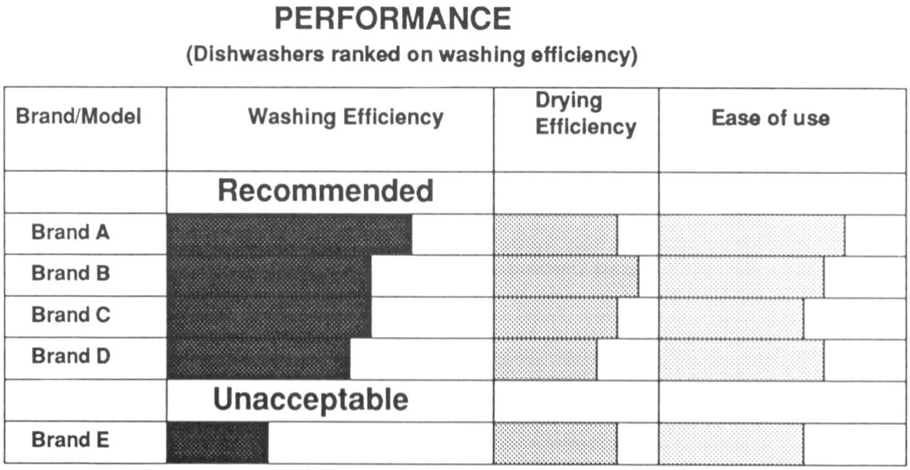

PERFORMANCE
(Dishwashers ranked on washing efficiency)

Brand/Model	Washing Efficiency	Drying Efficiency	Ease of use
	Recommended		
Brand A			
Brand B			
Brand C			
Brand D			
	Unacceptable		
Brand E			

Figure 3.6 Testing dishwashers.

looked at the things that most concerned the user of a dishwasher. Did the device clean dishes, could you follow the instructions, was it done in a reasonable time for a reasonable cost, could it fit in the kitchen and not make too much noise, was it safe and how did it compare to doing the dishes by hand? There are direct parallels with the testing objectives for dishwasher testing and the points at the start of this chapter. There are also direct parallels in the methodology *Choice* takes to do the tests. They do laboratory testing under controlled conditions, run surveys and do tests in people's kitchens. They summarise the results as in Figure 3.6 to make the results accessible to their readers.

In this testing and all other testing we have certain conditions that always apply. These are:

- Something to test.
- An idea of what it is we are testing.
- A method of testing.

To test a dishwasher we have to buy one, work out what is important and then devise a way of testing those characteristics. The following sections expand on these ideas as they apply to computer products. They give a few of the available methods, but as a general rule better results are obtained if tests are done simply, often and during development, rather than waiting until the product is completed, then trying to test exhaustively.

3.4.1   Something to Test

To test a computer product we must have it, or a substitute representation, available. Testing cannot be done unless there is something to test. This is easy when we have a completed product, but it is expensive to create a complete system before doing any usability testing. An important principle in creating usable systems is to test often and early. Try to test from the first day of design.

In the first stages of a project we only have ideas and we are often not even sure of the users. To have something to test we produce, as part of the design process, partial representations of the complete solution and use these as test vehicles. Chapter 2, on design, argues for quick sketching of possible solutions. Test these sketches with users to see which ones match their concept of the problem. Do similar

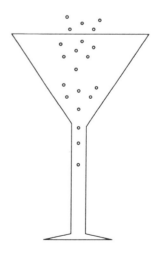

Figure 3.7 Eliminate distractors when testing.

exercises throughout system development and you will find that most testing is done with substitute or partial system representations.

As well as being expensive, a complete system is often not the best vehicle for testing. The complexity of a complete system often interferes with the testing procedure. One strategy in testing is to isolate and change a particular variable on its own. This becomes difficult with complete systems. If we wanted to test the taste of wine we would not test in different restaurants, with different foods, and with different companions. To judge a wine we eliminate distractors by setting up a special wine tasting. In the wine tasting wines are served in standard glasses with no external identification. The surroundings, at best, are austere. Similarly, when testing parts of computer systems, try to eliminate distractors by simplifying or by testing separate elements of the problem.

Instead of creating a complete system for testing, some of the following approaches should be tried first:

- Looking at competitive systems.
- Investigating previous systems.
- Building paper models.
- Creating video mock-ups.
- Creating interface prototypes.

Competitive Systems

Competitive systems can be other computer systems or other ways of doing the same task. These systems are relatively cheap to obtain, although they suffer the disadvantages of complexity. Running through a set of usability tests, such as those we give later in this chapter, is an excellent source of ideas on both what to do, and what not to do. Competitive systems have the advantage in that they exist and are used in the work environment. If a product already exists, and it does the same job as the one being designed, then perhaps it is better not to create yet another one. However, there are many cases where products exist that do a similar task, but perhaps in different ways. Analysing and doing

```
KI/TN/KJ

A22MAYDRWCBR0900

AV:DRW CBR 22MAY NOOP

0700 1325 TN 565 *DRWSYD FJYHM 733 M WE23 AAAAL

1550 1630 TN   7 SYDCBR FJYHM 72S S      AAAAL
```

Figure 3.8 Part of an airline booking dialogue.

usability testing on competitive products will help the understanding of the problem, show the differences in systems, and indicate how users operate this type of system. To tune usability measures, work out the mechanics of testing and apply them later to the product.

If designing a travel system, then investigating an existing travel agent's computer system should be a first step. Try to get an inexperienced user to try the system. Most on-line airline systems are difficult to operate and require considerable training and getting a novice to use it soon shows why this is so. These systems require a knowledge of arcane command language structures, an idea of how flights are connected around the country, and the ability to remember previous results for comparison purposes. Such systems are unusable for untrained operators.

Figure 3.8 is a typical screen input and output for an airline's booking system request. Even if the screen is understandable, it does not give the information needed to make a rational choice of flights. Nowhere does it tell that the flight from Darwin to Sydney goes via Gove, Cairns and Townsville. Nowhere does it tell that this is $100 more expensive than flying via Alice Springs and Adelaide. Nowhere does it give other possibilities. What is needed is the ability to try out different things and to experiment with other arrangements. Problems with this booking system become apparent when observing people trying to make real bookings with real customers. A new system should be designed to overcome some of these problems.

We have suggested exercises at the end of this chapter to give practice at usability testing on existing products.

Previous Systems

A completely new system is rare in most organisations. The tasks required for the new system are either being done with an existing computer system or being done manually. In any systems investigation check the existing system for usability. Doing this is more than an academic exercise. It will give an understanding of what problems to solve. It is an excellent systems investigation tool. Usability testing of existing systems gives a disciplined method for determining system requirements and usability goals.

Paper Models

Paper and blackboard models are the simplest, cheapest, most adaptable and often the most effective tool for usability testing. They are effective because when we use them we can concentrate on one issue at a time. They are simple, cheap and adaptable because of the medium and the way we create them by sketching and drawing. In Chapter 2, we gave examples of the use of this technique in design; you can also use sketches and drawing for testing.

Give people different pictures of the general layout of screens and see if they can understand the overall concept. Get programmers to see how easy it is to translate the tasks into programs by showing them a picture of the structure of the tasks. Write descriptions of tasks and ask the users if the descriptions match the tasks to be done.

Most design methodologies use pen and paper to express ideas. In usability testing we take these representations and, as far as possible, we check with the user if the models are reasonable.

Video Mock-ups

The video mock-up is a powerful, relatively cheap way to show the dynamic nature of a user-interface. It allows us to take static pictures and simulate a changing screen. Use a cartooning technique in which videos of pictures are filmed, the filming stopped, the pictures changed, and the filming started again. Doing it carefully makes the resulting video a form of animation.

This is particularly important for those applications where the change in the system display is important. Changes are difficult to explain with either words or static diagrams. In the case of the Crossword Designer we might wish to experiment with different ways of showing the "current slot" by simulating movement. In Figure 3.9, if we film half a second of each of the different items 1,2,3,4 and repeat the pictures another 7 or 8 times and then replay the video we "see" the apparent movement of slots around the perimeter in the first set, the flashing on and off of the second set, and the moving strips in the third.

The video will give a good idea of how the "slot" will look. It is possible to show other ways of highlighting the slot, such as the use of colour or hatching. Making a cartoon style video of some simple drawings will give a good idea of how the system will look. Now ask the users which ones they prefer.

A video can be complex, with cardboard mock-ups of whole terminals and computer systems. This will be much cheaper than building real terminals, and making real dialogues but it will still show users how the system will look.

Prototypes

People use the word prototype to mean different things. In many cases prototypes are sophisticated models of the final system. They may be complete systems, but constructed to throw away after use as a stepping stone to the final implementation. We build them because they are cheaper than building the final system, yet they allow us to test many things as though they were the final system. Other forms of prototyping are where people implement

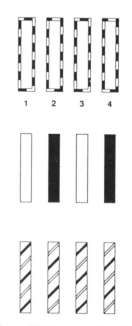

Figure 3.9 Diagrams for video.

representative parts of a system before implementing the whole system. In systems with fifty different tasks perhaps five will be implemented. In a system with a wide geographic distribution perhaps we will implement one fully functional district as a prototype.

For usability testing we do not recommend fully functional prototyping but user-interface prototyping. When building a demonstration user-interface, as described in Chapter 8, do many usability tests as though a complete system was available. One way is the development of the video mock-ups described above. One of the most successful computer programs for personal computers (Figure 3.10) has been the Flight Simulator game. This gives a prototype interface for different aircrafts and allows testing for aircraft navigation and instrumentation procedures. Many procedures can be learnt without ever leaving the ground. The full-scale simulators used by the Air Force and commercial flying schools take simulation of the user-interface as the next step. While these devices are best known for training users they also allow aircraft designers to experiment and test different user-interfaces, without the expense or danger of building and flying a real aircraft.

Similarly, we can build a prototype of the interface for a computer system, but not write any programs or code to implement any part of the system. Doing this is often better than creating fully functional prototypes, as the fully functional systems have a tendency to stay as operational systems with people unwilling to throw them away and treat them as genuine prototypes.

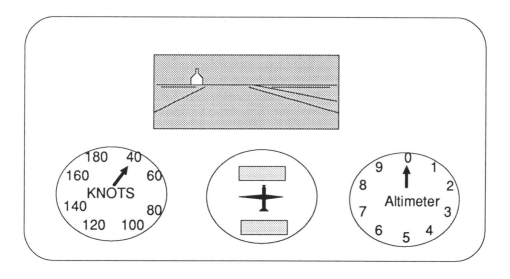

Figure 3.10 Prototype for testing pilots.

---

1. Choose a user task

2. Can I find all the objects to do the required task?

3. Can I recognise the objects?

4. How difficult is it to find the actions for the tasks?

5. When I do an action is there understandable feedback on the action result?

6. How quickly can I do the actions?

7. Are there too many actions to do the task?

8. What mistakes can I make and what happens when I make them?

Figure 3.11 Steps for testing with yourself.

3.4.2   Someone to Test With

As well as something to test we need a user to do the testing. Finding a *real* user is diffi-cult; even defining a *real* user is difficult. Is a user a person who has never seen the appli-cation before, or is a user someone who has used it continuously for twelve months? Once a person has done one test can they now be used for other tests or has the testing procedures made them atypical of the final users? Real users are hard to find and if they are found it is difficult to run controlled experiments using them.

   If people are used in tests, there is a moral obligation to treat them correctly. Use the set of guide-lines in Figure 3.21 to help determine appropriate ethical behaviour.

   Even though we would like to use real users we will have to make do with substi-tutes for most testing. Who and what are these substitute users? Substitute users can be ourselves, other members of our team, members of our family, experts in user-interface design or they can be books of user-interface standards and guide-lines.

   In practice, almost all users, in almost all tests will be substitute users. This does not matter, provided the problem is known and allowed for when interpreting results. In the same way that testing a product substitute can be better than testing a final product, so testing with substitute users can be better than testing with real users. However, at some stage you should test with real users in a real work environment. When this is done issues and points that never arise with substitutes will appear.

The Developer as User

In the same way that programmers can remove most of the logic errors of a program through tests run by themselves, so designers can remove many user problems by testing for usability with themselves as subjects. The main requirement is an appropriate attitude of mind. Try to imagine yourself as a user with a user's knowledge. When designing an interface run through a set of usability tests on yourself. Many designers do this automatically without ever having heard about usability testing. However, formalising the procedure helps guarantee it is done and helps develop the technique. Figure 3.11 gives a set of tests to run against a new piece of dialogue. Later evaluate how well you test with yourself as user, by comparing the efforts with results obtained from testing genuine end users.

Colleagues and other members of a design team can also act as users. Managers, who are not involved in day-to-day development, are a good source of substitute users. This often helps a project in other ways as it keeps management informed of progress and helps them understand the application. People who have moved out of an application area, and no longer have a vested interest in preserving the status quo, are often good substitute users. This type of person knows about the application and is in a position to discuss the new system and the existing system openly.

Current users often have other agendas. They may not wish to change anything as it is too much bother, or they may be afraid of the impact of anything new on their status and work prospects. Consider these aspects in the total system implementation, but isolate them from the user-interface design. On the other hand, real users are the best people to ask because they know the tasks the computer system is going to help with. They are the authorities on usability and they should always be the first consideration.

Experts as Users

Use the organisation's in-house user-interface experts or use external expert consultants. Experts, who see many different products, are often the best substitute users. They help quality control across applications and they can quickly test areas that ordinary users might take many months to discover. Experts testing a word-processing package will try such areas as indexing, importing and exporting data, handling of graphics and different fonts, all areas that new users are unlikely to try.

Experts have more confidence in their opinions and will tell you if something is wrong. Users often believe any problems are problems with themselves and not with the product. How often have we heard people using everyday gadgets say "I cannot use it because I'm not mechanically minded" or "I don't understand mathematics and so I can't use this package". In most cases it is not the person who is at fault; it is the gadget or program. The self-assured, competent user who knows it is a product fault, not their fault, is difficult to find.

Experts can see beyond the application and visualise what could happen. They can make constructive suggestions on how to solve a problem, as well as identify that a problem exists. When we created the diagrams for this book we tried several drawing packages. One package was particularly difficult to use. We found it hard to use and so did other users, however, we recognised that the problem was caused by the modal nature of the package dialogue. The package moved automatically between different modes at the

---

Mouse Selection

Click for Single Choice Selection: Clicking mouse button-one once without pressing any modifier keys, such as Ctrl, selects a single choice and de-selects all previously selected choices. This allows users to return quickly to a single-selection state, regardless of the number of previously selected choices.

Single Range Selection: There are two techniques available for creating a single range of items. Drag select provides an implicit technique, allowing users to press and hold the mouse button while moving the mouse pointer to select a range of choices. An explicit technique, Shift, is also available, using the Shift key as a spring-loaded mode to establish a range.

Figure 3.12 CUA guide-lines for mouse
selection.

slightest provocation, and with little visible indication. This meant that we often did the wrong operation because we thought we were drawing something, not selecting it or we thought we were in text entry mode but we were in a view mode. Because of our experience we could tell the designer not only that the package was hard to use, but why it was difficult and how to correct it.

Standards and Guide-lines as Users

As well as people we can test by comparing products against user-interface standards and user-interface guide-lines. Check-lists (Figure 3.12) given in books such as IBM's Common User Access Advanced Interface Design Guide, are an excellent, cheap method of usability testing. They give us a rapid means of eliminating many obvious mistakes.

People who have little colour sense and tend to create gaudy applications which offend the user's visual sensitivity, should look up guide-lines on the use of colour. Remove the browns, the juxtaposition of blue and green, reduce the number of colours on the screen from twelve to four and use different shades of the same colour instead of different colours for subtle highlighting.

If there is a problem with fonts for text look up guide-lines on fonts. If the text looks like this paragraph there is something wrong but what should be done? Should a san-serif font be used, when should highlighting be in **bold**, how many *different fonts* should be used, when are CAPITALS APPROPRIATE? Write down the rules for the application and do routine checks to see if they are obeyed.

The guide-lines on fonts say to use only one or two different font families in a document. Get variation, for emphasis, through the use of different forms of a font, such as italics, bold, underlining and different sizes. Be consistent by always using the same style and font for the same purpose. This document uses bold for headings, has a serif font for the main text and a san-serif font for text in diagrams. Use the same principles in selecting fonts for on-line dialogues.

3.4.3   The Environment for Testing

A computer application exists within a total user environment. *Physically* it runs within a level of ambient lighting, the computer sits on a desk, there are other items on the desk, the user sits on a chair, telephones ring and other sounds register on the user. *Functionally* the computer is only part of the user task. The computer might assist in calculations, or recording transactions, or help look up information. It is rarely the only part of any work task. *Organisationally* the user operates in a role within a total operation. Other people will depend on the work done, time pressures exist and there are other psychological expectations for performance placed on the user.

A program used in a noisy factory may be different from a program used in a quiet office. In the office we can expect users to hear warning noises, but we do not want an application that makes too much noise and disturbs other people. In a factory we may require a strident, distinctive sound to draw attention, or sound may be completely useless as a prompt.

For example, a computer terminal used by counter staff to help health insurance enquiries is only part of the query transaction. The counter staff using the computer must talk to the customer. Should the customer be able to see the transactions carried out by the operator? Perhaps in the total context of the transaction a more usable system will result if the customer can see the information kept about themselves. They may detect inaccura-

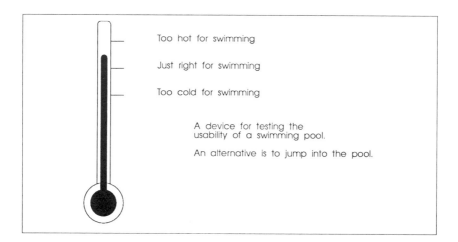

Figure 3.13 A tool for measuring usability.

cies in addresses, see invalid transactions and they may feel less threatened by the whole transaction. In this context the usability of the system is more than usability of the computer-operator interface.

The organisation context of program use will change usability criteria. A program used to check available airline bookings in a busy booking office will vary from a program doing the same task, but used at home. In one case the operator is under considerable psychological pressure to perform and not keep the customer waiting. In the other the user has time to experiment and try out different things. Some people perform differently under pressure and in those circumstances perhaps we need more guidance and less variability in the interface.

When doing usability testing be aware of the final environment for the application. Consider this environment when devising testing procedures and usability criteria. As with products and users an artificial or substitute test environment lets us isolate and test different environmental factors.

3.4.4   How to Test

Having specified a situation and invented something we would like to test, we now need a testing method. Testing requires measuring and comparing against expected results. Measurements may be quantitative or qualitative, we can compare with various mathematical procedures, we can check against different benchmarks, or we can simply compare against our users' expectations.

For example, we have a computer product and we want a usability test to show how easy it is to learn to use. To do this we must define some (quantitative or qualitative) measures that let us check the idea. The measure is always some user characteristic. To test for ease of learning, we might define usability as the average time ten users, who have never seen the product, take to learn a given task. Or we might define it as the number of functions a given population of users know after three weeks of regular use. Or we

• *PreDesign*	Full usability testing of competition and existing systems.
• *Conceptual*	Sketching ideas and trying out different pictures on users.
• *Task Design*	Checking to see if all tasks that need be done are done by working through user tasks.
• *Task Definition*	Validating against check-lists and guide-lines.
• *Implementation*	Usability testing with prototypes and with final system.

Figure 3.14 Tests at different stages.

might define it as the score on a standard attitudinal questionnaire given to learners after a two-week training course. In many cases the measure becomes the overriding evidence of how well the product performs and is more convincing than qualitative evidence. Figure 3.13 gives one a usability measure to test whether we should go swimming. Another method is to jump in the water and see if it is the right temperature!

We test usability by comparing the measure, either with a predefined goal, or by comparing it with measures from other products. We give examples of other usability measures and testing techniques later in this chapter.

3.5   When to Test

The user-interface design methodology, described in this book, includes testing in each stage. This section discusses the tests we might apply at different stages and outlines them in Figure 3.14.

3.5.1   Predesign Testing

As part of the system development methodology try to immerse yourself in the tasks being developed. Designing systems require a good understanding of the problem to be solved. One way to help achieve this awareness is to test competitive systems created by other people, and to test previous or current versions of the system. We can use the whole range of usability tests on these substitute products. The tests, as outlined previously, give us understanding, ideas for our own solutions and highlight strengths and deficiencies with existing systems.

3.5.2   Conceptual Stage

In the early stages of development try to define the idea of the system and its boundaries. Attempt to come up with a broad overview of the application and how it relates to the world. At this stage think of visualisations, analogies, or similar systems to get the idea of the system. We may visualise our time-tabling system as a white board, or use the "desktop" metaphor to describe the interaction of a group of computer applications, or say that a new booking system for the theatre is like the Qantas airline reservation system.

We need ways of testing whether our concept is acceptable and useful. It may be that the way we think of the system, as a system designer, is not appropriate for the end user of the system. Perhaps analogies are not needed to describe the system once it is operating? Perhaps the analogies are only useful in the training stages? However, if we can find useful ways of encapsulating the idea of the system that our users find helpful, we are well on the way to designing a usable system.

The techniques to test concepts at this stage are qualitative. Ask potential users to draw their idea of the system and see how well their ideas match ours. Give them different drawings representing different ways of thinking about the system and ask which ones match their ideas. Figure 3.15 shows some sketches representing ideas to use for a skills inventory of a group of people.

3.5.3   Task Design (Analysis and Design of User Tasks)

During task design we must test to make sure we include functions the user needs. Make sure to consider all the requirements, but be careful not to implement unnecessary features. Testing at this stage is for broad functionality. All the tasks users either do now or will want to do in the future, must be checked to see if they are possible. We can test by "scripting" the tasks and working through the steps to do them. In a pay-roll system, see if the interface allows the user to enter the salary, enter deductions, enter allowances, and

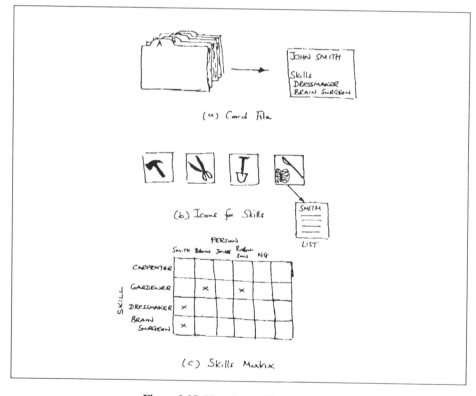

Figure 3.15 Ideas for a skills inventory.

print salary slips. They may also wish to change salary according to particular criteria. If this is so ensure the interface allows the inclusion of the criteria and has a way to ask for the calculation. The tests do not have to be detailed, only shown in principle, and can be done with sketches of screens, forms and reports.

A significant problem with many systems comes from feature creep. Feature creep occurs when designers and programmers put features into the systems because of a whim, or more dangerously, because it is easy to program. These features may not help the users at all, and may either mislead them, or make the application more complicated than necessary. A good example of feature creep is the interkey timing analysis in many keyboard training programs. With a computer program it is easy to calculate the time between different keystrokes. The temptation for the programmer is to calculate the times and display them to the user. With experienced typists the time between different keys varies widely and depends on the words typed and the juxtaposition of different letters. Displaying the keying time of the letter "A" to a learner will not help them become skilled typists and may even retard learning.

3.5.4 Task Definition (Detailed Development of Interface)

Develop the task definition by defining objects, actions and a model of how the system will work. Test it by seeing if the objects and actions make sense to the users.

This allows us to check for conceptual understanding. Do the users know the underlying structure of the system and how it works? In a pay-roll system there might be separate concepts for deductions and allowances. We might treat the two types of items as separate ideas, and build one set of rules for deductions, and other rules for allowances. However, the system design might have only one type of transaction that varies salary. This variation may be positive or negative, which corresponds to allowance and deduction. See Figure 3.16 for sample tables. Test to see if a person understands the system by asking them to do the data-entry for different variations in salary. If they put in positive values for things considered as deductions they have the first model, if they put in negative values they have the second model. Test for understanding by thinking of different ways people might misinterpret the system and ask them to do tasks that allows them to show their understanding (or conceptual model).

This style of testing is difficult to do as it is necessary to anticipate the different ways people might interpret the objects and actions. Set up testing procedures to eliminate the mechanical difficulties that may hide the conceptual problems. Show people pictures of screens and ask them what the different items mean to them. Ask them how they think they will perform a particular action, without getting them to do it. Give them questionnaires on their understanding of words used for actions. Testing done at this stage will often show how people misinterpret the system. However, be aware that misinterpretations are almost inevitable. The task is to try to understand and discover, through talking to the users, what it is they think is happening.

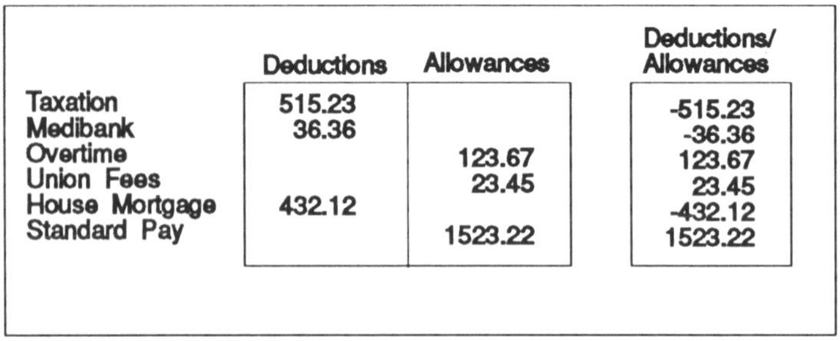

	Deductions	Allowances	Deductions/ Allowances
Taxation	515.23		-515.23
Medibank	36.36		-36.36
Overtime		123.67	123.67
Union Fees		23.45	23.45
House Mortgage	432.12		-432.12
Standard Pay		1523.22	1523.22

Figure 3.16 Two different ways of displaying
deductions and allowances.

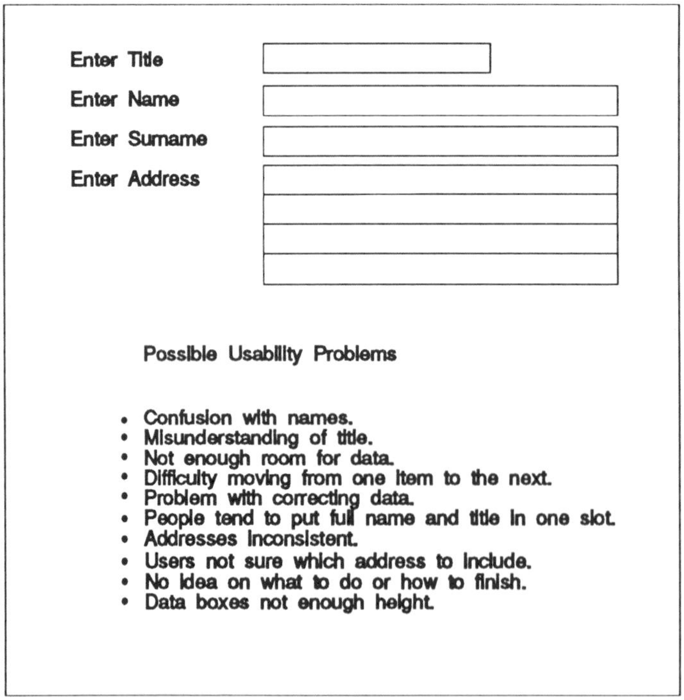

Enter Title

Enter Name

Enter Surname

Enter Address

Possible Usability Problems

- Confusion with names.
- Misunderstanding of title.
- Not enough room for data.
- Difficulty moving from one item to the next.
- Problem with correcting data.
- People tend to put full name and title in one slot.
- Addresses inconsistent.
- Users not sure which address to include.
- No idea on what to do or how to finish.
- Data boxes not enough height.

Figure 3.17 Sample form with possible
usability problems.

3.5.5   Implementation (Prototyping and Implementation)

The implementation stage is an easier environment to test. Here things are concrete, we have real computing artefacts to test, and we use common testing techniques. Once a user-interface exists on the screen, either prototype or implemented solution, people can operate it; they can do physical tasks as well as talk about what happens.

For example, it might be desirable to test how many errors people make when filling out a form. Put up a form on the screen and ask them to fill it out with typical system data. Now count the errors they make, analyse the errors, and determine the cause.

See how long it takes to perform a transaction. Start people working and time how long it takes to complete a task.

Another, relatively mechanical form of testing, is to check the interface against guide-lines and standards.

3.6   Testing Methods

Figure 3.18 lists different testing techniques described in this section. We have chosen a representative group of techniques rather than trying to be exhaustive. There is more information on usability testing methods in Helander (1988), Wright and Monk (1991),

Observations in controlled environment.

Co-operative user observation.

Observations in natural environment.

Automatic recording.

Constructive interaction.

Getting "experts" to evaluate.

Tests and Questionnaires.

Interviews.

Comparison to standards and guide-lines.

Automatic logging from applications.

Evaluate the aesthetics

Figure 3.18 Testing methods.

Figure 3.19 Pressures in the natural
environment.

Salvendy and Smith (1990) and in Nielsen (1989). Of all the methods we suggest the
most cost-effective method is the co-operative user observation method and we advise its
use for all systems. However, other methods are useful and should be used where appropriate. Before doing any testing, establish what the test should achieve and how it returns
the desired result. Where possible, establish quantitative usability goals for applications,
and measure to validate those goals.

Statements such as "our system is more user friendly", or "our new spreadsheet is
50 per cent more usable than LOTUS 123", have no real meaning. We must define what
we mean by "user friendly" and we must say what "50 per cent more usable" means.
Does it take 50 per cent less time to create a standard spreadsheet, or does it take 50 per
cent less time to learn to use the package, or do users make 50 per cent less errors?

3.6.1 Co-operative User Observation

All designers should use this method during the development and testing of any software
product. It is cheap and effective. It requires little expertise and little training on the part
of the tester. Other more controlled methods are outlined below, but designers should always use some form of co-operative user observations.

The method is extremely simple. The designer sits with a user and watches them
use the system. They may or may not have specific tasks to do. As they use the system
they are asked why they are doing actions the designer does not understand. If they have
questions they can ask what something means or how to do things. The designer notes

down the areas where there are misunderstandings or where the user does unexpected things. When users have problems they give their ideas on what they think might help them understand better. The idea is for the designer and user to co-operate positively to improve the product.

The method should be tried with different users. The number of problems discovered is more dependent on the users trying the system than upon any other factor. Try with different types of users and stop when no new significant problems are discovered. Normally only two or three different users are required to discover most problems.

We cannot overstress the importance of co-operative user observation. The method is simple, easy to do, yet so effective. There is no excuse for any system developer not to do this form of testing and it should always be done.

3.6.2 Observations in a Controlled Environment

Observing users can be done at various levels. As described above the designer can sit beside them and interact as they try the package, or they can be observed through a one-way mirror with no interaction at all. Ask the user to do specific tasks and to think aloud as they do the tasks. This thinking aloud takes the form of the users saying what they are doing and why they are doing it. For example, if testing a spreadsheet package, leave the computer turned off, leave a manual on the desk, and give people a printout of a simple spreadsheet and ask them to reproduce the printout. Record what happens on a note pad, tape recorder and/or a video recorder.

The measurements are broad ones. Can the user do the task? How many mistakes do they make? With a hand watch measure how long it takes to do a complete user task.

Observations have advantages of being cheap, easily replicated, adaptable and they give many insights into usability. The problems are that monitoring changes the users' behaviour, the tasks are "artificial", it is sometimes awkward to record what the user does, hard to reflect on what happens and difficult to see all the steps taken when users make errors and it may appear more rigorous than it actually is.

However, it does give us insights into why people take certain actions, it is relatively cheap and it can be effective.

3.6.3 Observations in a Natural Environment

Observing people using a package in the workplace helps the designer understand some of the external factors impacting the user. It is possible to see if they are under pressure, if they have many interruptions and how the physical surroundings influence their work. A good idea is obtained of the global conditions, and how the package might be better tuned to the work environment. Employ the same techniques as used with other observations.

How do you feel about using the computer system?

happy	:	:	:	:	:	:	:	unhappy
encouraged	:	:	:	:	:	:	:	repelled
eager	:	:	:	:	:	:	:	inhibited
secure	:	:	:	:	:	:	:	insecure
satisfied	:	:	:	:	:	:	:	unsatisfied

To me this question is:

: _____ : _____ : _____ : _____ : _____ : _____ : _____ :

Does this system meet your expectations?

always	:	:	:	:	:	:	:	never
completely	:	:	:	:	:	:	:	incompletely
consistently	:	:	:	:	:	:	:	inconsistently
adequately	:	:	:	:	:	:	:	inadequately
satisfactorily	:	:	:	:	:	:	:	unsatisfactorily

To me this question is:

: _____ : _____ : _____ : _____ : _____ : _____ : _____ :

How do you feel about the output you are getting from the application?

happy	:	:	:	:	:	:	:	unhappy
pleased	:	:	:	:	:	:	:	displeased
helped	:	:	:	:	:	:	:	bothered
good	:	:	:	:	:	:	:	bad
satisfied	:	:	:	:	:	:	:	unsatisfied

To me this question is:

: _____ : _____ : _____ : _____ : _____ : _____ : _____ :

Figure 3.20 Extract from a usability
questionnaire.

This testing is more difficult, as there are many external variables and factors influencing the operator. The presence of an observer changes the environment which may effect the operation. It may be difficult to know which external factors effect the operator. Use the same measures as in the controlled environment and use the controlled environment as a benchmark.

3.6.4   Automatic Recording

A variation on observations is to get the person to record their thoughts as they do the tasks, to record the screen state, the keyboard operation, mouse clicks and time. If this is on video tape it can be replayed and analysed in detail. It is expensive and should only be done after general observations have targeted particular problem areas.

It is difficult to analyse what has happened when replaying a session. Mistakes are easily seen but why people made them is difficult to understand. In the case of direct observation it is possible to ask a user what is going on if something they do does not make sense. It may help to have the user available during replay or try capturing the reason with a voice record of the user's thoughts. Usability testing is an active process and cannot be automated as it is necessary to get inside the mind of the person using the system, then think of ways to overcome their problems. It is not enough to observe problems. The designer must understand why the problems have occurred or at least what needs to be provided to users to prevent the problems.

Use this technique as the basis of series of experiments with many users. This is expensive and time consuming and is only justified for critical applications and then only for parts of the application. In effect this involves running psychological experiments and there is little evidence to show that the effort required is worth the results. The time is often better spent using simpler testing techniques and trying more user-interface variations. Details on how to conduct this form of experimentation are in Bailey (1989).

3.6.5   Constructive Interaction

Another variation on observations is to observe two or more users working on the same computer. This is particularly useful with children or with people who "freeze" when confronted with an observer. People who use the same package will talk to each other about the task and will explain what they think when they do things. Use this method instead of, or as a supplement to, the thinking-aloud technique.

3.6.6   Getting "Experts" to Evaluate

One of the most widely used usability tests is the expert review. Here we give "experts" a package and ask them to use it and to prepare a report on the package.

The review is a good testing technique. When asking for reviews, it helps to suggest to the reviewer areas and topics to cover. Ask people to comment on such things as learnability, effectiveness, flexibility, and comparisons with other products. Go through check-lists such as the guide-lines in Chapter 5. Try to get more than one reviewer to look at the product.

Be skeptical of some magazine reviews. We notice a disturbing tendency for most reviews to be "good" and to our cost we know the reviews to be wrong. We believe there are pressures for some commercial magazines and papers to only print good reviews because of libel problems and because software suppliers are often the magazines' advertisers. Some reviewers are ill-qualified to review as they do not understand the user tasks and others only review on short acquaintance and limited use.

3.6.7   Tests and Questionnaires

Use tests to find out how much people know about products. One of the usability problems with many products is that people do not know what the product does and rarely seem to discover or use its full potential. Use simple tests at different stages of a user's experience. For example, with a word processing package ask people to reset tabs to some new values. Test by giving people some output and asking if the package could produce it and if so how.

Questionnaires can elicit qualitative information as well as finding knowledge. Figure 3.20 is a page from a questionnaire to measure user satisfaction. Questionnaires can cover many people, and can elicit information that is difficult to find in other ways. Make sure the analysis of the responses is known before sending out the questionnaire.

Questionnaires are harder to construct than people imagine, and should be tested and validated. Proper questionnaire construction and analysis is expensive.

3.6.8   Interviews

An interview is like an interactive questionnaire. There is an analogy between questionnaires and automatic recording and interviews and direct observations. Interviews allow the same type of questions as a questionnaire, but allow a deeper exploration of the issues. This has the advantage of flexibility and finding hidden problems, but it has difficulties of interviewer bias and direction of interviewee.

3.6.9   Automatic Logging from Applications

A good technique for checking usability is to build automatic logging of usability measures into applications. Good measures are to count errors, to time tasks and to record re-

Never lie to your subjects.

Never knowingly put your subjects at risk without their informed consent.

Always tell subjects of any likely emotional or physical stress.

Always get the consent of subjects and always allow them to withdraw, without any penalty, from the test.

All test data must preserve confidentiality unless the subjects permission has been granted to release the data.

Figure 3.21 Guide-lines for experiments
with people.

sponse times. It is often easy to incorporate these measures when building applications. It is hard to add the measures, or to get the results in other ways, when the application is operational.

An interesting use of automatic logs is to look for maximal repeating pattern (MRP) of user actions. Such patterns often show interesting user behaviour. For example, if a user has to perform the same twenty actions several times the system might benefit from some short hand way to specify the actions. Ask programmers to log all error conditions and to write out a log of all instances of errors. Turn the log off when it is unused. One difficulty with automatic logging is the mass of data generated. Before starting logging make sure the measure and purpose is understood. If an organisation has standards for user-interfaces, or if it has guide-lines it is relatively easy to check for compliance with automatic checks and logs.

3.6.10 Evaluate the Aesthetics

What is attractive to some will not appeal to others. However, we should try to make our applications look good as well as be functional. When creating a horrible application people soon say if they are repulsed. We have no set of guide-lines on how to make applications attractive, other than the guide-lines on layout of screens and the use of colour. Look at other people's packages and rate them according to your feelings about their look. We believe it is good to strive to make applications look good and advice can be obtained from graphics designers and artists.

3.7   Ethics of Experimentation

When we run usability tests we involve users. Users are people and our usability tests are
a style of experiment. We should treat the experiments seriously and ensure we do not
transgress reasonable behaviour towards the subjects of the experiments. Figure 3.21 outlines our thoughts on the treatment of experimental subjects. These are loosely based on
the guide-lines from the Australian Psychological Society. Look to professional societies
to provide more discussion on this topic.

3.8   Bench-Marks for Usability

To measure we need something against which to compare our results. If we say that a
user makes ten errors per hour in using a package, does the measure show good usability
or poor usability? We cannot tell what the measure means, unless we have a comparison
bench-mark or reference point. We can do this by comparing to:

- Existing systems.
- Competitive systems.
- Manual systems.
- An absolute scale.

Note we are testing for usability not functionality. We assume the system has the required
degree of functionality and meets the requirements specification.

Existing System

Many applications are developments of an existing system. We already have a computer
package that does a similar task and we compare our new system directly with the old.
How quickly do we do tasks, how many errors are made, what measures do we get for
subjective satisfaction. We can test all the items mentioned in our check-lists and compare
them directly with the existing system.

Competitive Systems

The article by Pesot and O'Neill (1990) discuss IBM's approach to analysing competitive
systems. They list usability objectives of relative ease of use and ease of learning. They
define performance metrics of time to do tasks, steps to complete tasks, and problem
counting. The biggest problem facing the designer is the abundance of data and the analysis of performance measures.

In usability testing we have too many factors, too many variables, too many tasks, and too many ways of analysing. An important skill for the analyst is to select the points of greatest significance.

Manual System

The manual system is sometimes a special case of an existing system. For many systems we want to have a manual fallback if the computer system fails. If a manual system does not exist we might wish to create one for security and as a bench-mark to measure the performance of the existing system.

No comparable competitive system exists against which we can test Crossword Designer. However, checking the system against creating crosswords by hand shows an order of magnitude difference in speed of construction. For some people it was a case of making the task possible. This gives a good bench-mark against which to measure performance. This is something you can test for yourself. Try to construct a small crossword manually, then try it with Crossword Designer.

Absolute Scale

Sometimes we can use an absolute scale. With an air traffic control system we want to measure certain types of error performance against the absolute scale of zero. Errors that cause planes to collide are unacceptable. Other measures are not so stringent. Sometimes the measures are arbitrary; a word processor measure may be printing a ten-page document within one minute, or 50 per cent of all users give it a subjective evaluation better than satisfactory. These forms of measures are useful for comparing different systems.

3.9   Usability Check-lists

In this section we give five usability testing check-lists (Figures 3.22, 3.23, 3.24, 3.25, 3.26). The items and issues have been discussed previously in this chapter. The lists give a starting point for a testing regime. They are not meant to be exhaustive and the tests needed will depend upon the system and on the anticipated users of the system. We suggest building lists from experience and from reading other usability reports. Most organisations tend to create similar sorts of systems and know the important items to put into their check-lists. The book by Ravden and Johnson (1989) gives extensive useful check-lists.

The concept and task functionality list checks for broad functionality. It helps us see if the product covers the areas it should and if people understand what it will do.

The standards and guide-lines check if the syntax of the application conforms to organisational standards and guide-lines. The list is a sample derived from the CUA guide-lines.

Check if the users understanding of how the system works matches the way the system works.

Check if the package allows all tasks required by users.

Check if the package allows more tasks than needed.

Check if users know about task functionality.

Figure 3.22 Concept and task check-list.

Simple and natural dialogue.	Provides feedback.
Speaks the user's language.	Provides clearly marked exits.
Minimizes the user's memory load.	Provides shortcuts.
Consistent.	Provides good error messages.

Figure 3.23 User's language check-list.

Time to learn.	Number of errors.	Retention over time.
Speed of performance.	Subjective satisfaction.	

Figure 3.24 Quantitative measures.

Can all operations be done with keyboard.	Are the actions really actions or are they object selections.
Does mouse operation follow guide-lines.	Have windowing techniques been followed.
Do the action menus follow the recommendations.	Does Help work as suggested.
	Are dialogue boxes used correctly.

Figure 3.25 Sample CUA guide-lines.

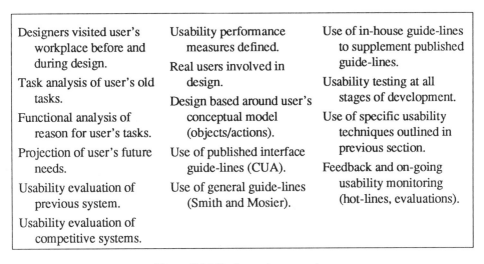

Figure 3.26 Design and construction

As well as the syntactic aspects we must check tasks against usability guide-lines. The article by Molich and Nielsen (1990) provides a good exercise and example of how to evaluate user tasks. We summarise the list presented in the article. We suggest reading the article and use it as the basis for task usability analysis.

Make quantifiable performance goals for the application. These goals will vary from system to system and user to user.

If there is access to the information, check the system construction. If designers and implementers value usability they would use the techniques outlined in this book during design and construction. Check how many were used for the package.

3.10 Usability Testing After the Product is Complete

Usability testing should not stop when the product is delivered. Worthwhile products evolve and develop and the best products of today are the result of evolution. It has been claimed that everyday consumer products need at least three versions before the designers finally produce a truly usable product.

As soon as the product is in the field there are many potential testers available. The important thing is to make sure there is a mechanism for hearing users and for reacting to their suggestions. Set up ways to gather user comments. In an early edition of this book we tried to elicit information about the usability of the book from readers. We included a tear-out questionnaire for people to fill out and send to us. We received one reply from over 1000 purchasers, and that was from a relative! Clearly that mechanism was not satisfactory. People will rarely say anything unless they have some reason. They might want a better product, they might be so dissatisfied that they wish to express their anger, or they might wish to obtain something else. To get feedback people must have a reason for giving it.

Use the simple marketing techniques of a free gift to anyone who sends something, or appeal to people personally to send some comments, or offer a reward to people who find problems with the product. Comments from users will normally not arrive unsolicited. It is necessary to set up ways to make it happen.

3.11   Design Guide-Lines and Usability Testing

This book has advice on how to design user-interfaces. It summarises the work of many other authors and has many guide-lines to assist designers. Where did these guide-lines come from and how can we refine and extend the guide-lines ourselves?

Few of the guide-lines came from traditional scientific experimentation. The psychological laboratories using standard experimental techniques have had a relatively small impact on the engineering of user-interfaces. Most of the information in this book, and in similar books, has come from an examination of invented user-interfaces. Progress in this field comes from an examination and investigation of inventions rather than an application of fundamental principles about the workings of the human mind. The art of user-interface design is driven by an examination of artefacts and the validation of designs is done through usability testing.

If this is so then all computer systems designers can participate in, and help develop the field.

This can be done by making explicit all the reasons for decisions and tradeoffs by writing them down as part of the systems documentation. Often assumptions can be tested in relatively simple ways. When it is uncertain how to present information to the user leave the choice to the user, but check what the users choose. For example, we constructed a program to help people learn Morse code. We were unsure of how to present the material to people and so they were given different presentation choices. Observations were made of users' choices which have now given us insights in how to present information for other computer aided instruction.

The crucial point is to make explicit the choices and tradeoffs and to devise appropriate testing methods.

Summary

Usability testing is a critical part of good user-interface design. To make good computer systems some form of usability testing is mandatory. The ideas in this chapter can be summarised by the following set of aphorisms which hold true for most situations:

- Usability testing requires a user.
- Usability testing is an important design tool and starts before any design is done.
- All testing requires something to test, something to test for and a way of doing the test.
- Critically watching a user use a product is the simplest most effective form of usability testing.
- Substitute systems make good test vehicles.
- Competitor's systems are a great source of ideas for new products.
- Always do usability testing of existing systems before designing a new system.
- Build user-interface prototypes instead of fully functional prototypes.
- Use yourself as a usability testing subject.
- Standards, guide-lines and rules give quick usability checks.
- Usability testing requires some form of usability measures.
- The main usability criteria is that the product does the task it was designed to do.
- Usability testing cannot be automated.
- Questionnaires are an expensive testing tool.

Crossword Designer Usability Testing

We ran usability tests on Crossword Designer throughout its development. The user-interface changed because of these tests. In this section we describe the development of the "Create your own grid" interface in Crossword Designer. In Chapters 2 and 5 we describe the ideas behind the package. The part of the package we discuss here allows us to make symmetric crossword grids.

During development the user-interface changed to better match the way users thought of the problem. Testing the conceptual model is difficult but getting the match between the user's ideas and the program is critical to success. The methods of testing were observation, expert evaluation and interviews with users.

The Problem

Figure 3.27 shows a typical newspaper style crossword grid. An important aesthetic characteristic of a crossword grid is the symme-

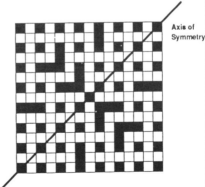

Axis of Symmetry

Figure 3.27 Typical crossword pattern.

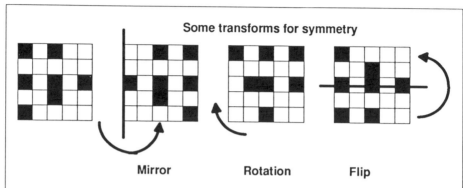

Some transforms for symmetry

Mirror   Rotation   Flip

Figure 3.28 Ways of generating symmetries.

try of the pattern. Most crosswords are symmetric about the diagonal axis shown in the diagram. However, they can be symmetric about other axes, and we can have rotational symmetry and mirror symmetry. The first attempt at an interface for Crossword Designer allowed users to generate patterns by manipulation of smaller patterns to make a bigger pattern. Typical steps to create a pattern are shown in Figure 3.28.

1. Create part of a grid - typically either the top left quarter or the whole top half. Make the pattern by clicking the squares with the mouse.

2. Mark any area and copy it with rotations, or flips to make the rest of the grid.

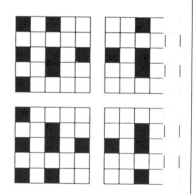

Figure 3.29 Pattern generated by transformations on top left corner.

The conceptual model was based on the idea of symmetry and gave the user ways of manipulating parts of the square to generate a symmetric pattern. This model is a typical programmer's model, as it concentrates on the mathematical idea of symmetry, and the implementation gave the user a way of generating symmetry through transformations.

A screen prototype of this method was created and users asked to create grids. The testing was simple observation and talking with users as they tried to create grids. Only one or two tests with non-programmers were enough to show that this method was unusable. It worked reasonably well with programmers and mathematicians who knew about transformations and rotations. However, most people did not view a grid this way at all. Their idea of a grid was not a set of rotations and symmetries. We tried to find how people viewed grids and soon discovered that most people did not even realise a crossword grid had symmetry, let alone the type of symmetry or how it was generated.

We tried other ways based on people generating larger patterns from smaller ones by applying the rules. None of these were successful.

It was clear that the conceptual model of the user was much simpler. Users did not see symmetry directly and did not think about transformations. Users saw black and white squares and they saw places to put words. They recognized the lack of symmetry but symmetry in itself was not consciously recognized. Their conceptual model of a crossword grid was a set of black squares defining places to fit words. The symmetry was desired but not part of the creation process. People just wanted it to "happen".

The solution (which came after several iterations) is shown in Figure 3.30. On the left we have the area where we create the grid. We click on blank squares on this area. When we click, the symmetry defined by the checked square, automatically puts

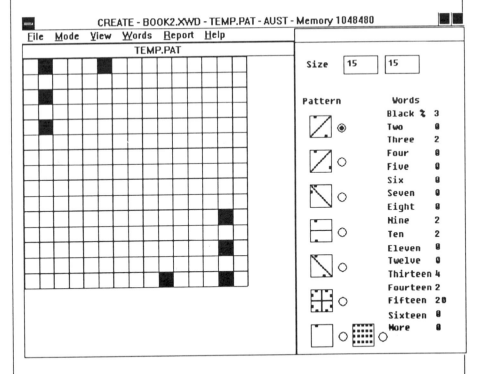

Figure 3.30 Pattern constructed by clicking
on squares.

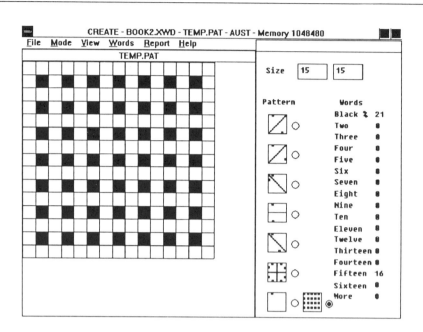

Figure 3.31 Quick way to construct a grid.

in the other squares to preserve the symmetry. In the Figure we have the top box selected and so that style of symmetry is preserved. People understand this not through explanation but by seeing it happen. When testing, as soon as someone clicks on an empty square and sees the result, they understand what has happened.

The list on the right shows the number of words of different sizes. A "good" pattern does not have small words of two or three letters and there is a relatively low percentage of black squares. Build the grid so these numbers change and monitor the progress.

The pattern shown in Figure 3.31 causes the whole grid to be filled as shown. This was added after seeing the difficulty people had in creating grids. In practise, many "good" patterns are variations on this basic pattern. By using this approach people can quickly create a new grid by using the concept of starting with an existing object and modifying it to create the new object. See the guide-lines Chapter 5 for a discussion of this principle in designing user-interfaces.

Some important points from this design exercise story are:

- Try to understand the way people think about the problem and get the interface to reflect those ideas. Although the grid pattern does have symmetries people do not think about it that way and so any dialogue based around symmetries will fail no matter how clever and easy to use they are. The underlying conceptual model did not match the typical user's model. Test for understanding through discussion with users and by observing them using the product. Failure to perform tasks is often a symptom of a mismatch between the implementor's conceptual model and the user's conceptual model.

- Try to get the program to reflect the user's understanding, rather than only concentrating on the syntax of the interface. It is better to change the user-interface than to try to change the users to match the interface. In the example we could have remained preoccupied with better ways to manipulate symmetry. However, this would never succeed as well as the current interface, no matter how well it was implemented and how much training we gave users. The users would still find generation of symmetries difficult and clever manipulation would only make marginal improvements to the interface. Major gains in productivity and usability are made at the conceptual level. Adjustments at the syntactic level help, but only give minor improvements.

- Test against the important criteria for the user. Users are interested in words - not patterns. The pattern should happen. The user should think in terms of making words of particular sizes. In this case they create the pattern but they control the creation by observing the size and number of words.

- Use the concept of starting with an existing object and modifying it to create a new object. In this case, and many others, it will prove to be a powerful simplifying paradigm.

Exercises

1. Test the most common spreadsheet in an organisation for usability for one user task. Find someone who uses the spreadsheet, find a task they do then check:

   - The user's understanding.
   - How quickly they get the job done.
   - How many errors, and what types, are made.
   - The user's feeling about the tool.
   - How well the application fits the organisation's interface standards.
   - How the application compares to user-interface guide-lines.

2. Take a task in an organisation that is not computerised. Think up some different ideas on how this task might be done and might be represented on the computer. Sketch these ideas and get other people's reactions to the sketches. For example, the organisation might have a paper telephone directory. Think up ways this might be done with computer assistance and sketch the approximate interface.

3. Do a usability test on a locally supplied paper telephone directory from a telecommunications company. Devise some tests to see if it is functional by asking people to find the telephone numbers for such things as, an ambulance, a local school, information on child care, the local member of parliament, a government organisation, an organisation which has several different names, a person with a name such as McClean, a person with a common name but one whose street or suburb is unknown. Devise some tests to see how long it takes people to find information.

4. Take any common household appliance and devise some usability tests. Go through the steps outlined in this chapter and write down all the tests to carry out. Compare the tests with those in a consumer magazine for the same product.

5. PageMaker and Ventura Publisher are two common desktop publishing packages. However, both have different internal structures and ways of organising data. Ventura puts formatting information in as TAGS in the text, and keeps separate files for the text, graphics, and drawings. This means Ventura can import text files from other packages, format the text, and yet it is possible to still go back to the originating package and view and manipulate the text with that package. PageMaker puts all the text and graphics together into one file and hides the tag information from the user. Devise ways of testing users, by inventing tasks, that show if people have the correct conceptual model for the packages. Think of tasks that might work in unexpected ways if people have the incorrect conceptual model.

6. Set up a video tape, with a user's permission, and film them in their work environment using a computer package. Do the recording automatically without being present and try to choose a busy environment. Choose a busy secretary doing word processing, or any computer application done at a "counter" such as a bank teller. On replay, observe and list the external factors impacting the user. Set up a similar task in a controlled environment and see how the performance varies.

7. Set up automatic data logging on video tape with recording of user voice comments. Give a user a new package and get them to install the package on their computer. Do the same thing with another user, but sit beside the user and observe what they do. In the second case ask the user questions during the installation, but try not to assist them. Compare the two methods of observations. Which method gave better insights and why?

8. Take two reviews of the same computer package from two magazines. Go through the reviews and list the usability problems identified by the reviewers. Before read-

ing the reviews try the package yourself and see how many usability problems you can identify.

9. Devise a questionnaire to evaluate a computer package for ease of learning. Test the questionnaire on a small sample, revise it, then try it on a larger group. Test the results of the questionnaire by direct observation of people learning to use the package. Compare the two approaches.

10. Take an in-house application and devise a usability measure to build into the application. It may be an automatic logging of errors, a response time measure, or the timing of a task. Implement the measure and analyse the results.

11. Take the most common word processor in an organisation and compare the HELP facilities against the CUA interface design guide-lines. After the analysis make suggestions on how to improve the HELP for this application.

12. Take a task from an application (for example, adding a word to a Crossword in Crossword Designer) and analyse it with the Molich and Nielsen (1990) check-list.

13. Make a copy of the next questionnaire sent to you before filling it in. Is it possible to see how the questionnaire supplier will analyse the responses? Do you think the questionnaire will get true answers to the questions? Did the questionnaire explain what it was trying to achieve? Will it achieve its objectives?

14. Take a poll among users of applications to find which application they think is the most attractive. If there are clear winners and losers see what makes some applications attractive and others less so.

Chapter 4

Objects and Actions

In this chapter, we develop the formal framework for the dialogue model. We will discuss what we mean by objects and actions, and how we can specify them. We then give examples of the more common types of objects and of how they can appear in a dialogue, and we discuss how sets of objects come together in an application.

4.1   What are Objects?

The dialogue model is made up of a set of *objects* to represent the data to be displayed to the user, plus a series of *actions* (or operations) which the user can perform on those objects. These provide the user with a set of building-blocks which they can use to perform the functions of the system.

Figure 4.1(a) gives an abstract picture of a user-interface object and the actions applicable to it. Figure 4.1(b) gives two actual objects: data on a person called Bill Smith, for whom we want to be able to perform the actions of Change Address and Change Telephone Number and on a vehicle ZZA109, for which we want to record a renewal of its registration. Each of these objects has a number of properties, e.g. Bill Smith has a *name*, an *address*, a *telephone number* and a *year of birth*, and YAA000 has a *registration number*, a *make* and *model*, and the *expiry date* of the registration. These properties are commonly referred to as *attributes*. One or more attributes usually have a special role, in that they are used to specify a particular object. Here we would use the name *Bill Smith* or the registration number *ZZA109*. These attributes are known as *identifiers*.

The *representation* of an object is the way in which it is displayed on the screen. Objects can be represented in many different ways, as we have seen, e.g. with the airline flight information. Two common ways are shown in Figure 4.2.

120

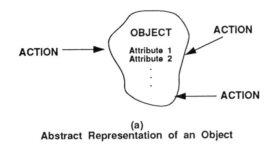

(a)
Abstract Representation of an Object

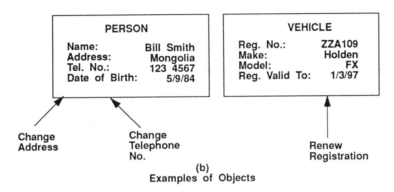

(b)
Examples of Objects

Figure 4.1 The idea of an object.

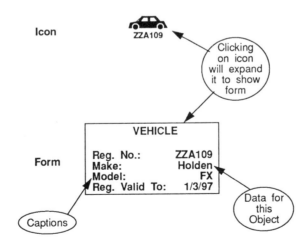

Figure 4.2 Representation of objects.

A *form* contains a set of *captions* with the attribute names and corresponding *fields* with the values of those attributes. Actions such as *Change Address* and *Change Telephone No.* are easy to perform with a form. The user moves a cursor to the field that they want to change, and enters the new value, e.g. if Bill Smith had moved to Vietnam, we would move the cursor to the address field and replace Mongolia with Vietnam. A form is useful when we want to know all about an object, but because it is textual rather than graphic in form, it is not always the most suitable representation.

An *icon* is a small graphic representation of the object. An icon can contain a limited amount of information. Our vehicle icons show the type of vehicle by being pictures of cars, trucks and buses, while the driver icons are coded using shading to show the licence type. An icon is easy to manipulate. In the vehicle pool system, we allocate drivers by dragging the driver icon to the appropriate place on the schedule.

It is often important to be able to move between representations. Very often, we will display an icon, but if a user wants more information, they can expand the icon (e.g. by double-clicking on it, or choosing a *zoom* option on a menu) to display a more detailed representation, such as a form. This happens, too, with lists of information. We may only show a limited amount of information about each object on the list (e.g. its identifier), but more information can be obtained by expanding it out.

Building a system around specific objects such as Bill Smith or ZZA109 is of little value, since they will not work for Julie Jones, Jason Minogue and BUS785. However, we can consider Bill Smith, Julie Jones and Jason Minogue as being *instances* of a *class* called *Person*, while YAA000 and BUS785 are instances of another class called *Vehicle* (Figure 4.3). Note that only the class names and object identifiers have been shown for clarity.

A class is an abstract definition of a particular type of object which contains:

- A definition of the data contained within the object, consisting of a list of the names, properties (e.g. allowable values) and meanings of the attributes of the object.
- A description of the allowable actions on the object, consisting of a list of the names by which the actions are to be specified, parameters required (e.g. data to be supplied by the user) and the processes performed by the action.

In Figure 4.4 we give formal definitions for the Person and Vehicle classes. The style of these definitions is based on the *protocols* used in the object-oriented programming language *Smalltalk*. We will discuss other ways of defining actions later in this section. In addition to the actions shown, every class has an action *Create*, which creates a new instance of the class (i.e. a new object), and an action *Destroy* which gets rid of an object of that class, but these may not be available to all users.

The implication of this distinction between classes and instances (objects) is that the class definition does not contain any data, merely definitions of what the data looks like. The actual data is held in the objects, in which the various attributes have been

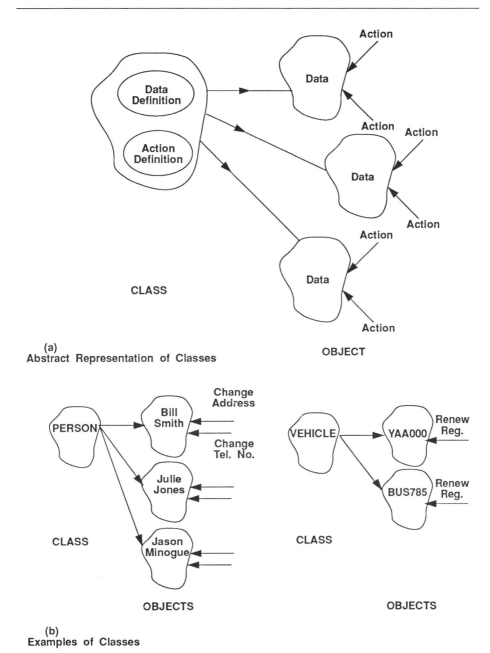

Figure 4.3 The idea of a class.

given values. However, objects do not store information about actions. Since the same actions are applicable to all objects of a given class, each object merely stores information (e.g. the class name or a pointer to the class definition) that enables it to use the action definitions stored in the class definition.

This means that when we are developing (defining) a system, we are defining the classes, i.e. we are saying what the data should look like and what we should be able to do with it.

When the system is actually running, we are working with objects, i.e. with specific instances of the classes containing actual data. The way in which these are implemented in a conventional computing environment is shown in Figure 4.5. The data definitions are data structure definitions (e.g. Pascal or Cobol record structures), and the action definitions are procedures. When the program is running, instances of the data structures are created on the stack or the heap, and actions are performed on them via procedure calls. At the user-interface level, the instances are displayed on the screen, and the user performs actions by means such as modifying data on the screen, selecting from a menu or pressing function keys.

Class PERSON	
Attributes	
Name	Person's Name, Surname First
Address	Person's Address
Telephone No.	Telephone Number
Date of Birth	Date of Birth
Actions	

Change Address
   To: New Address
	Change Address to address supplied in
	   New Address

Change Telephone No.
   To: New Telephone No.
	Change telephone no. to telephone no.
	   supplied in New Tel. No.

Class VEHICLE	
Attributes	
Registration No.	Vehicle Registration No.
Make	Manufacturer's Name
Model	Model Name given by Manufacturer
Registration Valid To	Date of Expiry of Registration
Actions	
Renew Registration	Increment Registration Valid To by one year

Figure 4.4 Class definitions for PERSON
and VEHICLE.

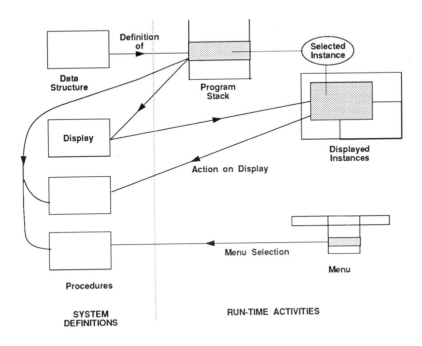

Figure 4.5 What happens when a system
is running.

The way that we work with objects is always the same: we *select* an object, and then perform one or more actions on it. All of the actions for an object are always available, i.e. we can find an object and, having found it, decide what to do with it. This is how we work with manual systems. Even if we have a fairly specific idea of what we intend to do with an object, we often change our mind once we see it, e.g. in the vehicle pool system, we may be intending to allocate a vehicle to a driver, but on seeing that it is overdue for maintenance, we decide to schedule it for a service instead. Systems that work in this way are known as *modeless*. This contrasts with *modal* systems, where the action is selected first. Many computer systems employ modal dialogues, often resulting in an unacceptable degree of rigidity. The idea of modeless dialogues was discussed in Chapter 1.

In informal discussion, the terms *class* and *object* are often used interchangeably, e.g. in our design methodology, where we talk about selection of objects to represent a particular system, we are really talking about what classes we should define, but when the system is up and running, we are manipulating instances involving actual data, i.e. the objects themselves. Provided that we can make the distinction between classes and objects when we need to, this is not a problem.

4.1.1   How Do User-Interface Objects Relate to Data Objects?

Superficially, some aspects of our discussion in the previous section sound very much the same as those in a book on data modelling. Conceptual data models such as the Entity-Relationship Model discussed in Chapter 2 rely on the identification of *entities* which represent data objects in the system, and the *relationships* between them. Each object has various *attributes*. Each object class (*entity set*) is commonly implemented as a file or as a table in a relational database.

There are, however, a number of differences, which we will discuss in more detail below:

- Data which a user might want to work with as a unit is often split over a number of entities.
- The data entities do not incorporate actions.

These arise from the fact that, as a user, we need to see our data in relation to other (relevant) data, and in terms of what we can do with them, while a data model is an abstrac-

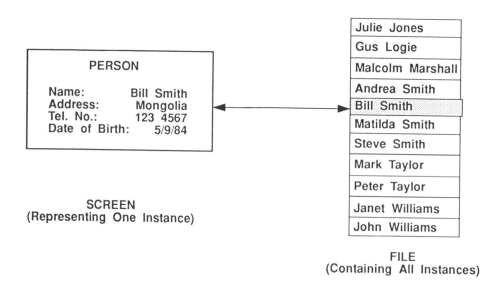

Figure 4.6 A simple filing system.

tion which breaks the data into as simple as possible units independently of the processes to be performed on it.

These differences are particularly obvious when we are dealing with visual representations of objects. A data model of a map would have the cities in one table (with their latitude and longitude), the coastline in another, and the roads (or airline flights) between them in a third, while as a user, we want to see them in a single coherent picture.

Early attempts (and this includes many of the current generation of CASE tools) at specifying user-interfaces attempted to use the data entities as the user-interface objects. This works well for simple systems in which there is only one type of object, for example a mailing list (where the object is *Person*), a library catalogue (where the object is *book*) or a file of recipes. Most simple filing systems (e.g. *Personal Filing System, Microsoft File*) work in this way (Figure 4.6). The user designs a screen layout which contains all of the fields in the file record (i.e. the data about one person, one book or one recipe), and this is used to generate a file definition. (The converse, which is for the user to define the file and allow the software to generate the screen layout, is also found, but is less satisfactory from a user-interface point of view, because the user no longer has control over the screen layout.) The user is then supplied with a series of commands (actions) to manipulate the file, e.g. to insert a new record, modify or delete an existing record, move to the next or previous record, select records based on field values or the position in the file. Some packages (e.g. *PC-File*) have modal dialogues, e.g. one must go into *Delete* mode and then locate the records to delete, but many incorporate a correct object-oriented paradigm, in that they let the user locate a record and then decide what to do with it. A reporting facility allows users to view and print data in a different format from that on the file, but not to enter or modify it in this form.

This approach runs into trouble once there is more than one type of data entity. Most current approaches to data storage (e.g. relational database management systems) encourage the fragmentation of data into a series of *flat files* or *tables*, i.e. files with fixed-length records in which each record is of an identical structure with no repeating items or groups. From a data storage point of view, there are good reasons for this approach. Data is stored in a way that is independent of the peculiarities of any particular application, thus making it equally accessible to all applications; each data item is stored only once (i.e. there is no *redundancy*), thus eliminating the possibility of inconsistencies which would arise, e.g. if a person's address is stored in two places and then only one copy is updated when they move; and the rules for manipulating these tables (e.g. for searching or combining them) are simple, easily programmed and easily expressible in command languages, e.g. the relational database language SQL. However, when we are designing the user-interface for a specific application, these criteria may not be the most appropriate.

Figure 4.7 illustrates a typical situation, based on the Vehicle Pool example introduced in Chapter 1. Part of the system concerns maintenance records on the vehicles. There are two types of data entity: one representing data about the vehicles themselves, a second containing maintenance details. The reason for the split is that, for each vehicle,

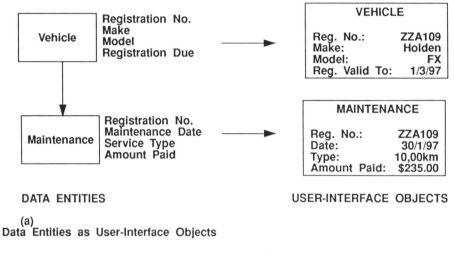

DATA ENTITIES   USER-INTERFACE OBJECTS

(a)
Data Entities as User-Interface Objects

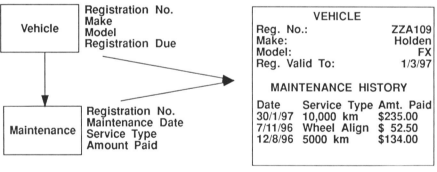

DATA ENTITIES   USER-INTERFACE OBJECT

(b)
Data Entities Combined to Make a More Useful
User-Interface Object

Figure 4.7 Representation of data entities
at the user-interface.

there are many maintenance records, each referring to a different service or repair. On the database, these maintenance records would contain no information about the vehicle except for an identifying number (we have used the Registration Number, but it is often an internally allocated *Fleet Number*) which allows one to look up the appropriate vehicle record. If we used separate screens for each file, as shown in part (a) of the figure, we get two problems:

- In looking at the maintenance record for the vehicle with registration number YAA000, the user has no idea (unless they have remembered the details) whether it is a MAN articulated bus, a bulldozer or the chief executive's limousine.
- There is the possibility of inconsistency between the two files, e.g. by inserting a maintenance record for a vehicle that does not exist, or by deleting a vehicle and leaving its maintenance records still there.

Although it is possible to build in checks at the database level to prevent the second of these from happening, their implementation is clumsy from a user point of view, since the user must go from what they are doing to another screen in order to make the necessary corrections (which are not always obvious) before returning to perform the original operation.

A much more satisfactory approach is shown in part (b) of the figure, where the user is given a single screen on which the vehicle data and the maintenance history are displayed. The user can scroll the list of maintenance data, modify fields on the display (where it makes sense to do this), insert new lines corresponding to additional services, and insert an entirely new vehicle, with attached maintenance records if desired. This gives the user all of the relevant data, and the ability to perform the necessary operations on that data, in one place. Problems of inconsistency are eliminated, because a deletion would delete everything on the screen (i.e. records from both files), and any attempt to insert maintenance data while the top half of the screen is blank (i.e. no vehicle is defined) both looks stupid to the user, and is easy to detect and prevent.

Conceptually, what happens is: in (a), the user was given two objects, *Vehicle* and *Maintenance*, which they had to manipulate independently, in spite of the relationship between them. In (b), this relationship was made explicit by supplying a single object (which to us is still called *Vehicle*) which contains the vehicle data, plus maintenance data from not one but all maintenance records for that vehicle. From the user-interface point of view, (b) is by far the better. This does not mean, however, that the underlying file structure should be changed, since, as we discussed above, the criteria for a good file or database design are different. Rather, what we are seeing is an application of the idea of *logical data independence*, in which the underlying data structures are mapped on to structures (often referred to as *subschemas* or *views*) appropriate to a particular application. Although in most database management systems these subschemas or views are highly restricted in form (often being subsets of underlying structures), there is no con-

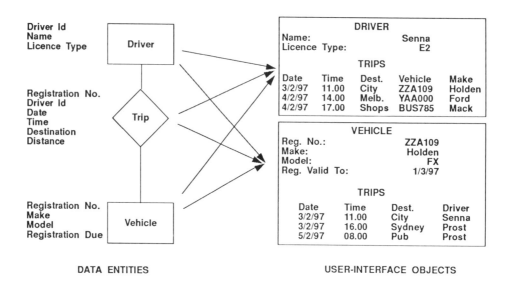

Driver Id
Name
Licence Type

Registration No.
Driver Id
Date
Time
Destination
Distance

Registration No.
Make
Model
Registration Due

Driver

Trip

Vehicle

DRIVER
Name: Senna
Licence Type: E2

TRIPS

Date	Time	Dest.	Vehicle	Make
3/2/97	11.00	City	ZZA109	Holden
4/2/97	14.00	Melb.	YAA000	Ford
4/2/97	17.00	Shops	BUS785	Mack

VEHICLE
Reg. No.:   ZZA109
Make: Holden
Model: FX
Reg. Valid To: 1/3/97

TRIPS

Date	Time	Dest.	Driver
3/2/97	11.00	City	Senna
3/2/97	16.00	Sydney	Prost
5/2/97	08.00	Pub	Prost

DATA ENTITIES   USER-INTERFACE OBJECTS

Figure 4.8 Multiple user-interface objects
for the same data entities

ceptual reason why they should be, provided that a mapping can be found between the object presented by the user and the underlying database, which should be possible if the objects chosen are sensible.

Figure 4.8 illustrates the way in which the same data can be seen in different ways. We are now concerned with the part of the system which records vehicle operations. There are three types of data entity: vehicles (as before), drivers, and an entity representing each vehicle trip, containing identifiers for both the driver and the vehicle to relate them back to the driver and vehicle files. However, the user is more likely to want to work with objects representing a particular vehicle (with a list of all its trips, including information such as the driver's name, which is only to be found on the file of drivers) or a driver (with a list of trips, including information such as vehicle type which can only be found on the vehicles file). The objects now combine information on three files in a way that overlaps between these two objects, and with the original *Vehicle* object in Figure 4.7(b).

This ability to provide different views of the same or similar data (often at the press of a button) is crucial to the design of good user-interfaces, because it allows us to look at the data in a way that is appropriate to the problem at hand, thus making it easier both to perform routine tasks and to make correct decisions.

4.1.2   Associations between Objects

In many systems, the major task involves establishing relationships between objects. This is true of both of our major examples: the crossword maker involves the association of words with positions on a grid; the timetabler involves organising teaching sessions (classes) in suitable locations at times convenient for both staff and students.

There are three distinct kinds of association (Figure 4.9):

- *Cross-references*, where an object refers to another object.
- *Inclusion*, where an object is part of a larger object.
- *Inheritance,* where a class of objects is a specialisation of a more general class.

We discuss these relationships in the following sections.

4.1.3   Component Objects

We argued above that we need relatively complex user-interface objects so that we can see the things that we are working with as a whole. If we analyse the actions on these objects, however, it becomes clear that we need sometimes to manipulate specific parts of the object, e.g. in the *vehicle* object in Figure 4.7, we need to be able to insert new vehicle maintenance records, and to select and modify existing ones. These actions still need to be performed within the context of the larger object, e.g. the maintenance records are still maintenance records for a particular vehicle.

The implication of this is that we sometimes want to look at *Vehicle* as an object, and sometimes at *Maintenance Record* as an object, but in such a way that *Maintenance Record* is still part of *Vehicle*. In other words, an object can contain other objects (Figure 4.10).

There may be only a single instance of an included object, or it may be possible to have multiple instances of objects of the same class. We could, for example, regard the *Engine* of a vehicle as an object in its own right with its own class definition, and include that object in the *Vehicle* class. In this case only one instance would be allowed (since vehicles such as cars and buses only have one engine). The *Maintenance Record*, on the other hand, can have multiple instances within the same vehicle object.

We need to supply the relevant actions to manipulate the included objects. The most basic requirement is a *Select* operation to specify the required object, e.g. a *Select Maintenance Record* action (which is usually implemented by allowing the user to move a highlight to the appropriate line in the display). Once this is done, the user can perform

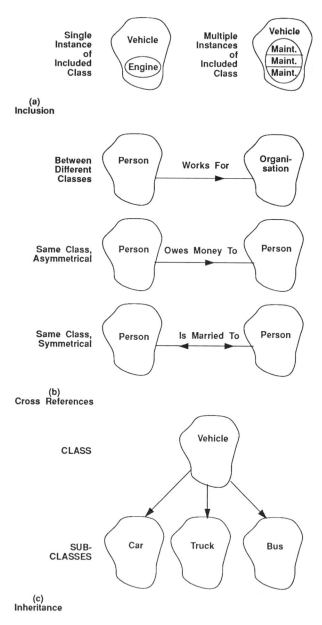

Figure 4.9 Relationships between objects.

the update actions defined within the *Maintenance* class. Similarly, there is a *New Maintenance Record* operation which creates a *Maintenance* object and includes it within the *Vehicle* object.

4.1.4 Cross-References

We build composite objects such as those discussed in the previous sections when we need to work with the data in those objects as a unit. Very often, however, we do not want to do that. Instead, we want to either view some related data briefly, or move on to working with that data, leaving our current data object behind.

We do this through the use of *Cross-References* (Figure 4.11), a familiar concept to readers of Library Catalogues and Encyclopaedias. We include in one object enough data (usually the identifier of the second object) to locate the other object, e.g. we might in-

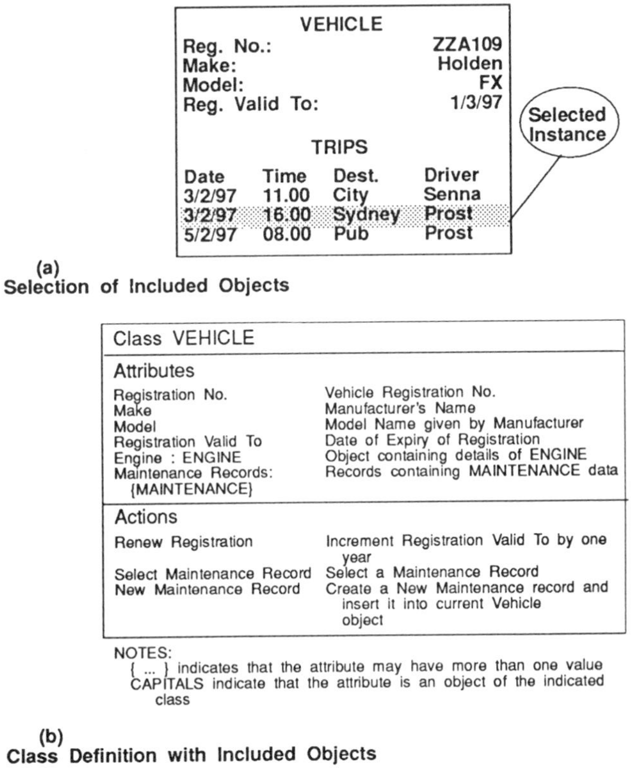

```
                  VEHICLE
    Reg. No.:              ZZA109
    Make:                  Holden
    Model:                     FX
    Reg. Valid To:         1/3/97       Selected
                                        Instance
                   TRIPS

    Date    Time   Dest.    Driver
    3/2/97  11.00  City     Senna
    3/2/97  16.00  Sydney   Prost
    5/2/97  08.00  Pub      Prost
```

(a)
Selection of Included Objects

```
Class VEHICLE

Attributes

Registration No.            Vehicle Registration No.
Make                        Manufacturer's Name
Model                       Model Name given by Manufacturer
Registration Valid To       Date of Expiry of Registration
Engine : ENGINE             Object containing details of ENGINE
Maintenance Records:        Records containing MAINTENANCE data
  {MAINTENANCE}

Actions

Renew Registration          Increment Registration Valid To by one
                              year
Select Maintenance Record   Select a Maintenance Record
New Maintenance Record      Create a New Maintenance record and
                              insert it into current Vehicle
                              object
```

NOTES:
    { ... } indicates that the attribute may have more than one value
    CAPITALS indicate that the attribute is an object of the indicated
        class

(b)
Class Definition with Included Objects

Figure 4.10 Inclusion of objects in other
objects.

clude the name of the garage at which the vehicle maintenance was performed, but other details of the garage are in a separate object because we do not usually need them.

Cross-references can be to objects of the same class or to different classes, e.g. a person (Bill Smith) may work for an organisation (the Sydney Waste Water Recycling Board), owe money to another person (Jason Minogue) and be married to yet another person (Julie Jones). These references can be stored in appropriate attributes in the object, e.g. the *Person* object would need attributes of *Employer, Creditor* (which can have multiple values) and *Spouse*. Note that some of these references are symmetrical (e.g. the spouse attribute in the object Julie Jones must be Bill Smith) but others are not (e.g. Jason Minogue might owe money to Kylie Ceberano and Kate Joel), and the reference from *Organisation* back to *Person* (if it exists) would be in an *Employee* attribute.

From the point of view of implementing a dialogue, cross-references are different from ordinary attributes, in that the dialogue must facilitate their use. A common way of doing this is to allow the user to select the cross-reference (e.g. with a mouse or by highlighting it) and then perform an action (e.g. double-clicking the mouse or using an *Open* command) which displays the referenced object (Figure 4.12). It is also useful to be able to display the structure of the cross-references explicitly, as in the family tree in part (b) of the figure. Here, only the object identifiers (the people's names) are given, but more detail could be obtainable by expanding them out. In some situations (e.g. hypertext documents) the user will follow a chain of cross-references through a large number of objects. In this case, the ability to pull back and see the structure of the system is vital if the user is not to get lost.

Class PERSON	
Attributes	
Name	Person's Name, Surname First
Address	Person's Address
Telephone No.	Telephone Number
Date of Birth	Date of Birth
Employer: Ref. to ORGANISATION	Cross-Ref. to Employing Organisation
Creditors: Ref. to PERSON	Cross-Ref. to Persons owed Money
Spouse: Ref. to PERSON	Cross-Ref. to Spouse
Actions	

Change Address
  To: New Address
	Change Address to address supplied in
	  New Address

Change Telephone No.
  To: New Telephone No.
	Change Telephone no. to telephone no.
	  supplied in New Tel. No.

Change Employer
  To: New Employer
	Change Employer cross-ref. to
	  New Employer

Add Creditor:
  New Creditor
	Add New Creditor cross-ref. to
	  list of Creditors

Delete Creditor:
  Creditor
	Delete Creditor cross-ref. from list of
	  Creditors

Change Spouse To: New Spouse	Change Spouse cross-ref. to New Spouse

Figure 4.11 Class definition including
cross-references.

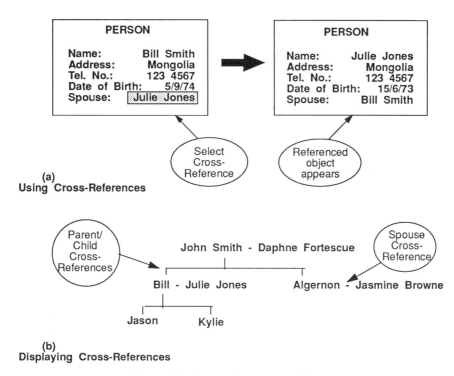

(a)
Using Cross-References

(b)
Displaying Cross-References

Figure 4.12 Cross-references in a dialogue.

Notice that a cross-reference is very different from including an object in another object. The cross-reference merely says where the extra data is to be found, while inclusion places the actual data within the including object.

4.1.5   Inheritance

Inheritance is different from reference and inclusion, in that both reference and inclusion refer to actual objects (although provision for them must be made when classes are being defined), while inheritance, on the other hand, refers to classes. Inheritance relies on the idea of classification, e.g. when we say that a cat *is a* mammal (i.e. the class of cats is a subset of the class of mammals), we also infer certain things about cats, e.g. that they are warm blooded, are covered in hair and (in the case of females) suckle their young. These things are properties of the class of mammals, and are regarded as being inherited by the class of cats.

When we talk about vehicles we have a similar situation. If, in our system, we need to store different information regarding trucks, buses and cars (e.g. a truck may have a maximum load, while a bus has a seating capacity), we need to create separate classes for *Truck, Bus* and *Car*. However, there may also be contexts in which we would like to use the fact that they are all vehicles (e.g. they all need drivers, consume fuel and have to be registered). We can achieve both these ends through the use of inheritance.

We first define the class *Vehicle* as in Figure 4.4 or 4.10. Then we define classes for *Car, Truck* and *Bus* which specify that their *Parent* class is *Vehicle* (Figure 4.13). These definitions include only the attributes and actions which are different from or additional to those in the parent (e.g. for *Truck* we have an additional attribute *Max. Load* and an additional action *Set Max. Load*), since the classes acquire all the attributes and actions of the parent *Vehicle* class.

This means that if we create a new *Truck* object, it will have all the attributes of *Vehicle* (*Registration No., Make, Model* and *Reg. Valid To*) as well as those specifically declared in *Truck* (*Max. Load*), and all actions applicable to *Vehicle* (i.e. *Renew Registration*) and specifically declared in *Truck* (i.e. *Set Max. Load*) will be applicable to it.

Inheritance is not limited to a single-level hierarchy. Most classification systems have many levels (e.g. that for living things) and inheritance operates throughout that hierarchy, so that, e.g. the class *cat* inherits properties from higher-level classes such as living thing and animal as well as from *mammal*.

When we are inheriting, we sometimes need to redefine an attribute or an action, e.g. whales are mammals but do not have hair. If we give a new definition in the new class, it overrides the definition in the parent, e.g. we could redefine the action *Renew Registration* in *Truck* to increase the *Reg. Valid To* attribute by three years instead of one, but do nothing in *Car* or *Bus*). If we then performed *Renew Registration* on a truck, it would increase the expiry date by three years, but if we performed it on a car or a bus, the action in the *Vehicle* class would be used, and the date would be increased by one year.

There exists more than one way of classifying objects in most systems, e.g. we could classify our vehicles into land vehicles, water vehicles and air vehicles, but we could also distinguish between powered vehicles (i.e. those with engines) and manually propelled vehicles. A given type of vehicle, e.g. a car, a bicycle or a rowing boat fits into

Class TRUCK	
Parent: VEHICLE	
Attributes	
Max. Load	Max. Allowable Load on Vehicle (tonnes)
Actions	
Set Max. Load To: New Max. Load	Change Max. Load to New Max. Load

Figure 4.13 Class definition involving
inheritance.

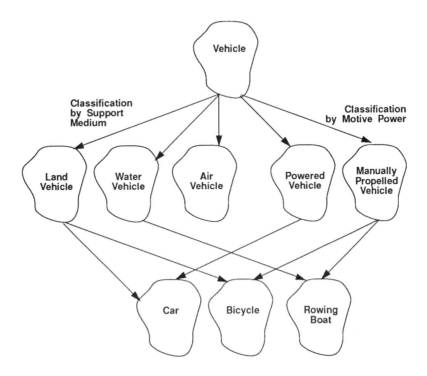

Figure 4.14 Multiple inheritance.

both classifications (e.g. a car is a powered land vehicle) and so inherits characteristics from more than one parent (Figure 4.14). This is known as multiple inheritance.

Inheritance has two major uses in dialogue design:

- It allows us to take generic ideas such as lists and forms (and objects themselves) and apply them to specific cases by adding additional features.
- It allows us to tackle more general problems with confidence, because we know that we can specialise in this way.

4.1.6 Specifying Actions

Specifying actions is, in some ways, more difficult than specifying objects. With objects, we can draw a picture. To show actions pictorially, we must draw a series of pictures (a *storyboard*), or a series of steps on one picture. We often do this (see, e.g. Figures 1.16 and 2.15), but it is often useful to have a more formal method of specifying actions. The main value of this is a "head clearing" function: so that when we change our representations of the objects, we still know what the actions were supposed to do. It also assists in the later programming of the system.

We have already discussed one method of specifying actions: their inclusion as protocols in the class definitions. This is probably too formal a way of doing it for many of our purposes, since these declarations are not the sort of thing that one scribbles on a whiteboard in the heat of an argument. We use two other methods to specify actions:

- *A command language.*
- *State diagrams.*

The command language contains essentially the same information as the protocols, and is as precise, but seems to be easier to use. One reason for this is that most designers are familiar with command languages, and so do not have to learn a new tool. The protocols, on the other hand, form a close link with the declarations needed for object-oriented programming languages, and so might be preferred for that reason. Our preference is for the command language. We have presented both, however, because we feel that both are useful. It is up to the designer to use whichever they prefer.

Command languages and protocols specify *what* the action is to do, and are adequate provided that the implementation of the action is hidden from the user, although the specification must include any parameters (additional data) passed to the action. In some cases, however, the action must invoke a modal sub-dialogue (e.g. a dialogue box) in order to obtain additional information. In this case, the structure of the sub-dialogue must be specified, i.e. we must know *how* the action is to be implemented. The state diagrams provide a method of doing this.

CAPITALS "..."	Literals (appear as written)
lower case	Names of objects, attributes, actions
[...]	Optional item
(.../.../...)	Alternatives (/ is separator)
{...}	Repetition
+	And (used to link syntactic components)

Figure 4.15 Symbols used in command language syntax definitions.

The syntax of a command language statement takes the form:

action name + object { + parameter name + parameter value}

where there can be any number of parameters. The symbols used are shown in Figure 4.15.

The *Renew Registration* action in Figure 4.1 would be written as:

RENEW object

an example of which would be

RENEW ZZA109

where the command name is RENEW and the object is ZZA109. The *Change Address* action would appear as:

CHANGE object ADDRESS TO new address

e.g.

CHANGE BILL SMITH ADDRESS TO VIETNAM

where we have a general CHANGE action that will change any attribute, so that the parameter name is the attribute name (ADDRESS) and the parameter value is the new address (VIETNAM). The use of "noise" words such as the TO in this example is a good idea if it lends clarity.

A common use of repetition is where an action can take a number of parameters, e.g. if we have an action

SHOW + object { + attribute [+ ","]}

which will display all the attributes specified, i.e.

SHOW ZZA109 MAKE

would display "Holden", while

SHOW ZZA109 MAKE MODEL

would display "Holden" and "FX". If names (e.g. object names and attribute names) contain spaces, it is often necessary to introduce punctuation to avoid ambiguity, e.g. we might want to be able to write:

SHOW ZZA109 REG VALID TO, MAKE, MODEL

This is the reason for including the optional comma in the syntax. The comma is in quotes (because it cannot be in capitals) to show that it is a literal. The alternative would be to impose a programming language type rule which says that there cannot be spaces in names, and which results in names such as RegValidTo or reg_valid_to, which are considerably less readable.

When specifying the actions, the syntax of the command (e.g. the form RENEW object) is used, and not actual instances, but in testing, it is very easy to generate instances of the commands, since all that is needed is a substitution.

One objection to the command language approach is that, by placing the action first and the object second, it in some sense runs counter to an object-oriented approach, which requires that we select an object and then perform actions on it. We could get around this by splitting the commands into two: a SELECT command, which contains the object; and a further action in which it is implied, e.g.

SELECT object
RENEW

The problem with this is that we might forget to specify the SELECT, so that our command definitions would be ambiguous. When using an actual dialogue, this is not an issue (we soon find out if we have no object or the wrong object selected), but in command language definitions, it might slip through unnoticed (or worse, lead to the person with whom you were discussing the dialogue thinking that you were referring to a different object) so it is better not to take the risk.

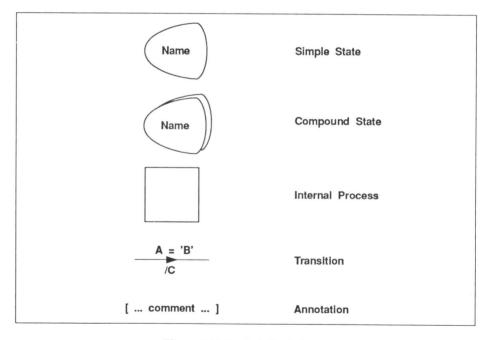

Figure 4.16 Symbols for dialogue
representation diagrams.

Command languages and protocols are not adequate to specify how an action is to be performed. In this case, we must use alternative techniques. Two common approaches are the use of formal grammars, and the use of state transition diagrams. The idea of a state model was introduced briefly in Chapter 1, and will be used here, because it lends itself to a visual picture of the process.

There are many different conventions for the symbols in state diagrams. The diagrams that we will use (which we refer to as Dialogue Representation Diagrams) consist of three main elements (Figure 4.16):

- A *(simple) state* of the system, which is a screen, an active window or a command prompt on display awaiting input.
- A *transition* from that state to another state on receipt of input. The transition is labelled by the input that causes it, e.g. A = "B" means the value B entered into field A. The A = and the quotes are omitted unless to do so would cause ambiguity. The text of any message to be displayed in the transition is shown, prefixed by a slash. Annotations can also appear on the transitions to indicate minor differences in the state of the screen or window resulting from entry via this particular path.
- Internal processes, which are significant items of internal processing which the designer needs to take into account, and which can alter the course of the dialogue (e.g. a NOT FOUND condition on a search which requires explicit action).

In addition to the simple state described above, the notation also allows for the specification of *compound states*. This is a state that is a complete sub-dialogue in itself, and which appears in another diagram. It is equivalent in function to the "levelling" of data flow diagrams, and is of use more in modal dialogues where there are deep menu hierarchies than in modeless dialogues. An example of its use is given below.

In Figure 4.17 we show how a state transition diagram can be used to represent the sub-dialogue involved in opening a file. This is a reasonably standard sub-dialogue that appears in virtually all systems, and as such does not really need to be specified as part of any normal design process (except that it is required), but it is useful as an example here because of its familiarity. When OPEN is invoked from the menu, a list of directories (subdirectories of the current directory on the current device, .. to return to the parent of the current directory, and the identifiers of the other devices) and the contents of the current directory (the file list) are obtained. The OPEN dialogue box is then displayed. If a different directory is selected (either from the list or by typing it in), then the directory list and file list are updated. If a file name is selected (either from the list or by typing it in), then, unless it contains a wildcard, an attempt is made to open the file. If the file is opened successfully, the dialogue box is closed and control returned to the calling window with data from the opened file on display. If the open fails, control returns to the

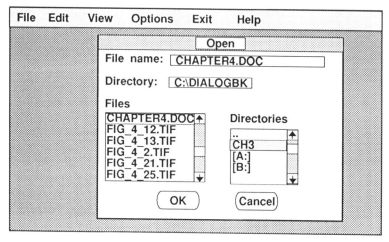

(a)
The OPEN Dialogue Box

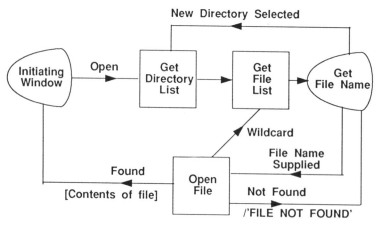

(b)
Dialogue Representation Diagram

Figure 4.17 Sub-dialogue for the OPEN action.

dialogue box with an error message "FILE NOT FOUND" displayed. If the filename contains a wildcard, the file list is redisplayed using the search criteria specified.

The state diagram differs from the actual implementation in the error handling. The "FILE NOT FOUND" message would in practice be displayed as a dialogue box with a single-exit option (OK), but this is an implementation detail that it is not necessary to specify here.

Another area in which we might want to specify a dialogue sequence is in the creation of new objects. Figure 4.19 shows the creation of a new trip in the vehicle pool system. It works by selecting a vehicle, moving to the time (as displayed on the schedule) at which the trip is to start, depressing the mouse button, and dragging the mouse to the end time, at which point the mouse button is released. Selection of the vehicle highlights it. While the mouse is being dragged, a dotted line appears, which becomes a solid line when the button is released. At this point, the vehicle is unselected.

This dialogue is not modal, since the user could perform other actions once they had selected the vehicle, but it does constitute a distinct series of steps which need to be spelled out in some way.

It could also be argued that the dialogue is overly complex, because clicking on an empty space on the schedule should be a clear enough indication that you want to create a new trip. A problem arises, however, if one is trying to select an existing trip (e.g. to move it) and one "just misses" and clicks on empty space. This way, the two procedures are distinct enough for inadvertent confusions not to arise. We also need to ask whether the vehicle should stay selected or not at the conclusion of the action. The reason for unselecting it is so that the trip creation process is terminated, and so additional trips are not inadvertently created if, for example, the user attempts to change the trip just created.

There is little need to use compound states in describing modeless dialogues. Their main value is where there is some significant subsystem which is not of interest in displaying a particular part of the dialogue. Figure 4.18 shows a situation where this might arise. A login procedure has been provided which directs users to different parts of a sys-

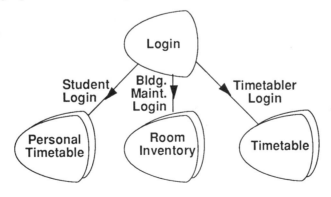

Figure 4.18 A login procedure.

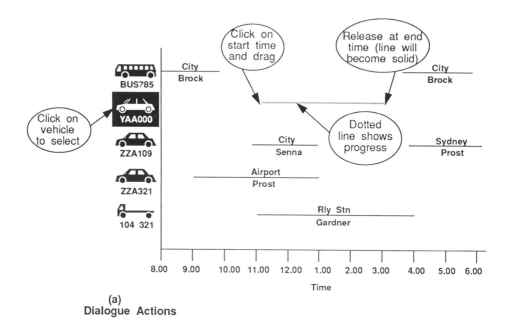

(a)
Dialogue Actions

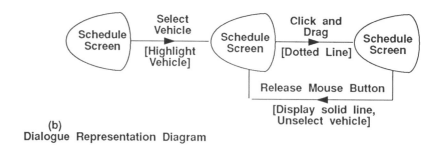

(b)
Dialogue Representation Diagram

Figure 4.19 Scheduling a new trip.

tem (the Personal Timetable system, a Room Inventory system and the full Timetabling system) depending on the user-Id that they enter. Since we are not interested in the details of the three systems, they can be represented by compound states.

It must be stressed that the level of detail embodied in a state transition diagram is only needed when a significant sub-dialogue is entered. For most actions, the command language specification is quite sufficient.

4.2 Common Objects and Actions

4.2.1 A Toolkit of Objects and Actions

One of the greatest assets of an experienced designer is the ability to recognise a familiar situation and to use (or adapt) tried and true solutions when such a situation arises. One of the strengths of object-oriented techniques is that they encourage the designer to break the problem down in such a way that familiar situations appear, and then provide the tools, in the form of predefined objects and actions, which can be readily incorporated in the design.

In the following sections, we discuss some common cases that turn up again and again. We start by looking at actions that are common to all or most object classes, and then look at some frequently occurring object classes.

A naming convention for some common actions has developed over time, and is incorporated in the Common User Access guide-lines. At times, the conventions seem awkward, since they are built around the handling of document and graphics files, but they are widely used and reasonably well understood, and will be discussed here.

4.2.2 Common Actions

Certain actions are applicable to all objects, to the extent that we often do not explicitly specify them unless their effect for the class under discussion is significantly different from the norm. These actions are:

(i) *Selecting an Object.* The ability to select an object underlies the whole object/ action model. This is represented by the command

SELECT object

Selection is usually by pointing, e.g. by placing the cursor on an object (and clicking the mouse if necessary). Figure 4.20(a) shows four common cases: selection of an object on a list by moving a highlight, selection of an icon by clicking on it, selection of a graphical object by clicking on it, and selection of a field on a form

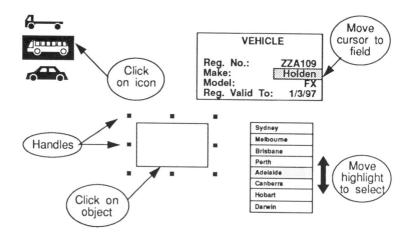

(a)
Selecting a Single Object

(b)
Selecting Multiple Objects

Figure 4.20 Selection of objects.

by moving to it. In situations were more than one object can be selected, selection techniques used include the *marquee* select, in which a rectangle is drawn around the required objects with the mouse, clicking on more than one object, and dragging a highlight over adjacent objects in a list [Figure 4.20(b)].

Other commands may leave an object selected as a side-effect, e.g. creating a new object usually leaves that object as the selected object, as does a Find command that retrieves a single object.

(ii) *Unselecting an Object.* This is represented by the command

UNSELECT object

Unselecting can be done implicitly or explicitly. Selecting another object usually cancels the previous selection. Explicit cancellation is usually done by repeating the process used to make the selection, e.g. clicking on an object a second time may unselect it. Sometimes the designer may have to decide whether to unselect an object at the end of a modal dialogue sequence.

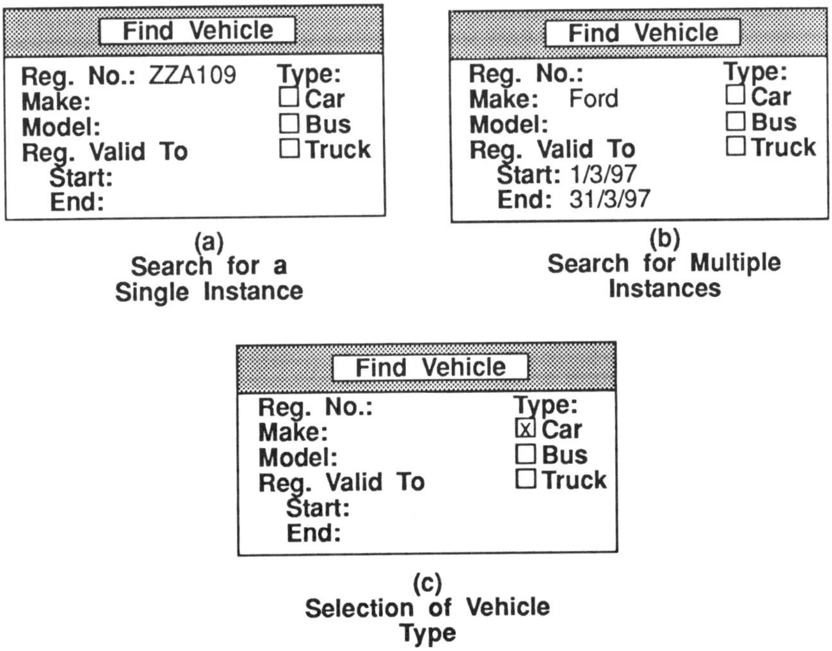

Find Vehicle	
Reg. No.: ZZA109	Type:
Make:	☐ Car
Model:	☐ Bus
Reg. Valid To	☐ Truck
Start:	
End:	

(a)
**Search for a
Single Instance**

Find Vehicle	
Reg. No.:	Type:
Make: Ford	☐ Car
Model:	☐ Bus
Reg. Valid To	☐ Truck
Start: 1/3/97	
End: 31/3/97	

(b)
**Search for Multiple
Instances**

Find Vehicle	
Reg. No.:	Type:
Make:	☒ Car
Model:	☐ Bus
Reg. Valid To	☐ Truck
Start:	
End:	

(c)
**Selection of Vehicle
Type**

Figure 4.21 Finding objects.

(iii) Finding an *Object or a Set of Objects*. This can involve locating a single object, or a number of objects that satisfy a particular set of criteria. A typical form of *Find* might be

FIND class WHERE {attribute = value(s) [AND/OR]}

in which we are looking for all objects in the given class which have the appropriate combination of attribute values. The values can include ranges or sets of discrete values, and conditions on different attributes can be linked by AND or OR conditions.

FIND VEHICLE WHERE REG NO = ZZA109

will locate a single Vehicle object with Reg. No. ZZA109.

FIND VEHICLE MAKE=Holden AND REG VALID TO = 3/97

will locate all Holdens whose registration expires in March 1997.

Find can be implemented in a number of ways. Figure 4.21 shows one common way. The user is given a form on which they can fill in search conditions. The form can be the standard representation of the object, or a special form invoked

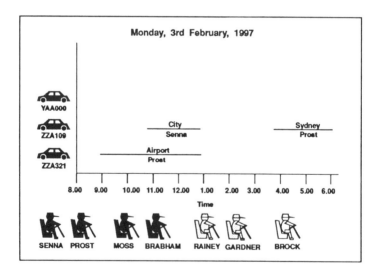

Figure 4.22 Vehicle pool display after
FIND CARS command.

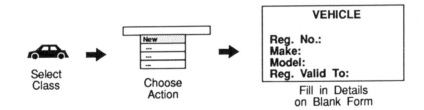

(a)
Creating a New Object from Scratch

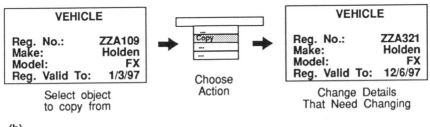

(b)
Creating by Copying

Figure 4.23 Creating a new object.

through a modal dialogue. The latter approach is usually more powerful, because it allows specification of value ranges for a field and of combinations of conditions, where the standard representation of the object does not. In cases where more than one object is retrieved, the Find action often brings up a list from which further choices can be made.

Find provides a very powerful means of determining which objects we are to work on at a given time. In Figure 4.22 we show the vehicle pool schedule, but with cars only displayed. This corresponds to the use of a FIND CAR command (remember that CAR is a sub-class of vehicle). This option is implemented as one of a series of check boxes (the others being TRUCK and BUS) on the search screen.

The Common User Access implementation of *Find* is the Some ... option on the View menu.

(iv) *Creation of a New Object.* New objects can be created in two ways (Figure 4.23). The *New* action operates on the class to create a new member of that class, i.e.

NEW class AS object

e.g. NEW VEHICLE ZZA321 would create a new instance of the class *Vehicle* called ZZA321. The new instance should, if possible, be given a default set of attributes. The alternative to the *New* command is to create the new object by copying (or cloning) an existing object:

COPY object TO new object

e.g. COPY ZZA109 TO ZZA321 would create a vehicle object ZZA321 with the same attributes as an existing object ZZA109. The user can then change any of the attributes that are different. This is usually far easier than creating new objects from scratch, to the extent that in many systems this is the only way to create new objects.

(v) *Destruction of an Object.* This is usually called *Dispose* or *Destroy*:

DISPOSE object

e.g. DISPOSE ZZA321 would get rid of the object created in the previous paragraph. The most common way of implementing *Dispose* is through a menu option (e.g. *Delete* or *Clear*) acting on the selected object.

Under CUA there are a number of variants on *Dispose*. For objects which are part of a larger object, there are two actions which appear on the *Edit* menu:

*   *Clear* removes an object from the screen but leaves the space occupied by it.
*   *Delete* removes the object and also the space occupied by it.

Clear is used, e.g. for drawings, where deleting a component should not affect the layout of other components, while *delete* is used, e.g. for text, where deleting a word or a paragraph causes the remaining text to move up to fill the space.
If an object occupies a window in its own right, the CUA option is *Close*, which appears on the *File* menu. To destroy an object stored on disk, it is *File Delete*.

(vi) *Moving and Copying Objects. Move* takes a number of forms, e.g. relocating an object on the screen, transferring data from one part of an application to another, moving an object from memory to disk or vice versa. The basic form of the *Move* command is

MOVE object TO location

e.g. in the Vehicle Pool, MOVE TRIP 5 TO 13.00 USING YAA000 would describe the movement of a trip on the schedule to a time of 13.00 and the line corresponding to vehicle YAA000. This would be implemented by dragging the appropriate line on the diagram (Figure 4.24). A very common method of moving objects is by cutting and pasting (Figure 4.25). A temporary storage area called the *Clipboard* is used to hold the object being moved or copied. The CUA commands appear on the *Edit* menu and are:

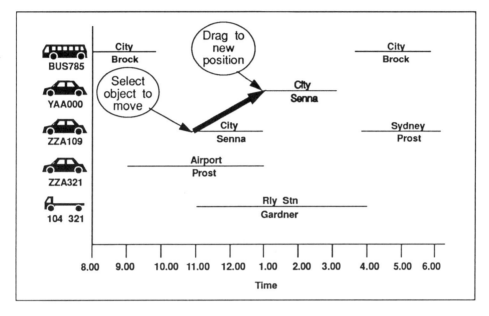

Figure 4.24 Moving an object.

- *Copy* - make a copy of the selected object on the clipboard.
- *Cut* - make a copy of the selected object on the clipboard, and perform either a delete or a clear action on the original.
- *Paste* - place a copy of the object on the clipboard at the position indicated by the user.

To move an object, it is selected and a *Cut* (or *Copy*) action executed. The place to which it is to be moved (which can be in the same or an entirely different window) is then selected and a *Paste* command invoked. The object remains on the clipboard until another *Cut* or *Copy* command is executed, so other actions can be performed between the *Cut* and the *Paste* commands, or multiple copies can by made using multiple *Paste* commands.

The common transfer operations to and from disk (e.g. *Save* and *Retrieve*) are, in fact, copy operations, since the original object (on disk or in main memory) is not destroyed. We tend to think of this form of copying as different from the cloning operation discussed above, in that we see this as creating two copies of the same object, rather than creating a completely new object. For this reason, different verbs are used:

      SAVE object
      OPEN object

Under CUA guidelines, these appear on the *File* menu. Notice, however, that there is a version of *Save* with an additional parameter

        SAVE object AS new object

which is a genuine copy command. Under CUA, this appears on the *File* menu as *Save As ...* Other variants are *Import* and *Export*, which make copies of objects which are in different formats, e.g. a word processor may use *Export* to create a file in the format used by a different word processor. However, the usage here is not consistent, since another package may use an option under *Save As ...* to perform this task.

(vii) *Obtaining or Changing the Value of an Attribute of an Object.* Words commonly used for these actions are *Show* (or *Enquire*) and *Set*, e.g.

        SHOW ZZA321 MAKE

would give the value of the attribute MAKE, i.e. Holden, while

        SET ZZA321 MAKE = Porsche

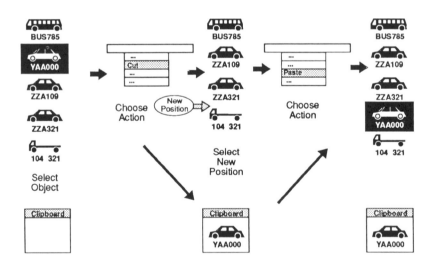

Contents of Clipboard

Figure 4.25 Using the clipboard to move
an object.

would change the value of MAKE to Porsche. These are commonly implemented by displaying a form or a dialogue box containing the attributes of the object (Figure 4.2). The user may then change the attributes in an appropriate manner, e.g. by typing in a new value, choosing a value from a pick-list, or by making a selection using check-boxes or radio buttons. These techniques are described in more detail in Chapter 5.

(viii) *Displaying an Object.* This makes an object visible to the user:

DISPLAY object

e.g. DISPLAY ZZA109 would display the object ZZA109 on the screen. There are various ways of asking that an object be displayed. The most common is expanding out an icon (Figure 4.2).

The reverse of display is:

UNDISPLAY object

This corresponds to shrinking the object back into an icon.

In addition to *Display* itself, there are usually a set of *Display Options* commands, which the user can use to decide how an object is to appear. In Figure 4.26 we show a number of ways in which the *Vehicle* object might appear. The user could choose these options from a menu. Similarly, in Figure 4.27, we show how the display of the vehicle schedule could be rearranged so that it was organised by driver instead of vehicle. The vehicles now appear as a list at the bottom of the display, where the drivers were before. This again could be chosen as a menu option.

```
┌─────────────────────────────┐
│          VEHICLE            │
│                             │
│  Reg. No.:       ZZA109     │
│  Make:           Holden     │
│  Model:              FX     │
│  Reg. Valid To:    1/3/97   │
└─────────────────────────────┘
```
Vehicle with No
Trips or Maintenance

```
┌─────────────────────────────┐
│          VEHICLE            │
│  Reg. No.:       ZZA109     │
│  Make:           Holden     │
│  Model:              FX     │
│  Reg. Valid To:    1/3/97   │
│                             │
│    MAINTENANCE HISTORY      │
│                             │
│  Date    Service Type Amt. Paid │
│  30/1/97 10,000 km    $235.00   │
│  7/11/96 Wheel Align  $ 52.50   │
│  12/8/96 5000 km      $134.00   │
└─────────────────────────────┘
```
With Maintenance
Records Only

```
┌─────────────────────────────┐
│          VEHICLE            │
│  Reg. No.:       ZZA109     │
│  Make:           Holden     │
│  Model:              FX     │
│  Reg. Valid To:    1/3/97   │
│                             │
│            TRIPS            │
│                             │
│  Date    Time  Dest.   Driver │
│  3/2/97  11.00 City    Senna  │
│  3/2/97  16.00 Sydney  Prost  │
│  5/2/97  08.00 Pub     Prost  │
└─────────────────────────────┘
```
With Trip Records
Only

```
┌─────────────────────────────┐
│          VEHICLE            │
│  Reg. No.:       ZZA109     │
│  Make:           Holden     │
│  Model:              FX     │
│  Reg. Valid To:    1/3/97   │
│                             │
│            TRIPS            │
│                             │
│  Date    Time  Dest.   Driver │
│  3/2/97  11.00 City    Senna  │
│  3/2/97  16.00 Sydney  Prost  │
│  5/2/97  08.00 Pub     Prost  │
│                             │
│    MAINTENANCE HISTORY      │
│                             │
│  Date    Service Type Amt. Paid │
│  30/1/97 10,000 km    $235.00   │
│  7/11/96 Wheel Align  $ 52.50   │
│  12/8/96 5000 km      $134.00   │
└─────────────────────────────┘
```
With Trip and Maintenance
Records

Figure 4.26 Display of different parts of the VEHICLE object.

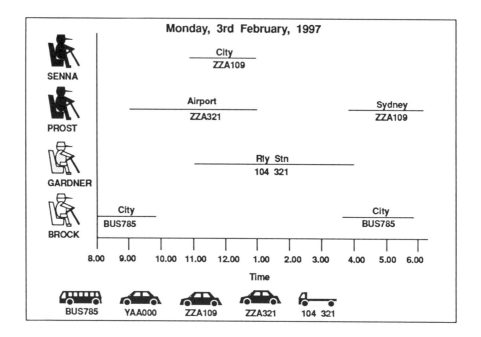

Figure 4.27 The vehicle pool schedule
organised by driver.

Under CUA, these actions appear on the *View* menu. These options are obviously highly application-dependent. We include them here because, in almost every system, there are actions of this type. It is these actions that give the user much of the control over their environment that a good dialogue requires.

One way of thinking about these common actions is to regard them as properties of a class called *Object* (Figure 4.28) which contains only those features that are common to all classes. The other classes then inherit from object. Object itself has only one attribute, *Object Name*, which is the unique identifier given to the object. The existence of the Object class means that we do not have to constantly redefine what we mean by things like *Move, Copy, Display, Find* and *Select* which are the same for most if not all objects, but where there are special requirements (e.g. a *New* command for a particular object class may have to set up special default values) we can always override the inherited action with a special one for that class. The class hierarchies in languages such as *Smalltalk* are implemented in this way.

In most of the class definitions in this book we will not explicitly include a parent class if that class is *Object*, but it is implied.

4.2.3 Slots

A *slot* is an object that can contain another object [Figure 4.29(a)]. The most common use of slots is when we are building some sort of a framework into which we wish to place other objects, e.g. in a timetable, we have a series of timeslots (designated either by the time of day or by some number, e.g. the period number) into which we schedule classes, while in the Crossword Designer, the crossword frame is made up of a series of slots into which we place words. Slots can be of equal or of unequal size. A sophisticated version of a slot appears in an organisation chart, where each position is in effect a slot into which a person can be placed. In many applications, one uses collection objects made up of slots, e.g. the timetable grid or the crossword frame.

Slots may be defined so that they can hold only a single object, or multiple objects. The timeslot in Figure 4.29(b) allows for multiple objects.

The actions on a slot include placing objects into the slot and removing them from the slot, and also checking whether a particular set of parameters (e.g. a time) lie within the bounds of the slot.

Class OBJECT	
Attributes	
Object Name	Unique name given to the object
Actions	

New:
    Object Name
	Create a new instance of the selected class
	    with name Object Name

Dispose	Destroy the selected object
Copy To: Object Name	Copy the selected object to Object Name
Move To: Location	Move the selected object to Location
Show Value Of: Attribute Name	Show the value of the attribute Attribute Name

Change Value
    Of: Attribute Name
    To: New Value
	Change the value of attribute Attribute Name
	    to New Value

Display	Display the currently selected object

Find
    {Attribute: Attribute Name
      Value: Value   }
	Find all objects with the stated values of the
	    named attributes

Select:
    Object Name
	Make the object Object Name the currently
	    selected object

Unselect	Unselect the currently selected object

Figure 4.28 Class definition of the OBJECT
object.

4.2.4 Collections

In many situations, we are concerned not with one object, but with a collection of objects: a crowd of people, a gaggle of geese, a hit list, or a road network. This is illustrated schematically in Figure 4.30. *Collections* are important in dialogue design, because they often form the basis for an overview.

Since a collection is in itself an object, all of the common actions described in the previous section apply. In addition, there are four basic operations that we can perform on any collection:

- We can *add* an object to the collection.
- We can *delete* an object from the collection.
- We *find* an object in the collection (i.e. we can test for *membership*).
- We can *count* the number of objects in the collection.

We can classify collections in two different ways (Figure 4.31): by the types of object that they contain, and by the relationships between the objects in the class.

In the first classification, we distinguish between *homogeneous* and in*homogeneous* collections, i.e. ones in which all objects are of the same class (e.g. a payroll made up of people, or a fleet list made up of vehicles), and ones in which objects can be of different classes (e.g. an assets register, which can contain vehicles, buildings, typewriters and tea urns). Depending on the way that you wish to view the problem, these distinctions can often be reversed, e.g. the fleet list could be viewed as being made up of car, truck and bus objects (i.e. is inhomogeneous), while the assets register could be made homogeneous by introducing a *Possession* class (with attributes *Possession Number, Possession Type, Value, Description*) to which all assets belong. This apparent discrepancy arises because, somewhere in our classification system, we can always find a class (even if it is the most general class *object*) to which all the objects belong.

The types of collection that occur in most practical problems are either homogeneous collections, or inhomogeneous collections where there are some attributes in common (e.g. the value in the assets register) which can be manipulated in some useful way, so that the treatment of homogeneous and heterogeneous collections is much the same.

The second type of classification is concerned with the relationship (or lack of) between objects.

The simplest collections are the *set* and the *bag*, which are unordered collections, i.e. there is no concept of a position of an object in the collection. In a set, a given object can only appear once. The membership of a club is a set of people: there is no particular ordering (e.g. no member is in no way superior to another or has special privileges based on some notional position), and any given person can only belong once. The four operations described above are the only operations on sets.

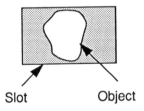

Slot   Object

(a)
A slot

Class TIMESLOT	
Attributes	
Slot Identifier Start Time End Time Occupant: {OBJECT}	Id. for slot (e.g. period no.) Start of Timeslot End of Timeslot Occupant(s) of slot
Actions	

In Timeslot?:
    Time
Fill slot:
    Object
Vacate slot:
    Object
	Does the specified time fall within the
	    timeslot?
	Place object Object in slot
	
	Remove object Object from slot

(b)
Class definition for a timeslot

Figure 4.29 Slots.

In a bag, the same object may occur more than once. This often occurs when we have a number of objects of the same type and do not want to distinguish between them, e.g. we might have three apples and four oranges. The roster in Figure 4.33, although not a bag, illustrates another situation where the same object might appear twice in a collection. There is one additional operation on a bag: to *count instances* of a particular object in the collection.

Ordered Collections are characterised by there being relationships between the objects (commonly described by links) which specify the order in which they appear.

In a *list* (Figures 4.31-2) the objects appear in a set order. This order may be specified from the data in the object (e.g. a list of names in alphabetical order) or it might come from an external source (e.g. a waiting list ordered by when the objects were placed on the list, or a list of stations on a railway line). If an attribute (or a group of attributes) is used to order the list, these are known as *sort keys*.

Since a list is ordered, there is a concept of a "next" object (after the current one) and a "previous" object, with *Next* and *Previous* actions to allow movement along the list. *Insertion* in a list has to be in a particular position. The convention is that it is following

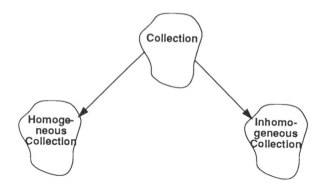

(a)
Classification by Types of Object

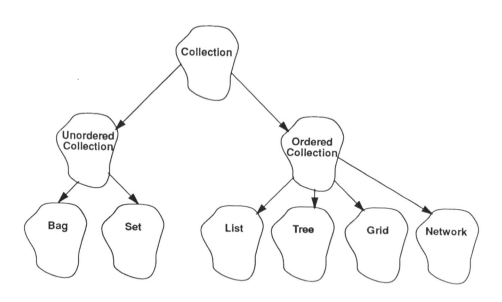

(b)
Classification by Relationships between Objects

Figure 4.30 Types of collection.

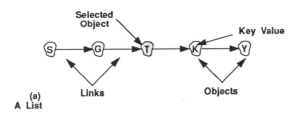

(a)
A List

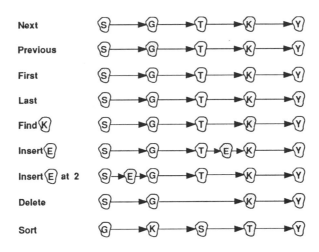

(b)
Effect of Actions on the List in (a)

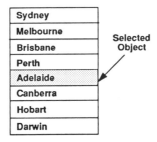

(c)
Representation of a List

Figure 4.31 Lists.

the currently selected object, but that a particular position (e.g. second) can be specified. The latter option is the only way to insert at the front of the list. If the list is ordered using a sort key, the correct position can be obtained by using a *Find* action, which, if the object is not found, by convention selects the object prior to where the looked for object should be, and then the *Insert*.

Representations of lists commonly do not show the links explicitly, but simply list the objects in order. An object can be selected by moving a highlight.

A variation on a list is a *circular list*, in which there is no start or finish, the "last" node being connected to the "first".

A *grid* (Figure 4.33) is a two-dimensional version of a list. Users of spreadsheets will be familiar with grids, since a spreadsheet is merely a blank grid. Each cell is a *slot* object waiting for other objects (numbers, text and formulae) to be placed in them. A roster works in a similar way: the grid squares represent *tasks* to be performed in a specified *timeslot*, and peoples' names are then attached to these squares. As with lists, the links are rarely shown. To move around a grid, actions *Left, Right, Up* and *Down* need to be implemented to move from cell to cell. Insertion must be a row or a column at a time.

A tree (Figure 4.34) represents a hierarchical organisation of objects. At the top, there is a single object called the root (trees are always drawn upside down or on their side). This is linked to a series of objects below it (its children), and these in turn are linked to further objects (their children). Typical uses of trees are to represent organisa-

Class LIST		
Parent: COLLECTION		
Attributes		
Contents:		
{Object: OBJECT	Object in list	
Position}	Position of object in list	
Ordering Keys	Attributes (if any) on which list is ordered	
Actions		
Next	Select next object on list	
Previous	Select previous object on list	
First	Select first object on list	
Last	Select last object on list	
Find:	Select indicated object. If not found, select	
Object	previous to correct posn. (key ordered list)	
	or first in list	
Insert:	Insert OBJECT after currently selected object	
Object	and make it selected object	
Insert:	Insert OBJECT at specified POSITION in list	
Object	and make it selected object	
At: Position		
Delete	Delete selected object	
Sort	Sort list in key order (key ordered list only)	

Figure 4.32 Definition of the class LIST.

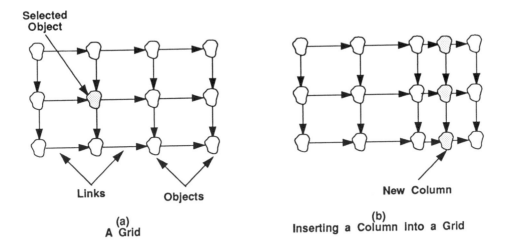

Selected
Object

Links   Objects

(a)
A Grid

New Column

(b)
Inserting a Column into a Grid

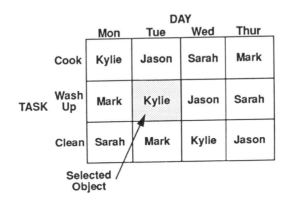

DAY

	Mon	Tue	Wed	Thur
Cook	Kylie	Jason	Sarah	Mark
Wash Up	Mark	Kylie	Jason	Sarah
Clean	Sarah	Mark	Kylie	Jason

TASK

Selected
Object

(c)
Representation of a Grid

Figure 4.33 Grids.

tion charts, and directory structures on computer systems. Complete trees are usually represented in a very similar way to the diagram, showing all the links, as in the family tree in Figure 4.12. The other option is to represent a path through the tree, in the form of a list of all the objects on a direct route from the root to the current object. A directory path, e.g. C:\DIALOGBK\CHAP3\ is such a list. To move around a tree, one needs actions to move to a parent node, and to a specified child node. Sometimes the children of each parent are organised on a list, in which case actions such as First Child and Next Sibling are available.

Graphs and networks (Figure 4.35) are the most general form of ordered collection, in that each object can be linked to as many other objects as desired. This is handled by keeping a list of the other objects pointed to. The links can be one-way or two-way: in a directed graph, links are one-way, i.e. a link from object A to object B does not imply a link from B to A, unless it is explicitly shown. The data flow diagrams in Chapter 2 are directed graphs, as was the critical path diagram used to model the airline flight information. In an ordinary graph, links are two-way. In a network, weights are assigned to the links, e.g. if the network represented a road system, the weights would be distances between towns.

Because of the complexity of the links, the best way of representing graphs or networks is to reproduce the appropriate picture of it as closely as possible, so we would represent the network in Figure 4.35 exactly as it looks.

4.3   The Structure of an Application

So far, we have been talking about individual objects, or special kinds of collections of objects. An *application* is a different kind of object. It is the collection of objects that we supply to a user to perform a specific task or set of tasks (Figure 4.36).

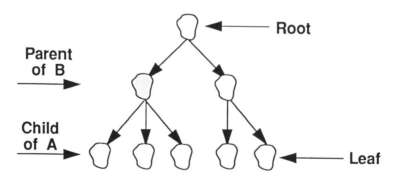

Figure 4.34 A tree.

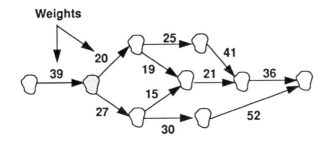

(a)
Schematic Picture of a Network

Class NETWORK	
Parent: COLLECTION	

Attributes
Contents:
  {Object: OBJECT   Object (Node) in network
  { Link To   Cross-Reference (Link) to another Object (Node)
     Weight   } Weight attached to Link
  }

(b)
Part of the Class Definition for NETWORK

Figure 4.35 Networks.

An application normally consists of a number of objects. As a rule, each of these objects is contained in a separate window (Figure 4.37) and the user moves between objects by moving between the windows. If all the windows are displayed, then the user can select a different window by moving the cursor to it and clicking the mouse. If the window is represented by an icon, then clicking on the icon can expand it. A third method is the use of a *window* menu, which gives a list of the windows and allows the user to select whichever one they want.

The job of the application is to facilitate the user's task by:

- Providing any necessary links between the objects.
- Displaying, or allowing the user to display, the objects in appropriate forms for the different tasks.

The user will enter the application from the operating system (or an overlay to it, such as the Windows Desktop) either by invoking the application directly, or by attempting to access an object created by the application. When an application starts up, there is usually one window available for each class of object. One of these is active. The choice de-

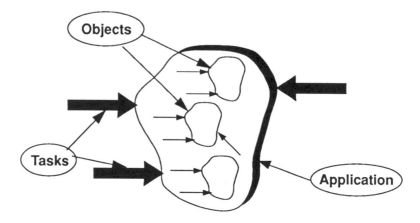

Figure 4.36 An application.

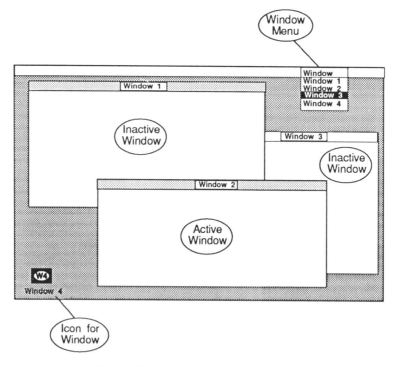

Figure 4.37 Screen display with windows for
each object.

pends on the application: it may be an overview or the most commonly used or "main" object; it may be the last active window the last time the system was used, or it may be the one nominated by the user as their initial window. The use of an overview as an initial window is discussed below. Most word processors display their "main" window (the document window) on startup. Further objects of the same class (and their associated windows) are created using actions such as *Create* or *Copy* (implemented, e.g. as *File New* and *File Open*) on the appropriate window.

In many applications, the windows are not independent, but are linked, e.g. by overview-detail relationships, or because information about two different types of object are required at the same time, and so must be displayed together.

In our Vehicle Pool application, there are four main objects: *vehicle, driver, trip* and *schedule*. The tasks to be performed were given in the initial requirements specification, as processes on the data flow diagram (Figure 2.20) and are:

- Schedule trips.
- Arrange maintenance.
- Register vehicle.

The first requirement of a user entering a new application (even a familiar one) is to orient themselves. This requires some sort of overview. In the Vehicle Pool system, the schedule screen (Figure 4.38) performs this function. It contains three objects: the schedule itself, a list of vehicles and a list of drivers. The schedule itself is a collection of trips.

The schedule appears as a Gantt chart. If the schedule is organised by vehicle, the vehicle list is incorporated into the chart (up the left-hand side), while the driver list appears at the bottom. If the schedule is organised by driver, the positions of the lists are reversed. The user can change the representation using a *By Driver/By Vehicle* option on the View menu.

The schedule contains information for one day. If it will not all fit, the schedule can be scrolled. Because most of the requests for transport are made on the day or only a day or two before, the schedule initially displayed is for the current day. The scheduler can move between days using *Next* and *Previous* options, or by overtyping the date at the top of the screen with a new date.

The user should then be able to perform operations on this overview (e.g. scheduling trips), or to look at and work on individual drivers or sets of drivers in detail. This gives the structure shown in Figure 4.40. The conventional way of bringing up a driver or vehicle object would be by double-clicking on it on the schedule screen. An alternative would be to select the object, and then use the *View* menu. This latter approach has the advantage that the user can specify display options, e.g. whether they want to view a single object or a list of objects, what form the object should be in (e.g. should there be trip and/or maintenance information) and what order they should appear in. Double-

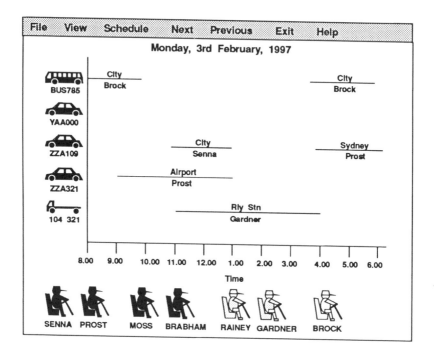

Figure 4.38 The main screen of the vehicle
pool application.

clicking would give the object in whatever form was specified the previous time it was displayed.

The menu structure is given in Figure 4.41. There are three variants on the *view* menu, depending on whether the schedule itself, a vehicle or a driver is selected. These would be combined into one with the parts that are not applicable dimmed. The *One* option displays a single vehicle or driver, the *Some* .. or *All* displays a list. *Some* .. brings up a dialogue box to specify search parameters. *Link* displays a list with the details of the currently selected list element alongside. *By* .. brings up a dialogue box to specify a sort order. *Trips* and *Maintenance* are toggles which specify whether trip and maintenance information is to be included in the objects. If any further tailoring was needed, these would probably be moved to an *Options* menu. *Maint. List* and *Rego. List* are discussed below.

Although general-purpose *Find* and *Sort* options (i.e. *Some* .. and *By* ..), along with the object-specific formatting options, would give all of the facilities required, some quite specific display options are likely to be used sufficiently frequently to require specific provision. These are:

- A Registration Renewal list, in which vehicles are listed in order of the Registration Valid To attribute, with the earliest dates first.
- A Maintenance Due list, in which each vehicle's last service, the mileage since the last service, and the mileage at which the next service is due are listed, with those closest to needing a service at the head of the list.

Note that, although we have not shown it, the current mileage and next service due fields should be included whenever maintenance details are displayed as part of the Vehicle object, so this second list is not a special format in any way.

How, then, can this system be used to perform the required tasks?

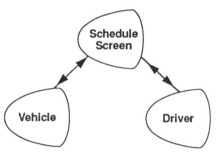

Figure 4.39 Vehicle pool dialogue structure.

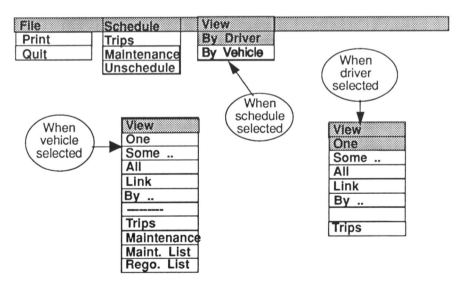

Figure 4.40 Vehicle pool menu structure.

VEHICLE LIST				
Reg.	Last Service			Next
No.	Date	Type	km	Serv
ZZA321	3/12/96	Rego	50123	50000
ZZA109	30/1/97	10000	13927	15000
BUS785	12/4/96	W.Al.	22967	25000
YAA000	11/9/96	15000	17422	20000
104321	15/1/97	10000	11500	15000

VEHICLE

Reg. No.:	ZZA109
Make:	Holden
Model:	FX
Reg. Valid To:	1/3/97

TRIPS

Date	Time	Dest.	Driver
3/2/97	11.00	City	Senna
3/2/97	16.00	Sydney	Prost
5/2/97	08.00	Pub	Prost

MAINTENANCE HISTORY

Date	Service Type	Amt. Paid
30/1/97	10,000 km	$235.00
7/11/96	Wheel Align	$ 52.50
12/8/96	5000 km	$134.00

Maintenance list   Details of selected vehicle

Figure 4.41 The maintenance list.

The *Schedule Trips* function can be performed on the Schedule screen, using the actions to schedule and move a trip that we have described previously (Figure 4.18, Figure 1.16 and Figure 4.24). To remove a trip, one double-clicks on it, and to remove a driver (or vehicle if the schedule is arranged by driver) one double-clicks on it where it appears against the trip. Menu options can also be provided. To unschedule, this involves selecting the trip (or driver) and using an Unschedule option. To schedule, a dialogue box would be needed to gather the necessary information on start and end times, and driver and vehicle allocation.

The *Arrange Maintenance* function is based on the maintenance list described above. The user uses the list to select candidates for maintenance. For the purposes of this discussion, it is assumed that a vehicle requiring maintenance is out of service for a full day or a number of days. Unless they arrange maintenance so far ahead that no vehicle is scheduled, they need to check the trips currently scheduled for the vehicle and find a free day. The most convenient format for this is the Vehicle object with the trips listed, and not the schedule, since the schedule only covers one day. Again, this could be done with the features already provided, but it would be nice to make it simpler for the user.

The best approach is to use two windows: the list, and the full details of the object currently selected on the list (Figure 4.41). These two windows keep in step: if the user moves down the list, the object in the second window changes. This mode of viewing is a particular case of the *link* mode provided on the view menu, rather than being a special feature provided for this function. Only the invocation (from the Maintenance List) option is automatic.

Once the user has found a suitable date, they use the *Maintenance* option on the *Schedule* menu. This will put up a dialogue box asking for the date. It will also result in the vehicle icon on the schedule for that date being dimmed, so that it cannot be selected. Any clash with trips scheduled would, of course, result in an error message, but note that this procedure would avoid most errors because the user can see what they are doing.

Renew Registration involves two distinct aspects: presenting the vehicle for a roadworthiness inspection, and recording the renewal. The first of these is essentially a maintenance operation, and could be handled in the same way, i.e. the *Registration List* is just the maintenance list organised by registration date. Recording the renewal can be done by typing a new date into the vehicle object, however displayed (e.g. if there were more than one per day, the renewal list would be the obvious choice).

The point of this example is to demonstrate the way in which quite powerful functions can be provided through the provision of a small number of objects and an equally small number of actions, provided that the objects can be presented in the right way at the right time. Most of the ideas about how the system works would have been developed during the initial visualisation of the system, with the actual objects and actions being developed from this.

There are two main errors which designers make in putting together systems in this way:

- They provide *only* the general-purpose facilities (such as Find and Sort, and the ability to display a single object and a list), and do not address the frequently used special cases (such as the maintenance list), which makes the resulting system too clumsy to be easy to use.
- They concentrate too much on the special cases, providing different facilities for each, but no general-purpose facilities, thus making the system complex and inflexible.

The happy medium is half-way between these positions. The special cases must be provided as instances of more general facilities, but there must be short-cuts (e.g. "canned" definitions) to provide them. Where additional special cases are required, or existing ones have to be treated differently, these can be added reasonably simply by adding or changing the short-cuts. Note that this approach is not the same as providing a *macro* facility on top of general-purpose facilities, since macros have to be programmed by the user, and programming is a difficult task.

The structure discussed here is very different from the deep menu hierarchies encountered in many mainframe systems. These are built around tasks (or actions) rather than objects. Problems often arise because a user may want to jump across a menu hierarchy, e.g. to perform an enquiry in the middle of a transaction. Because these systems are highly modal, the designer must make explicit provision for any such jumps, i.e. they must explicitly build flexibility in the system. This is not a very flexible way of providing flexibility, since it is limited both by the designer's imagination and by problems of complexity.

Some designers encounter problems in what object to show first, because there are two or more independent objects which could be accessed and they are unable to decide which is the "right" one. There are two rather different reasons for this situation occurring:

- The visualisation is incomplete, with ideas for detailed objects but no overview. This is a common problem with people trained in areas such as data analysis, where the emphasis is on breaking down the problem into its smallest components.
- The user genuinely wants to approach the problem from different directions. In this case, the most commonly accessed object should appear first, with a rapid access path to the others, the user should be allowed to specify (via a *preferences* menu) which object(s) they want displayed first, or the system should display the last object accessed.

Summary

In this chapter, we developed the formal framework for the dialogue model. This model is made up of a set of *objects* to represent the data to be displayed to the user, plus a series of *actions* (or operations) which the user can perform on those objects. These provide the user with a set of building-blocks which they can use to perform the functions of the system. Each object has one or more *attributes* which represent properties of the object. One or more attributes (known as the *identifier*) are used to specify a particular object.

The *representation* of an object is the way in which it is displayed on the screen. Objects can be represented in many different ways. Two common ways are as *forms* (containing all the attributes) and as *icons* (a stylised picture representing the object).

Objects are grouped into *classes*, which define a particular type of object. A class is an abstract definition of a particular type of object. The class definition contains both the attributes of that type of object, and the allowable actions on that object. Although these ideas of classes and objects are related to some of the concepts used in data modelling (e.g. *entities*) they are not the same, since data which a user might want to work with as a unit is often split over a number of entities, and the data entities do not incorporate actions. Dialogues whose objects are obtained purely by looking at the data model usually contain only very detailed information, and lack any form of overview.

There are three distinct kinds of association between objects: *cross-references*, where an object refers to another object; *inclusion*, where an object is part of a larger object; and *inheritance*, where a class of objects is a specialisation of a more general class.

To show actions pictorially, we must draw a series of pictures (a *storyboard*), or a series of steps on one picture. More formal methods of specifying actions include: the use of *protocols* in the class definitions, a *command language*, and *state diagrams*. Command languages and protocols specify *what* the action is to do, and are adequate provided that the implementation of the action is hidden from the user, although the specification must include any parameters (additional data) passed to the action. When we must know *how* the action is to be implemented, e.g. with a modal sub-dialogue, state diagrams are of more use.

One of the greatest assets of an experienced designer is the ability to recognise a familiar situation and to use (or adapt) tried and true solutions when such a situation arises. One of the strengths of object-oriented techniques is that they encourage the designer to break the problem down in such a way that familiar situations appear, and then provide the tools, in the form of predefined objects and actions, which can be readily incorporated in the design.

Some commonly occurring actions are:

- Selecting an object.
- Unselecting an object.
- Finding an object or a set of objects.
- Creation of a new object.
- Destruction of an object.
- Moving and copying objects.
- Obtaining or changing the value of an attribute of an object.
- Displaying an object.

These common actions can be regarded as properties of a class called *Object* which contains only those features that are common to all classes. The other classes then inherit from object.

Two commonly used types of object are:

- Slots, which are objects into which other objects can be placed.
- Collections of other objects, e.g. sets, lists, grids, trees, graphs and networks.

An *application* is the collection of objects that we supply to a user to perform a specific task or set of tasks. As a rule, each of these objects is contained in a separate window and the user moves between objects by moving between the windows.

The job of the application is to facilitate the user's task by providing any necessary links between the objects, and displaying, or allowing the user to display, the objects in appropriate forms for the different tasks.

The window initially active when the application starts up depends on the application: it may be an overview or the most commonly used or "main" object; it may be the last active window the last time the system was used, or it may be the one nominated by the user as their initial window.

In many applications, the windows are not independent, but are linked, e.g. by overview-detail relationships, or because information about two different types of object are required at the same time, and so must be displayed together.

The essence of good application design is the provision of the required functionality through the judicious choice of a small number of objects and actions, linked so that the objects can be presented in the right way at the right time. Common errors involve provision only of very general features, making the resulting system too clumsy, or an excess of special-purpose facilities, thus making the system complex and inflexible.

Exercises

1. Peoples' names are always a problem in computer systems. If we store the full name in one field, we do not know which is the surname, yet if we store the surname separately we do not know whether it goes first, last or somewhere in the middle. A person's preferred mode of address (for use, e.g. on a conference tag) may not be obvious, e.g. it could be an abbreviation or a second given name. Titles, degrees and decorations might also have to be included.

   Devise a name object that can be included in a person object to handle these problems. Show how a user can define the relevant parts of the object as part of a dialogue. If you think that certain attributes (e.g. degrees and decorations) are not really part of a name, show how these fit in the context of the larger person object.

2. Vector graphics software is based on the construction and manipulation of geometric objects, e.g. lines, connected sets of lines, circles and rectangles. Although there are significant differences between the different types of objects, there are also similarities, both in properties and behaviour.

(a) Show how inheritance can be used to build a class hierarchy of different types of geometric objects; and

(b) Using sketches, show the various actions possible on geometric objects (e.g. resizing, reshaping, changing fill), and investigate the changes required for the more specific classes.

   You may want to look at a vector graphics package (e.g. Macdraw, GEM Draw, Corel Draw) to get some ideas as to the possibilities.

3. A small business computer application might be defined by the following set of relations:

   CUSTOMER NO*, NAME, ADDRESS

   PRODUCT NUMBER*, NAME, PRICE, UNITS

ORDER*, DATE, PRODUCT NUMBER, CUSTOMER NO, QUANTITY

INVOICE*, DATE, PRODUCT NUMBER, CUSTOMER NO, QUANTITY

INVOICE*, DATE*, PAYMENT

DELIVERY*, DATE*, PRODUCT NUMBER, QUANTITY, PRICE

What objects can best represent this system, what are the characteristics of the data and what actions will be performed on these objects.

4. Using the dialogue representation symbols in Section 4.1.6, specify the dialogue steps to cut and paste text in a word processor.

5. Take an application with which you are familiar and see if you can classify all the actions and objects with the set of common actions and objects defined in this chapter. Are there any actions which do not fit? If so, can you generalise these actions and extend the set of common actions?

6. See how many of the actions you have identified in the previous question could be re-expressed as a variation on a move operation. For example, we can change a Dispose Object to a Move to Garbage action.

7. Find a command language dialogue (UNIX shell or DOS command line), identify the objects and actions manipulated by these applications and describe the system using the approach in this chapter. Does this help you think of a better user-interface for the system?

8. Consider a document such as a memo or a short report.

    *   What objects can be used to represent this document and its component parts? What attributes should they have? What actions should be available to manipulate each of these objects?
    *   You will probably find that you have a large number of possible objects. A typical word processing package will regard some of these as important, and build its operation around them, while relegating others to a minor role or ignoring them altogether. Using a word processing package that you know, identify these "important" objects, and suggest why they are important.
    *   How does this choice differ from that in a desktop publishing package, and why?

Chapter 5

Guide-lines for User-Interfaces

This chapter outlines rules and guide-lines for user-interfaces. Chapter 1 outlined the design approach, Chapter 2 discussed the ideas of objects and actions and Chapter 4 discussed the development of a conceptual model for the user-interface. In Chapter 3 we gave usability rules and guide-lines on how to test computer systems. Those ideas are the most crucial in developing usable computer systems. This chapter contains similar, practical advice to that given in most other texts on the design of computer systems. The advice is useful and necessary, but you must have an overall framework within which to apply it. You do not design by applying guide-lines. Guide-lines help you check your designs, but they are not magic formulae to generate systems.

The advice is given as a set of rules, some supported by research, some from accumulated wisdom on the part of designers. We make no claim that they are the final word on guide-lines, but you will find them a useful starting point. We give references for you to find more detail on particular aspects. Much of the material comes from two major sources. First the work on the Xerox Star user-interface and second the IBM Common User Access guide-lines.

5.1 Rules from Xerox Star

The work at Xerox Parc in the 1970s influenced the style and shape of present day user-interfaces. The article by Smith *et al.* (1982) describes the rationale behind the interface. We start with these rules because they are simple and easy to apply, yet their application helps produce usable computer systems. Many of the same ideas appear in different guises in other parts of this book but their historical and practical importance justifies their emphasis. Figure 5.1 shows a list of easy and hard principles to use when designing a user-interface. The ideas on the left are easy and those on the right are hard.

5.1.1   Concrete versus Abstract

As discussed in Chapter 8 it is suggested that we make interfaces concrete rather than abstract and give examples as well as rules. In the design of the airline's timetable system we used the map representation of Australia rather than a matrix. Concrete things are easier to show visually than abstract ideas. You can test this by trying to think of ICONS for an aeroplane, electronic mail documents, heat, and usability. The more concrete it is, the easier it is to represent, and hence the easier it is for people to manipulate visually.

5.1.2   Visible versus Invisible

An easy way to make a difficult user-interface (and this is a good objective for some games and quizzes) is to keep things hidden from the user. Put up prompts, then make them disappear while they are still needed; even worse, put up messages onto part of a virtual screen that is invisible to the user. Hiding information and forcing people to remember ensures a hard-to-use interface.

5.1.3   Copying versus Creating

This idea is an extremely powerful one and is the foundation for many of the ideas in this book. Do not generate new solutions; take old ones and modify them. Rather than creating a new document take an old one and change it. Never require people to invent from scratch. Always give them something they can modify. Thinking this way changes the approach to user-interface design and it applies to many other work situations. The idea makes copying intellectually respectable. Plagiarism is only a problem if another person's work is passed off as your own without appropriate acknowledgement.

Easy	Hard
Concrete	Abstract
Visible	Invisible
Copying	Creating
Choosing	Filling in
Recognising	Generating
Editing	Programming
Interactive	Batch

Figure 5.1 Easy and hard operations.

5.1.4   Choosing versus Filling In

This is a variation on copying. Instead of requiring people to remember what to type, give them lists of things from which they can choose. Use pick-lists extensively in dialogues. Make a rule that if data is in the system then a user need never type it again. Somehow they should be able to choose the item and put it into the machine. (However, do not require them to select, but give them the option of typing in.) In some cases it is obviously impractical and a poor way of inputting data. To produce this book it would be clumsy to select every word from a list rather than to type it in.

Recognising versus Generating and Editing versus Programming are other instances of a similar idea. Always try to start from something and work to a new solution by modifying the old.

5.1.5   Interactive versus Batch

This is no longer the issue it was in the 1970s. People have accepted that interactive computer systems are normally better than saving transactions, keying them away from the computer, then entering them in a batch. This was an issue once. Batch systems may be better where the computer is not as good a tool as other methods. For example, sketching is often better done by hand than with a computer because it is quicker and the current computing technology is not as free or easy to use as a pencil and paper.

Sometimes data is prepared as the result of some other operation and, when convenient, it can be entered as a batch. This often happens in retail stores where preprinted tickets are collected and then entered later as a batch. However, for most applications, it is often best to use the computer as an interactive tool that assists the end-user input the data instead of collecting data for some later batch operation.

5.2   General Principles

Chapter 3 on usability suggests ways to evaluate a user-interface. Those rules will help your design efforts as you want your product to pass any usability test. We will not repeat the rules here, but ask you to review the material. The principles presented here come from a variety of sources with several coming from the Xerox Star project. They give ways of thinking about applications and give strategies to help test designs. The principles are suggestions, not absolutes and it is still necessary to test designs on users and design with imagination and intuition.

5.2.1 Design Systems to Fit the User's Conceptual Model

This idea is the central idea behind this book. The Xerox project pioneered the idea of building from the user-interface out, rather than start with hardware, design software and then add the user-interface. They began with the tasks that users wanted to do and invented objects and manipulations to model those tasks, then tested users to see if they understood.

5.2.2 Consistency

Consistency in user-interfaces seems a self-evident virtue. On the surface it appears that consistency will make it easier for users to move from one application to another, it means we stop reinventing the wheel, and it makes it easier for people to learn a new package. In general this is true, however, we must be careful in the way we are consistent. If we decided that we would always have green screens with brown writing then the fact that we were always consistent would be bad, because brown on green is hard to read. We must make sure our standards are good ones.

When we look closely at consistency and what it means we find that the concept is difficult to apply. The difficulty is that we have many variations, many differences in environment, many ways of interpreting the same thing. Take the simple case of how to indicate that the computer is processing and that you have to wait. The Windows guide suggest you display an hour-glass (Figure 5.2). Should the hour-glass "sand" move to indicate the amount of time left, or should it put in the estimated time until completion, or should it flash (and if so, at what rate). Do we need to standardise at the detail syntax level or is it enough to say "some form of hour-glass should appear"? Do we even need to standardise on the symbol or is it enough to say: "if the system is working there should be a visual indication"? The level at which you are consistent requires judgement; in this example we think you should be consistent at the level of always having some recognisable hour-glass representation. We think this because the shape of the hour-glass becomes the idea of waiting. The details of the representation (or rendering) is less important than the idea represented by the hour-glass.

Do we always want to be consistent? Inconsistencies can show differences that are helpful. One of the difficulties with hypertext systems is user orientation. If all screens "look the same" then we get no location feedback from the shape or appearance of the screens. Perhaps it

Figure 5.2 Standard time passing symbol.

would be better to make the screens different depending on where you are in the hyper-text database?

If we are too consistent then perhaps our applications will become too boring. Perhaps we want some variety to prevent users becoming tired of the same old visuals. Do some inconsistencies matter? Does it matter if I use different fonts for my screen displays as long as I am consistent within an application?

Sometimes you have two consistency rules conflicting. Our first rule might be that the same actions will do the same sort of things. We might say, for a particular application, that a double-click on the mouse will delete the object on which it is positioned. However, another rule for double-clicking on the mouse could be: "do the action the user is most likely to want to do on this object at this particular time in this particular context". The idea is consistent, but the particular action could vary wildly. In fact, the second rule seems to make for better dialogues.

Treat consistency, like all the other rules in this chapter, with care. As a general principle it is better to be consistent, but do not be pedantic. There can be good reasons not to be consistent.

5.2.3   Universal Commands for Consistency

The Xerox project found several commands that were used in many of their applications. The commands operated in the same way no matter what type of object was manipulated. These same commands apply to many other applications and should be carried out in the standard way. The commands are in Figure 5.3.

Of these commands the most fundamental is the *Move*. It is surprising the number of different operations that are variations on the *Move*. For example, in the Xerox list the *Copy* command can be replaced by moving an object in a different way, e.g. with the mouse button down and the *Delete* command by moving an object to a rubbish bin. However, the list in Figure 5.3 is a useful starting point for the commands needed for many systems.

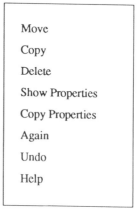

Move

Copy

Delete

Show Properties

Copy Properties

Again

Undo

Help

5.2.4   User Control

If a user-interface is prescriptive, with little control by the user, then unless it is a simple product it will probably be a poor interface. One of the themes in this book is to make systems that the user controls. Poor systems require the user to react to the computer rather than the user ask-

Figure 5.3 Universal commands.

ing the computer to do tasks. If users are required to get information in one way only, and the system has several screens with required responses, the application will almost certainly have problems. Users have different ways of operating, they have different tasks from those thought of during design, and they will want to do things in different ways from the way envisaged.

Forcing people into a straightjacket of responses causes them to become frustrated and annoyed with the product. A program that always shows an initial screen (slowly), that always requires confirmation of actions, that assumes data-entry in particular ways, soon becomes tedious. Where possible, allow the users to vary the way they use the system. A simple example is the entry of dates into a form. A poor computer system will require people to enter dates as dd/mm/yy. This is consistent and will work, but only applies to some countries. The computer knows what year it is and what month it is so if a single number is entered the system should supply the month and year. If nothing is entered then put in today's date. Allow the entry of dates as 3 December 1940. A poor interface will only allow one format, it will have to be correct and it will probably require the typing of 03/12/40 with mandatory leading zeros on single digits. A side-benefit of this particular example is that a flexible date entry may even work in the year 2000!

5.2.5   Modeless Interaction

Modeless dialogues tend to give the user more control. The idea of modal and non-modal states was discussed in Chapter 1. A more formal definition of the same idea is given by Tesler (1981):

"A mode of an interactive computer system is a state of the user-interface that lasts for a period of time, is not associated with any particular object, and has no role other than to place an interpretation on operator input."

When using modes in dialogues make sure the user can see that the system is in a different mode by changing the display in some obvious way or by restricting the user actions. For example, if users must see a message and respond before continuing, give them the message in a modal dialogue box and require them to respond before allowing any other operation.

5.2.6   User Modifiable

No matter how much testing is done and how much user input is obtained, users will often want different things in an application. Some people like icons, others like words. Some prefer pale, almost monochromatic colours, others like more variety on their screens. One way of solving this problem is to make applications tailorable. Allow users to adjust the way information is presented. The problem is that flexibility can make an interface more complicated. One way is to make changes to presentation and style separate and distinct from the regular dialogue.

The keyboard training package KEYCOACH provides an interesting example of user adjustment. Initial versions of the package had one way of presenting lessons and exercises. This was tested with different instructors. It was found that different instructors had incompatible requirements. Some instructors believe that when using a keyboard training package (to teach typing) the student should be stopped as soon as an incorrect key is pressed and required to press the correct key before continuing. Others believed that the student should be allowed to continue. Some instructors wanted the keyboard displayed on the screen, others did not. Some instructors liked students to type from the screen, others wanted them to type from hard-copy. Some people liked beeps others did not. There is no way of reconciling these differences. The solutions are either to force people to all adopt the one approach, or to make the application tailorable. We suggest the latter is the best strategy.

5.2.7   Short-cuts for Experts

When we design a user-interface we take into account both new users and experienced users. Unfortunately, different users are more comfortable with different dialogues. An expert does not need as many prompts; an expert can take short-cuts and still know what is going on. We can sometimes solve this problem by giving different ways of doing the same actions. The dialogues will now often work for both beginners and for experts. The simplest example are the *hot-keys* on pull-down menus. You do not expect beginners to use them but you find experienced users soon start to take the short-cut. You must ensure the short-cuts do not interfere with beginning users and you should ensure there is some way for users to discover the short-cuts.

Another common short-cut is to reduce the number of prompts. Many automatic bank tellers have the sequence of prompts shown in Figure 5.4. In that diagram the output from the teller is in a regular font and the user responses are indented and shown in italics.

An *expert* user of an automatic teller will discover that there are short-cuts (Figure 5.5). The expert has saved one prompt and does not enter the decimal value for the money. Of course, a *clever* teller program would only require the pin number and the amount in dollars. The OK confirmation message could also be omitted as a customer can recover from a mistake by redepositing money. However, this would have to be weighed against the difficulty of depositing.

```
Enter Card

Enter Pin Number and press OK

8923

OK button

Select transaction type

Press withdraw cash

Select account type

Press cheque account button

Enter amount as xx.xx

xx.xx

xx.xx entered. Press OK or Cancel

OK button. Withdraw card take
    cash and statement
```

```
Enter Card

Enter Pin Number and press OK

8923

Press withdraw cash

Select account type

Press cheque account button

Enter amount as xx.xx

xxOK

xx.xx entered. Press OK or
    Cancel

OK button. Withdraw card

Take cash and statement
```

Figure 5.4 Automated bank teller dialogue.

Figure 5.5 Expert user of automated teller.

5.2.8 Use the User's Language

Users and computer systems designers often have different vocabularies. For the computing person a RAM is not a sheep, nor does a PORT have ships. Be careful with your language and take particular care of abbreviations. Use the language of your users. If you have to use a technical term, make sure people have easy ways of discovering the meaning of the term. Computing jargon draws heavily on words in common usage and so it is very prone to misinterpretation.

5.2.9 Motivation

Poor applications destroy the motivation of users. Users often have discretion on whether or not they use a computer package as they sometimes have other ways of solving their tasks. It is surprisingly easy to destroy some users' confidence in a computer program. For example, if an application allows people to work for several hours and then lose all their work they will be loathe to use it again. Even if error messages are cute and/or sarcastic people soon become angry. If the machine constantly beeps, or if it takes an inordinate amount of time to do a seemingly simple operation, users lose patience and become critical and untrusting. Users must have confidence in the products they use and confidence is built on good experiences.

5.2.10 Feedback

It is hard to imagine a more fundamental principle than this, yet you will often find dialogues that violate the rule. When you get a user to perform an action you must let them know the result of the action. If people select an object by clicking on it, you should change the object in some way to show that it is selected. Imagine a dialogue with no response from the computer? It is almost unworkable.

Some cities have pedestrian-activated traffic lights. Probably for reasons of economy and reliability, on some buttons, pressing the button gives no indication that it is activated. When there is a long delay, people continue to press the button or press the button after they see someone else do it. The uncertainty produces an anxious reaction in people waiting. Some simple indication that the button was active would reduce button pressing and reduce anxiety. Unfortunately, it would not reduce all because some people keep pressing buttons even when they can see they are activated. They have a false model that more presses will cause the lights to change faster.

The most common case of lack of feedback is delay in feedback. The user performs an action and it takes several seconds before anything happens on the screen. If people experience such delays they will often assume the machine has not noticed their action and so they will do it again, and again.... You can easily experiment with this phenomenon by delaying your response on the telephone. In the middle of a conversation, delay your response. It can cause people to become quite agitated so make sure you do it with a forgiving friend.

5.2.11 Seeing and Pointing Versus Remembering and Typing

This is the way to realise most of the ideas in the previous section. The Xerox Star interface made applications visible. Everything the user needs to understand the application is shown. When the users want to do something they look and point, rather than remember, then type in a command.

5.2.12 What You See Is What You Get (WYSIWYG)

WYSIWYG makes for more than just easy-to-use systems. What you see becomes the new reality. People understand the application by the way they see it and by the way the objects change on the screen. The appearance of objects on the screen becomes the user's understanding of what the object is. The way we change it on the screen becomes the user's understanding of the actions in the system. Thus a drawing is firstly a drawing on the screen and later we might print it on paper as the final rendering, but while it is in the computer the screen image is the reality. The ability to change all the greens to reds is now part of the understanding even though it cannot be done on paper.

It is not possible to make a complete mapping between a computer model and some other reality (that is represented on a computer). WYSIWYG operates on the computer model and only represents the things being modelled. A crucial design decision is how to show the problem. There is a tendency for computer systems to use more sophisticated visual rendering to make computer models look more like external objects. This may or may not be important to the task. Generally it isn't. When designing a house with traditional paper plans, the plans look quite different from the house when built, but are similar in the important aspects. The plans show relationships of rooms to each other, the relative dimensions, and the positioning of features. What is important is showing the parts that help the user carry out the required tasks. The critical decisions are the things represented, not whether they look the same as some other reality.

5.2.13 Simplicity

Keep things simple. This is hard to achieve. It is simple for the authors of this book to write programs, but difficult for an untrained person. If a problem requires programming then the simplest way may be to require the user to write a small program. However, if they cannot write programs the task becomes difficult.

All designs require a series of tradeoffs. When considering simplicity designers have a genuine problem as it is difficult for them to understand that other people think in different ways to them. Thus what is simple for an artist might be difficult for a computer professional and vice versa. Creating simple solutions and not trivial or difficult solutions is difficult. Success requires the designer to be continually aware of usability issues.

5.2.14 Closure

Closure means that at certain points in the dialogue the user can *close* their minds to the previous steps. An interaction sequence is divided into self-contained independent sets and there is some way of showing people when a set is completed. This means users only need to remember the end-state and they can forget the steps. Typically this is shown by changing the system to indicate something is finished. If the object is moved from one part of the screen to another the object display may change as it moves. When the movement has stopped it changes to its static state. The user can forget how it moved and get on to the next part of the dialogue.

There is an interesting example of closure with drop-down menus. A drop-down menu may be opened by either clicking on the main menu bar or by simply moving the cursor to the menu. The menu stays open until the system decides the operation is activated when the menu closes. Many packages leave the menu open (dropped down) even if the cursor moves away from the menu. They wait for the user to do some other operation before removing it. Other systems close the menu as soon as the cursor moves away from it. Either way the system tells when the action has started or been abandoned by closing the menu and this allows the user to concentrate on the next step in the dialogue.

5.2.15 Easy Reversal

Allow people to easily change their mind. If someone does something and then decides that is not what they want then allow them to change it. Most applications should have an "undo" operation. One of the advantages of a word processor over a pen and paper is the ease of changing the text. It is often easy to undo the completed work, not with an undo operation, but by deleting and then reinserting which is an example of the undo operation without undoing.

If it is easy to reverse operations, the application is easier to use and easier to learn. If people know they can reverse operations they know they can make mistakes without penalty. This reduces stress when using the product and people are more likely to experiment. Experimentation without punishment leads to faster learning.

5.2.16 Simple Error Handling

When an error occurs the user has done something the program did not expect. Error is not the best word to use when this happens as it implies fault. The user has misunderstood what was required and attaching blame is inappropriate. Because there is a misunderstanding, or the system is used in an unexpected way, the user needs easy ways of recovering or being shown what was expected. Error messages that say "Incorrect user response" with no further information were created by designers with a punitive attitude. Error messages should help the user and error correction should be an easier operation than the operation that caused the error. In fact, *error message* is an inappropriate term. A better term is *misunderstanding* message. This gives both the user and the designer a proper perspective on what has happened.

5.2.17 Prevent Errors

Dialogues should guide in appropriate ways or allow common variations. Many people often type I
or lower case l instead of 1 (one). The program
could accept any of these keys as 1(one) instead of
insisting people type in the *correct* character. Look
closely at error messages that always give the users
the solution. Perhaps the program can accept the input instead of saying it is an error?

  Grid snap in a drawing program is a good example of how to prevent errors. When the grid snap
is ON lines must start and end at the intersection of
a grid (Figure 5.6). When drawing lines they normally connect to other lines. With grid snap this is
easy to do and so it prevents many drawing errors.

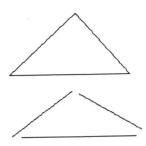

Figure 5.6 Grid snap prevents
connection errors.

5.2.18 Provide Clear Directions and Messages

One of the most frustrating things about many systems is not knowing what to do. It is
particularly annoying if there is no indication of how to exit from the package or from a
function. The user must know how to get out, and there should always be a way out. If
the program starts to do a long operation let the user know how long it will take and give
them a way of stopping it.

  When you give messages make sure they are well phrased and they tell people
what to do. Messages of the type

  ILLEGAL CHARACTER ENTERED

should never appear. The character is not ILLEGAL, just unexpected. You should say
what was entered and what the user should now do. Perhaps the message could say:

  A number was expected; an "A" was entered.

When reporting an error tell the user how the program interpreted the situation. In the
previous example the program detected an "A", so tell the user. Some might argue that the
error message is too long and is unnecessary. If this is a worry allow the user control over
the style (brief or long) of error messages. Use the rules of Plain English to help formu-

late messages on the screen. Use brief, simple sentences that people can immediately understand and act upon. Be non-anthropomorphic and make sure people know they are interacting with a machine and not a human. Look in the documentation chapter for further information on English usage. Chapter 6 "No easy answers: Investigating computer error messages" by Charney *et al.*(1988) has a description of an interesting experiment that elaborates on the difficulty of creating acceptable error messages for all users.

5.2.19 Easy to learn

Whiteside *et al.* (1985) showed that easy-to-learn products were also easy-to-use products. Hence one way of designing a usable product is to design an easy-to-learn product. How can you make your package easy-to-learn? In Chapter 8 we give some ideas on creating courses to teach people how to use packages. If products support those ideas then they will be easy to learn. Make sure people can see how to apply the computer program to their tasks, make the achievement of tasks self-contained and easily compartmentalised, allow people to build their expertise slowly without having to worry about all the features of the total package and make it easy to explore different areas.

5.2.20 Reduce Short-term Memory Load

Good computer systems put few demands on short-term human memory. It is hard to remember a string of digits. The human short-term memory of individual items of information soon fails. Make sure people have to remember few facts, numbers or words. People can remember strategies and techniques to find items, but have trouble remembering particular items. For example, an application that requires people remembering the names of files and typing them in will be hard to use. A simple, major improvement, to such programs is for it to remember the last few files worked on. When a user starts the word processor the program could display the last few files, allow selection from the display, and also allow the display of other files. This seemingly simple idea makes the program easier to use because it reduces memory load and fits in with the way people often work.

Another way to reduce memory load is to allow people to change the environment so that they work with different defaults. When compiling programs the compiler requires a set of parameters to tell it how to handle the source code. There can be dozens of parameters. If people have to enter these every time they run the compiler they will soon complain. Make sure the system supplies *sensible* defaults and make it easy for users to change them. The setting of inappropriate defaults is an area to watch during usability testing.

5.2.21 Guide-line Books

Smith and Mosier (1986) compiled a collection of user-interface guide-lines from various sources. Galitz (1989) has a collection of guide-lines related to screen design. Marcus (1992) translates principles of graphics design to the electronic media. Bailey (1989) has many guide-lines based on psychological principles. There are guide-line books for software development environments supplied with the manufacturers software. These are excellent sources of advice and where possible you should follow those guide-lines. This will tend to make all programs for a particular environment have a similar look and feel.

5.3 Common User Access

IBM's Common User Access guide-lines (IBM 1989) gives recommendations for the syntax of the user-interface for programs to run on the IBM range of computers. Provided the interface strategy follows the ideas in this book it does not matter which particular

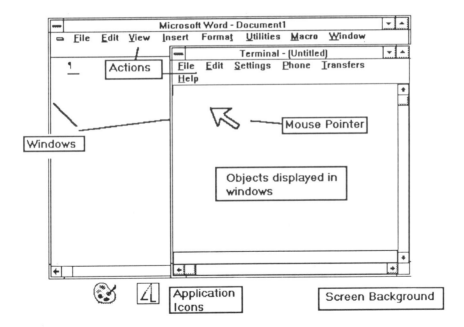

Figure 5.7 Screen components.

syntax is used, but applications should be consistent. Use the IBM suggestions, the Microsoft implementation of CUA, Apple guide-lines, or the Open Systems Motif for Unix systems. In this book we use CUA guide-lines and illustrate them with screens drawn under Microsoft Windows. We summarise the main syntactic elements of this style of interface, but leave the details for you to look up in your appropriate style guide.

5.3.1   Visual Components

The main screen components for applications are shown in Figure 5.7. All applications operate through windows. There is a free moving cursor operated by a mouse. Actions are always in pull-down menus, application objects always appear in application windows which are normally adjustable and movable.

Figure 5.8 shows the parts of a window. The title bar can have a system menu icon to allow you to access the system menu to perform operations on the window such as minimise. It has a title and window sizing icons. The window border allows resizing, the scroll bars allow the scrolling of information contents in the client area and the action bar holds the names of actions.

Figure 5.9 shows a list box, drop-down combination box, entry field, push buttons, radio buttons, and check buttons. Use these components to set parameters and conditions of objects.

A *list box* allows selection of an item from a list of items. If all the elements do not fit into the box then use scroll bars to allow movement through the list.

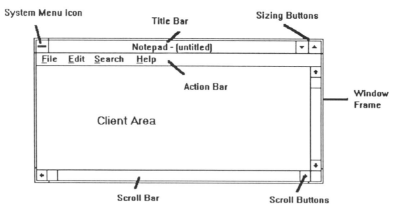

Figure 5.8 Parts of a window.

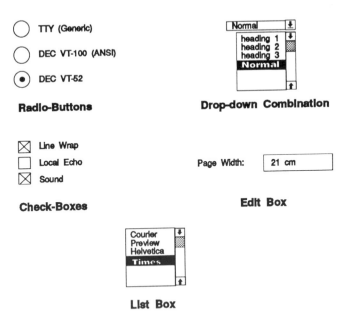

Figure 5.9 Standard dialogue components.

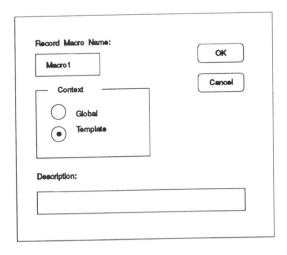

Figure 5.10 Modal dialogue box.

A *drop-down combination box* has the same functionality as a list box except it takes less space on the screen and shows the selected item. A variation on the drop-down combination box is to allow the user to type in their own data instead of selecting. Use the list box if screen space is available and if the user is likely to make a change. Use the drop-down combination when there is a premium on screen space and the item rarely changes.

Push buttons are used where there is one operation and it is to be done as soon as it is pressed.

Radio buttons get their name from the buttons on car radios. Button selecting is mutually exclusive for a group of buttons. Press a new button and the old button goes off. Use this where there is a set of choices but only one at a time is valid.

Check-boxes select a condition. They operate like a light switch. It is either on or off. A typical use is font style selection where there is bold, italics, underlined or any combination.

Entry fields allow text entry. Entry fields can have one or more lines.

Figure 5.10 shows a modal dialogue box. A modal box requires the user to act on the box before continuing. These will always have an OK button to exit from the box, but they may also have CANCEL.

5.3.2   The Mouse and Its Icon

Chapter 4 discussed the importance, to the user dialogue, of selecting objects and the manipulating of those objects. The mechanism by which this is done is the mouse or its surrogate. Use the mouse to point a cursor at an object. Click the mouse button to select the object at which it points. Selected objects change their appearance to show they are selected. Put the actions that can occur on the selected objects in the menu bar.

Some actions may be done with direct manipulation of the mouse cursor. Do this by holding the mouse button down on an object. The action that will occur on the object depends on the application and the object. The program can show what operation will occur by changing the mouse icon. See Figure 5.11 for example mouse shapes to indicate different operations. In some cases change the icon as soon as the mouse cursor moves onto an object. In other cases wait until the mouse button is depressed. One example of the former is when the mouse cursor moves to a window border. The cursor changes to a double arrow to show that the border may be resized.

Many objects may be selected together. Do this with a drag select. Put the cursor outside any object then drag it (move with the button down) over several objects, each of which will be selected. Actions now apply to all the selected objects.

Often there is a most likely action to do on an object. That is, after it is selected then the same action is often performed. The double-click of the mouse lets us do this with just the mouse. This is used in Crossword Designer to put words from a list into the crossword and to remove words from the crossword.

All operations should be possible with the keyboard and action menu and without a mouse. However, good dialogues tend to have a considerable number of mouse operations and the keyboard is rarely, if ever, used. Strive for a mainly mouse dialogue with single-mouse button operations. Restrict the use of the second (or third) mouse buttons. Use a keyboard mouse combination instead of the other mouse buttons. For example, many drawing programs use Shift plus Click for multiple selection, or Shift plus drag for duplication.

Make good use of changes to the mouse icon to indicate different operations. If the meaning of the button click changes because of the Shift key being pressed then change the mouse icon.

5.3.3 The Action Bar

Almost all applications will have a menu with one or more (in shown order) of:

File Edit View Options Help

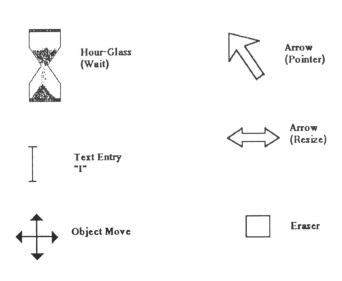

Figure 5.11 Different mouse icons for different operations.

New		Undo	Alt+Backspace	Help for help...
Open...		Cut	Shift+Del	Extended help...
Save		Copy	Crtl+Ins	Keys help...
Save as...		Paste	Shift+Ins	Help index...
Print		Clear (optional)		Tutorial...
Exit		Delete (optional)		About...

Figure 5.12 File menu.   **Figure 5.13** Edit menu.   **Figure 5.14** Help menu.

Samples of the expanded File, Edit and Help are shown in Figures 5.12,13,14. Applications may have other application-specific items.

An area that concerns many new designers is what to put in the action bar. If you follow this book then you will only put things that perform *actions* on objects. Do not put *object selection* on the menu bar. For example, in the vehicle scheduling problem described before, we selected a driver object, then changed the *view* of the object. It would be wrong to put driver and vehicle on the menu and select a view by selecting the object from the menu.

In most dialogues people select instances of a particular object. Do not select objects from the action menu, but use a pop-up list or some other mechanism. Sometimes it might appear you are selecting objects, but in fact, you are selecting actions. A common example is the selection of fonts for a piece of text. You might think of the fonts as objects, but in fact, you have selected a piece of text and then you apply the font as an action to the text.

All applications that manipulate files as single objects should have a *File* menu and it should include the items in Figure 5.14.

The *Edit* menu is used for applications, such as document processing and drawing programs, in which we can edit the object and act upon parts of the object. It should include the items shown in Figure 5.13.

The *Undo* operates on the last edit operation. The *Cut* moves the selected part of the object to the clip-board and compresses the object, *Copy* moves the selected part to the clip-board and retains the original, *Paste* puts the clip-board contents into the object at the cursor position. Note the use of accelerator (hot) keys of *Alt+Backspace*, *Shift+Del*, *Ctrl+Ins*, *Shift+Ins*, meaning we can do the operations by pressing the appropriate hot keys or by selecting from the action menu.

The *View* option allows the user to change the view of object without changing the object. In particular it allows users to select groups of objects to see on the screen and to change the way they are displayed. See the discussion on viewing the data in Chapter 4. *Options* allow users to customise the presentation of the application. For example, in a word processing application it might allow the toggling of the display of rulers or hidden text.

Help is an important option. F1 should always give help on the selected object and actions. The Help menu allows the user other access to help. The suggested menu is shown in Figure 5.14.

See the suggestions on help design in Chapter 8.

5.4   Screen Layout

One of the recommendations in some books on screen design is to keep the screen "un-cluttered" and not to make it too busy. Unfortunately, this is often interpreted incorrectly.

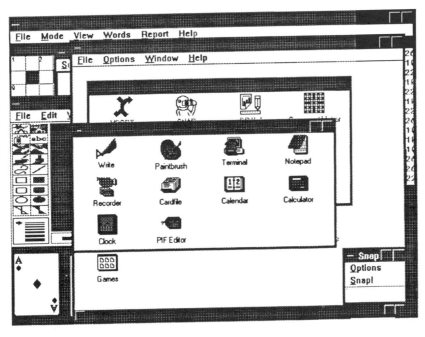

Figure 5.15 Screen with a lot of information.

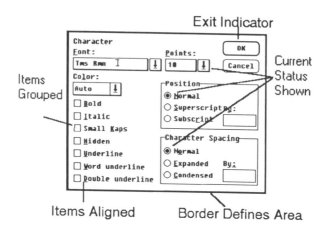

Figure 5.16 Form Layout.

The idea behind the advice is to make sure people can see what is happening on the screen. (One way of achieving this is to reduce the amount of information on the screen.) The correct advice is to make screen layout understandable. The screen can be filled with information and yet it is still usable. The important point is to group information into dis-tinguishable chunks, make the layout tell part of the story, and make sure the focus is on the appropriate information. Newspapers can be read without difficulty, yet on any meas-ure the layout of a newspaper is cluttered. However, the elements are easily recognised. Figure 5.15 is a screen which is completely filled up with bits of information yet it is clear what to do after a short period of familiarisation.

Layered windows is one technique for doing this. Within windows group informa-tion so that it is clear what the different parts do. Figure 5.16 shows a form on a screen. The captions give some important syntactic rules. Grouping and aligning items vertically makes for better looking and easier-to-use screens. The elements should have syntactic clues that tell the user what they are and how they work without reading instructions. People who are familiar with the Windows interface instantly recognise the different ele-ments in Figure 5.17.

Figure 5.18 summarises guide-lines from Galitz (1989) to make the layout visually pleasing. The book "Envisioning Information" by Tufte (1990) is an excellent source of inspiration for the visual presentation of information. It shows a rich diverse set of ways people have shown information on paper. Many of the ideas can be used on screens.

Balance.

Regularity (of elements), symmetry (axial duplication), predictability (no surprises).

Economy (enough to give the message).

Sequential (use in order you read).

Proportion (eg. golden rectangle 1 height: 1.618 wide).

Figure 5.17 Layout guide-lines.

For text use lower case with upper intitial letter.

For visual search tasks use UPPER case.

Use proportional spacing.

Stay with one font style.

Figure 5.18 Guide-lines for font use.

No jargon.

Use short familiar words.

Use complete words; avoid contractions, short-forms.

Use positive terms.

Use simple action words.

Avoid noun strings.

Do not stack or hyphenate words.

Do not include punctuation for abbrev mnemonics and acronyms.

Figure 5.19 Guide-lines for use of words.

Keep text to 30 to 35 characters width.

Use short sentences of familiar words.

Place a full stop at the end of each sentence.

Do not right-justify.

Separate paragraphs by blank lines.

Use paging not scrolling.

Figure 5.20 Guide-lines for text on screens.

5.4.1 Captions

Make sure people can tell the difference between captions and data. Figure 5.19 shows acceptable and unacceptable ways. Use consistent physical relationships. For single-data fields put the caption on the left and for repeating fields put the caption above . With multiple entries left justify both captions and fields or right-justify captions as in Figure 5.20. With forms on screens try to reduce the number of vertical "lines". Group the data and distinguish data-entry and captions.

5.4.2 Entering Data into an Item

Figure 5.21 shows a data-entry screen with captions and an area where the user types in data. The presentation and operation on these relatively trivial operations show the diversity that is possible in screen interactions. In practice guide-lines, or user-interface management software, make many of these choices for the designer. However, this example illustrates the diversity possible and the importance of standardisation. Even the seemingly simple operation of numeric data-entry has many variations. If every designer used a different way then it would make data-entry difficult and confusing for the user who moved between applications.

- When entering data it can go left to right or right to left. Hand-held calculators enter data right to left. Most computer programs enter data left to right.
- What does the program do with data in the field before the user starts typing? When entering the first character it might clear the existing data, or it might overtype, or it might insert the new character in the string. Figure 5.22 illustrates this variation.

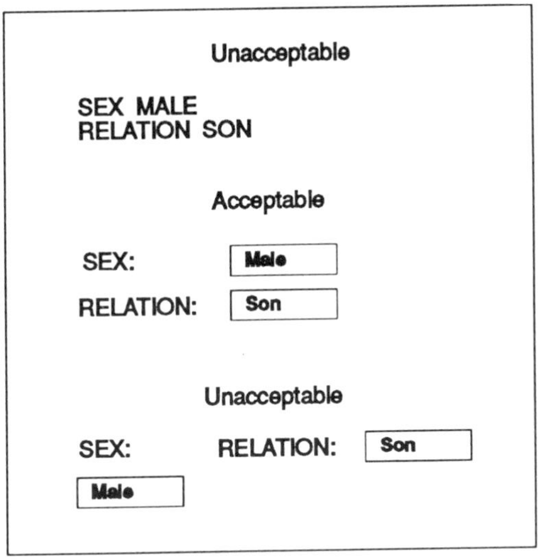

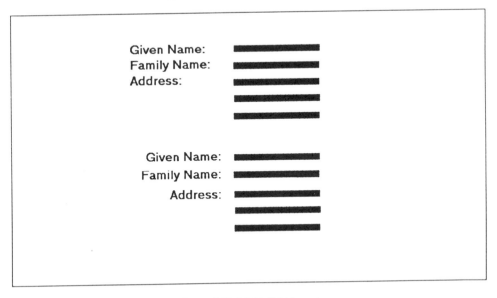

Figure 5.21 Positioning of captions.

Figure 5.22 Multi-field layout.

- If the data fills up the data-entry field what does the program do? Does it automatically move to the next field, or overtype the last character, or ignore all extra characters, or "enter" the characters but not show them, or push the data to the left so the user cannot see the beginning. What happens after the backspace character is pressed? Is a blank inserted, is the original data replaced, or is the data squeezed. Figure 5.22 shows possible variations.
- After entering the data the program discovers an error. What does it do? It can clear the original data and report the error. It can position the cursor on the first character that seems to be in error. It can require the users to enter valid data before going to the next field. It can insert the closest value that might fit.
- How does the program handle special keys such as left, right, up and down arrows. What does the TAB key do? What happens when the user presses the Home, End, Ins, Del or Esc keys?

5.5   Designing Paper Forms

Designing paper forms is similar to designing a screen-based user-interface. Paper forms in some ways are simpler, because the medium is static, but in other ways more difficult as the medium cannot help the user. To design a paper form think of it as a "conversation"

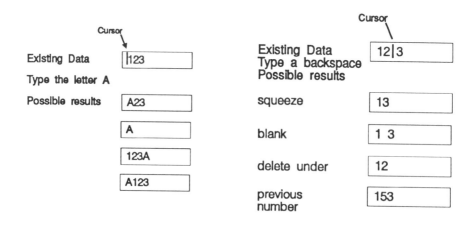

Figure 5.23
Changing existing data item.

Figure 5.24
Possible results after a backspace.

in which information is requested from people. Work out what information is needed, what people need to know, what they have to supply, how it will be processed, and how the form is filled out. After the form is designed it is tested for usability. Most organisations have skilled forms designers to help with typographical issues or similar information can be found from commercial printers.

5.6   The Use of Colour

Colour can improve the user-interface, but for many systems it has little measurable effect on users' performance. Its main value lies in making the displays more interesting for users. It is a similar phenomenon to television. The information content of most programs is the same in colour or in black and white, yet most people prefer watching colour. However, there are some occasions on which colour can help the user-interface designer. In principle it gives us another dimension to our highlights. Use colour for highlighting reasons. It helps group like items, it distinguishes groups, it calls attention to important fields, and it can be used as a visual code. For example:

- Make all captions one colour and all data-entry fields another.
- Make the active window a different colour from an inactive one.
- Make all addresses a particular colour.
- Put warning messages in red.
- When the status of item changes then change its colour.

The best way to design in colour is to first design in monochrome. The reason is that monochrome forces the grouping of items. It is not possible to use the colour crutch to overcome poor layout. After designing in monochrome go back and enhance it with colour. There is also the practical reason that many people have monochrome and do not have colour screens so applications that work with both extend the applicability of the product.
Be conservative with colours. People should notice the package and be undistracted by garish colours. Colour is a powerful visual stimulus which means that unfortunate choice and combinations will be noticed.

- Try to keep the number of different colours on any screen to no more than four.
- Choose different shades of the same colour and use the different variations for emphasis.
- Try to make colours useful and appropriate.
- Remember that different shades of grey are acceptable colour variations.

- Indicate action with warm colours and use brightness for emphasis. Black, blue or white background are best.
- Avoid incompatible combinations of colours. Examples are blue/yellow, red/green, green/blue and red/blue pairs.
- Use high colour contrast for character/background pairs. Examples are white on black, white on blue, or black on white.
- Confine light blue to background areas.
- Red and green are hard to see on the periphery of the visual field so do not use them for coding in areas away from the main centre of attention.
- Assign colours to user expectations. Blue for cold, red for hot and danger, green for go, amber for wait.

Different guide-lines give suggested colour combinations. Start with these. Experiment as the technology of colour is changing and better combinations may arise as new and better colours become available. Try colours out on users, find a set that works within the organisation, and define some standards.

5.7   Using Sound in Computer Systems

In most computer systems sound is a relatively unused channel of communication. The idea of desktops covered with chattering, beeping noisy computers makes some of us hope that this silence will continue. However, communicating with sound is so important to humans that computer systems will increasingly use sound as a way for people to interact with them. This section has ideas on using sounds in computer systems and discusses the role of computer speech input and output.

5.7.1   Sound as Confirmation

Almost all computers make noises and we use these noises subconsciously to help us operate the machine. Next time you turn on your friendly personal machine listen to the different noises it makes and think how they help you understand what is happening. Keyboards, for example, are designed to make a clicking noise when a key is hit. People do not like silent keyboards as the sound of the key helps them type. It is not as important to easy typing as the movement of the key, but people feel uncomfortable when it is removed. The sound acts as a confirmation that a character was typed. Computers give other aural signals that act as confirmation of actions or that indicate that it is operating correctly.

After using a machine for some time the noises it makes help people identify it and tell them what it is doing. When the sounds change they are aware of it. The sound from the movement in the disk drives gives a pattern associated with running particular programs. If it changes it is noticed and the user knows, without realising why, that something is different. If the fan noise varies there may be something wrong. If someone turns the beep sound off on a machine, without the users' knowledge, they may think the machine is malfunctioning. All these sounds confirm that the machine operates as expected. These examples are similar to other simple auditory feedback on which people rely in their everyday life. Stop reading this book and listen to the background noises in your current environment.

"Click"

"Thud"

- How many different sounds can you identify?
- Were you aware of them before reading this?
- If one of them stopped or changed do you think you would notice?

Figure 5.25
Sound buttons.

The characteristic of auditory input to confirm the state of the world is one way to use sound in computer systems. Simple everyday sounds can supplement, or even replace, visual confirmation in computer systems. Most computer systems have buttons on which to click. After clicking the button it visually changes. Instead of a visual cue an equally effective way would be for the computer to make an appropriate button pressing noise to tell that it has happened. Use one sound for OK type buttons and a different one for Cancel buttons (Figure 5.25). Many of the actions involved in most interactions could be enhanced with appropriate sounds. Try some of the design exercises at the end of the chapter to expand your view of the use of sound in computer systems.

5.7.2   Sound as State Information

Filling a bath with water can be monitored by listening to the sound of the water running into the bath. The sound changes as the bath fills and tells one how much water is in the bath. The sound represents the bath's fullness state. This ability to use sound to tell users about the state of operations can be a powerful tool for dialogue designers. For example, many computer systems often have background tasks such as printing, receiving mail, and automatic backups. Use low-volume everyday sounds to indicate the state of these activities. Perhaps a low-level printer noise for background printing which changes as the printing nears an end or different postmen's whistles for different types of incoming mail. These sounds also act as confirmation, but their variation tells us about the changing state. Such sounds soon fade into the background and people only notice them when they change or are absent.

5.7.3   Sound as Navigation Aids

Computer games use sound effectively. In adventure style games location is indicated by different sounds. In a cavern there is an echo, rushing water near the river, the snake pit has ominous hisses and birds are heard after managing to escape from the dungeons and tunnels.

Use the same principle to help show location in applications. Hypertext is notorious for its ability to lose people. Lost in Hyperspace is no longer a space fiction invention. Complex CAD systems which represent three dimensions on a two-dimension screen need ways to help users orient themselves. Sounds can help in applications in much the same way as in computer games. The sounds indicate place or proximity. The sounds themselves can be meaningless (non-iconic), but their association with a location in an application gives meaning. Often the sounds themselves and when to cause them can be left to the user who can use them in an analogous way to book markers. This use of sound is similar to using sound to show changes of state. In this case the changing state is the changing location.

5.7.4   Sound as Annoyance

A noisy machine could be an annoying machine. When including sound in an application make sure it will still work without the sound. Some users may have hearing difficulties, some may be in an environment where extra noise is unadvisable, some may want a quiet life. In the same way as we design applications which work without colour but use colour to enhance usability, so our applications should be able to work silently with sound included as an aid to usability.

If sound is present make sure users have control over it. We expect to have control over the colour in applications so we should expect to have control over the noises machines make. For example, we should be able to replace any bird noises with animal feeding noises or lower the volume or increase the pitch.

5.7.5   Speech and Computer Systems

Human communication is predominantly speech-based. It is the normal way people communicate. As a way of communicating with machines it has great appeal and potential yet most computers are deaf and dumb. There are significant problems involved in using speech in computer systems and so far no compelling application or reasons have appeared to require manufacturers to supply all computers with a vocal ability. It is only a matter of time before this does happen and when it does many other common applications will use both speech input and output in efficient natural ways. Most applications could use speech input and output to enhance usability, but most do not because enough hardware in the market does not support speech. In the meantime, to see how to use speech, look at those applications and environments where speech is necessary or where it has an overwhelming advantage as a method of human – computer communication. These applications show the way future computing will evolve and give ideas where it might be worth while investing in speech technologies.

It is inexpensive to make a computer say things through simple recording technology. Getting sound input and output is not a problem. The problems arise with what to do with it. Recognition of discrete words is available today. However, the recognition of continuous speech and a human-like interaction with computers is still an unresolved software problem. Still, even without full human capabilities, speech can be a valuable user-interface technique. Perhaps Figure 5.26 indicates a future usability problem?

5.7.6   The Role of Speech Input and Output

The human to human model of speech communication, in most cases, is not appropriate as a model for human to computer communication. When people communicate they often wish to explain what they feel or think so that they can develop an understanding of each other and of their wishes. In conversation people attempt to get the other person to be in a similar state to themselves so that they can know what it is they wish to communicate. When communicating with machines we do not wish to explain ourselves or to develop a rapport or understanding. We want to get the machine to do a task. Throughout this book we have emphasised the role of the computer as a tool to carry out the user's wishes. The

Figure 5.26 Human interference?

tool has no need to understand to do those tasks. In the future computers may have such capabilities, but for most of today's uses people need to understand what the tool is doing and not vice versa.

This means that the use of speech between humans is different from the use of speech between computers and people. Talking to a computer has the same purpose as using a keyboard, display or mouse. It is just a different method of input and output. However, because of its human-like qualities, computer speech can cause usability problems. People start to attribute human-like understanding to computer systems and this causes difficulties. It can even be argued that some forms of communication will never be possible between entities with different physical structures. How can an electronic circuit really understand the feeling of a sore toe? Hence, there is some merit in forcing computer speech input and output to be different from human speech so that misconceptions do not arise. Designers should certainly be aware of the dangers and should resist the temptation to make computers too *human-like*.

5.7.7   The Telephone and Computers

If a person wishes to communicate with a computer via a telephone connection, voice is sometimes the only form of computer output and may be the most efficient form of limited input. Certainly putting a computer on the end of a telephone is a cheap method of giving access to computing resources. Telephone companies and financial services commonly use telephones to provide access to computer databases of directories or financial information with speech input and output. The structure of their successful dialogues is stylised and brief. People adapt to the limitations and when the systems are limited and

Customer	Dials a computer
Computer	Hello, this is the XYZ Bank computer telephone answering system. What is your account number?
Customer	One, five, three, six, nine
Computer	What is your secret number?
Customer	Two, three, four, five
Computer	John Smith, your current balance is 23 dollars. If you would like to have your balance repeated, please say "once more". If not say "OK".
Customer	OK
Computer	Thank you for calling.

Figure 5.27 Simple human - computer dialogue.

focussed in scope they are more likely to succeed. See Figure 5.27 for a sample telephone computer conversation.

The main difficulties in these limited dialogues is the handling of errors. In ordinary text-based question and answer dialogues errors and backtracking give similar challenges to the designer. Here there are similar problems but with the added complexity of people sometimes attaching human-like qualities to the machines.

5.7.8 The Use of Speech in Everyday Applications

For most everyday computer applications speech output can probably be replaced with either sound icons or visual cues. Speech by its nature is transitory and the type of information required in most applications most of the time is better done visually. In those cases where sound is useful a sound icon will normally suffice.

Limited speech input has more application than speech output and can enhance the ease of use of most interactive computer systems. Most computer input is relatively simple, either being the activation of a command or the entering of simple data items. All the pull-down commands in any system can be supplemented with voice input. The voice commands can operate in the same way as short-cut function keys, except they are less obtrusive and easier for the operator. Single-word commands are easily recognised and the application leaves little scope for operator confusion. Almost all interactive applications would be enhanced with simple voice input of commands.

More complex input of spatial data or textual material is best done with more appropriate input devices such as the mouse or the keyboard. Designers should use the most convenient input method for the task at hand. Speech has a role, but normally as a supplement to other methods rather than as the dominant form of computer input and output.

Use voice input for data-entry tasks. The problems with such data-entry is the problem of recognition and error correction. When an incorrect letter is typed it is simple and easy to see and correct. When a word is spoken that the computer misinterprets it is difficult to correct it with only voice commands. The reason is the difficulty of positioning or pointing with voice commands. To correct something it is easy if we can point to something and say "fix this one" while it is difficult to tell which one to fix. Pointing is trivial with cursor keys and even easier with a mouse. Hence to use voice input for data we should recognise this intrinsic difficulty and work our way around the problem.

Do this by a mixed mode of input. That is, use voice to get the data in and use conventional techniques to correct the data. Do not attempt to position with voice but use a mouse for pointing. For example, if this paragraph was being dictated, the position of the cursor would tell the machine what to do with any voice input. If the cursor was on a word it would replace the word. If the cursor was between words it would insert a word. If it was at the end of the paragraph it would keep entering words. The cursor movement would be done with a mouse.

When we talk to people our language has much redundancy. If we miss several words we can still understand what was said. Look at the following set of words, which has several words missing and see if you can understand it. (The full sentence is shown at the end of this chapter):

This means use speech in applications tolerate mistakes.

Even if you failed to get the meaning from the above words the idea of this sentence can be found from the other parts of this and the preceding paragraph. Speech input is fine in those cases where there is either redundant information or the user can easily adjust to mistakes that are made. For example, when using voice input to select a pull-down menu it is easy to correct a wrong command by saying the command again instead of activating the selected menu. Another example could be in using speech to help search a database with keywords. If the machine could not recognise one of the keywords, say a synonym to help give the meaning.

Using speech input in applications which require accuracy and no misinterpretation of results is problematic. Unless speech input was backed by visual and aural confirmation it would be unwise to use it as a method of controlling an airliner or a weapons system. In contrast, as a means of entering quick notes for later editing it holds its promise as a sophisticated dictating machine.

Crossword Designer Use of Guide-lines

We have described different parts of the Crossword Designer in other chapters. Here we discuss the use of some of the guide-lines described in this chapter in the Cross-word Build dialogue option. We also show how usability tests indicate changes to be made and how we use our understanding of the guide-lines to suggest changes. The screen for this section of the dialogue is shown in Figure 5.30.

This part of the program allows people to create "crossed words" by typing in words. The computer tries to fit each new word into the existing pattern. It puts the word into the place it thinks is the best but shows the other places it might fit. The user can accept or reject the suggestion and continue typing in new words.

If words do not fit or you do not want them in the crossword you can put them into a list of "words still to fit".

This dialogue is relatively difficult in comparison with other parts of the application. The idea is essentially simple, but gets complicated when the user changes an existing crossword. If you go through typing in words and accepting the places suggested, then the dialogue is easy. This is in line with making things simple for begin-

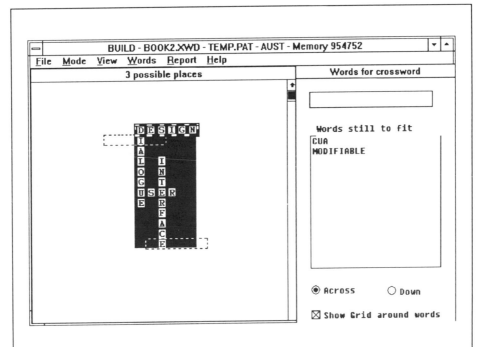

Figure 5.28 Build your own crossword.

ners. The idea of selecting a position for the word, but showing where else it can fit, makes the important decision elements visible and shows people options, rather than asking them to discover where else things might go. The shaded area shows the extent of the crossword.

If the user wishes to remove a word from the crossword they highlight the word by selecting it with the mouse, then double-click on the word. This is the most likely action people want to do on a word.

If they want to move a word outside the crossword they highlight the word and click on the screen where they would like the word to go. Our usability testing has found this to be a problem. People accidentally click on the screen, the word moves and they do not know what has happened. When operations happen "by magic" and people do not understand they become frustrated. A better solution would be to select a word then to "drag" it to its new position. This would require a positive action and would not happen by accident. This problem was not apparent when we first tested and constructed the system. It only became apparent with a few beginning users.

The check-box is an on/off indicator. If it is set then lines appear around each letter. The across/down button boxes position the words across or down when a word is moved.

The top-level action bar does not change throughout the application. In different screens at different times only some actions are valid. The actions that are not active are in grey but the action menus do not change content. Figure 5.31 shows the screen with the Words action dropped down. This means that people become used to the position of the actions and makes the application consistent. Another choice would be to remove the inactive items from the menus, but this would lead to an inconsistent varying menu.

This particular screen works almost entirely with the mouse. The main difficulty is with clues. We have a consistent way of entering clues through the whole application via the Words menu. Another choice would be to have an area of the screen devoted to clue entry. Any clue for the highlighted word would be shown. To enter a clue we would simply type in the clue. This was not done because of screen space. We felt the space for the clue would be better used to show more of the crossword. However, after some usability tests we find that people have more difficulty with clues than with any other part of the system. The next version will have space for the clue which will remove some of the difficulty. When a word has a clue it is coloured red so there is a direct visible indication of this fact.

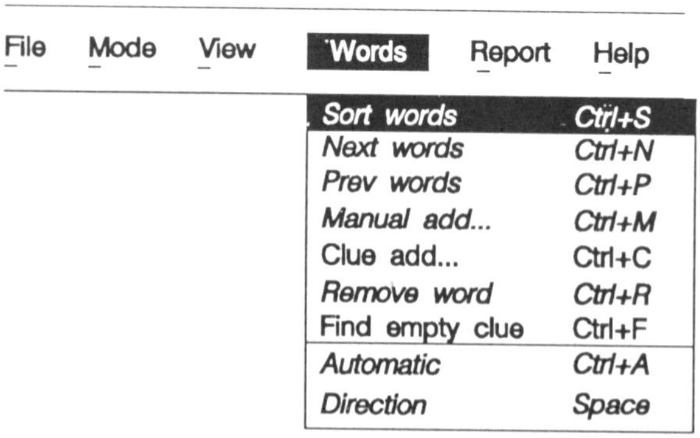

File	Mode	View	**Words**	Report	Help

Sort words	*Ctrl+S*
Next words	*Ctrl+N*
Prev words	*Ctrl+P*
Manual add...	*Ctrl+M*
Clue add...	Ctrl+C
Remove word	*Ctrl+R*
Find empty clue	Ctrl+F
Automatic	*Ctrl+A*
Direction	*Space*

Figure 5.29 Drop-down menu.

Summary

Guide-lines are of great assistance to designers. Whether we use them consciously or not they influence the shape and style of our user-interfaces. As well as formal guide-lines we also rely on folk proverbs to help us summarise and understand the processes we use. While the following might not qualify for immortality they may help consolidate our knowledge.

- Being consistently bad is worse than inconsistency.
- Use unobtrusive short-cuts for experts.
- To every action there should be a reaction.
- Divide your dialogues into digestible chunks.
- Do not punish users for making mistakes.
- The operation to correct a mistake must be simple.
- Make sure your error messages are correct.
- An easy-to-learn package is an easy-to-use package.
- Allow users to vary their interactions.
- Never require people to keep more than four items in short-term memory.
- Make your products safe, helpful and professional.
- Put pick-lists on data-entry items.
- Showing relationships is more important than exact rendering.
- Copy instead of creating.
- Use few colours and use co-ordinated colours.
- If you cannot decide on a feature leave it as a user option.
- Use sound icons, not speech, for sound output.
- Use sound input where precision is not required.

Exercises

1. Find examples of inconsistencies in user-interfaces. Are the inconsistencies good or bad?

2. Design an even shorter dialogue for the automated teller.

3. Take any spreadsheet program and work out the different ways of adding a column of numbers. If you were teaching someone to use the spreadsheet would you start with the longest (most keystrokes) way and move to the shortest?

4. Implement the automated bank-teller dialogue on your computer. Remove some of the prompts and ask people to use it.

5. Think of a cheap, reliable, understandable way to tell people the button is pressed on a pedestrian-activated light. Don't forget that people cross streets from both directions.

6. Examine a spreadsheet dialogue and see how the package uses the concept of closure to break the dialogue into parts with a visual ending.

7. Find a retail store with on-line data-entry of sales to a computer. Check if it assists the shop assistant or is it only for the benefit of store management.

8. Take an application which you have used extensively on a colour screen and try it on a monochrome screen. Can you still use it effectively or does the lack of colour hamper your use?

9. Take a programming package that allows you to vary colours. Change them in different ways. Try to make the "worst" combination for your eyes. Now try to get the "best" combination. Compare your sets with other peoples. Try to use the suggestions in this chapter.

10. Design an all-mouse dialogue using only one button to allow the following operations on an object. We want to be able to move the object, resize it, delete it and duplicate it. Can you now add the actions to recolour it and flip it over?

11. Design some auditory icons (similar to visual icons) to represent the following actions. Mail arriving in your electronic mail box. Saving a file. Resizing a window on the screen. Sorting a list. Finding a spelling mistake in a document. Resetting tab markers. Taking an item out of a list.

12. Use your favourite word processor or spreadsheet and think how you might use auditory feedback to supplement visual feedback for different commands.

13. How many common sounds can you think of that represent the state of an activity? For example, the sound of a car engine tells you how fast it is rotating.

14. What are some computer multi-tasking activities whose state we could represent with sound?

15. Take any question and answer dialogue that uses a keyboard and screen and see if you can turn it into a voice question and answer dialogue. What are the changes you needed to make to handle the lack of visual output and the greater variety of user responses?

Full sentence used in example on page 206:

This means we can use speech input in applications where we can tolerate redundancy and mistakes.

Chapter 6

Designing a Dialogue Model

The steps in the development of a dialogue were discussed in Chapter 2 and are summarised in Figure 6.1. In this chapter we are concerned with the first four steps:

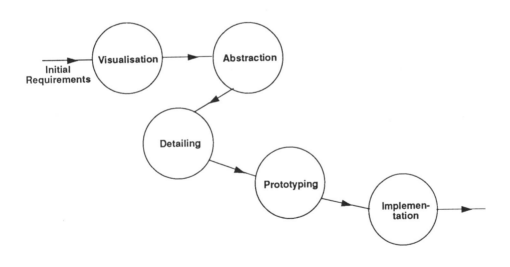

Figure 6.1 Dialogue development steps.

- The *visualisation* of the dialogue.
- The *abstraction* of this visualisation in the form of a set of objects and actions.
- The *detailing* of the model, in order to come up with a reasonably detailed specification of how the dialogue will look and behave.
- *Prototyping* of the system to produce a detailed mock-up of the interface for evaluation in conjunction with the user.

As we have already stressed, these steps merely form a guide to the sort of processes involved in the development of the dialogue, and so should not be regarded as a rigid sequence of activity.

6.1   Developing the Conceptual Model

6.1.1   Introduction

In Chapter 4, we developed a conceptual framework into which we could fit our design. We talked about objects and actions, and about how they fit together into a complete application system.

Before we address the design problem itself, it is worth while reminding ourselves of the sorts of features that we are aiming at in designing the system.

The first thing that we need to remember is that a computer screen is *visual*. We are *looking* at the screen, and are receptive to all the visual cues that are on the screen. To communicate effectively we use *pictures* as well as words; we use layout to draw attention to important things, to group related things and separate unrelated things, and to relegate marginal things to the margin. We make important things big and unimportant things small. We push things that we are not currently working on into the background. A pictorial representation of an object is both more immediate and more easily comprehensible than a text description of the same object.

The second point to remember is that it is easier to *point* to something than to explain what it is.

The third point is that individual objects in isolation are rarely of much use except for the most mundane tasks. Most significant decisions involve *comparisons*. This implies that we are more likely to be looking at *collections* rather than at individual objects. In other words, the data must be presented in such a way as to give the user an *overview* of what is happening, with the ability to explore detail on demand. Systems that show only one object at a time, or limit the user to a single type of object, tend to inhibit rather than assist decision-making.

The fourth point to remember is that it is the user that is making the decision, not the machine. This means that the system must be designed to assist the user, by presenting, or enabling the user to obtain information relevant to that decision. A criterion for a good system is that it comes up with the appropriate data at the appropriate time, yet makes it easy for the users to explore additional data. It should also place it on the screen in a way that allows them to make it part of the data display on which the decision is based, or to cull unwanted data from the display. In addition, the user must decide on the appropriate action, at any given time, and should not be forced to follow some sequence dictated by the machine.

This, then, is the framework within which we are trying to design.

Some of these criteria may seem to be overambitious. The designer of a system running on a text-based mainframe terminal that displays twenty-five lines of eighty characters in green or amber and updates the entire screen at once, may see little sense in ideas about pictures, pointing, and multiple objects on the screen. This is not the case. Although the full power of a graphical user-interface is not available, simple graphics and diagrams are possible, split screens can be used to show multiple objects, and cursor keys can be used to point to objects. It is far better to start with something exciting, imaginative and ambitious, and then to pull back to something that can be implemented, than to start with something that is already limited, e.g. a rigidly modal full-screen menu and full-screen forms system, and to restrict the system to that.

We have said that there are four main processes involved in the development of a dialogue design: visualisation, abstraction, detailing and prototyping. The first three of these are concerned primarily with the development of the conceptual model, and the last with the actual screen layouts and dialogue syntax.

We will discuss these in turn in the sections below with the help of two examples. The first is a club membership system, a brief formal specification for which is given in Figure 6.2. It is an example of a system containing personal information, and is in fact so simple that it would in reality be implemented using packaged software. We will use it to illustrate the use of forms and lists, which appear as components in much larger dialogues. The second example is the Airline Flight Information system introduced in Chapter 2, which is used to illustrate the formalisation of a relatively complex visual idea.

6.1.2   Visualisation

In the visualisation stage, we develop an overall picture of what our system will look like, and how it will work.

The first step is an exploration process, concerned with coming to terms with the requirements for the system. Even if there is a formal requirements specification, this is at best a guide to some features of the system, and must be discussed further with the users before any real understanding is obtained. For example, the specification of the club membership system in Figure 6.2 gives an indication of what the system is supposed to do, and of what data is to be stored, but no idea of how it is supposed to do it. In other systems, the initial requirements specification is developed as a part of this exploration process.

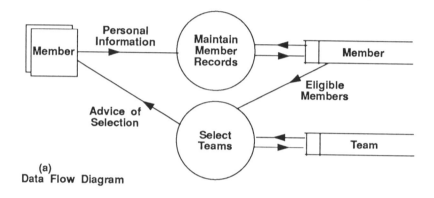

(a)
Data Flow Diagram

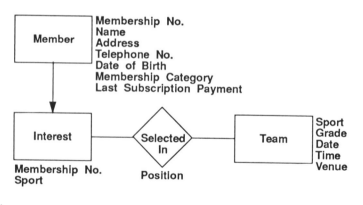

(b)
Data Model

Figure 6.2 Initial specifications for a club
membership scheme.

There are a number of sources of ideas:

- Defining the scope of the system. In finding out what the system is supposed to do (and more importantly, not to do), one often obtains a "feel" for how it should behave, and how people expect to be able to interact with it. Some things may be important, others slip into the background. A good example was the vehicle pool system. The data flow diagram has three circles of equal size, but, until the last section of Chapter 4, most of our effort was expended on one (Schedule Trips), because it was seen as the most important. The result of this was that the visual presentation of the system was based on addressing that process, rather than on the other two.

- Manual processes. Seeing how people perform the same or related tasks, and looking at the forms and documents that they use is a valuable source of ideas. Many representations (e.g. the schedule in the vehicle pool) are based directly on the representations used in manual systems. To obtain an understanding of the processes involved, it is best to actually perform them, e.g. building a schedule or a crossword by hand gives an idea of the thought processes involved, and so a clearer idea of the sort of information needed when, and of the way in which it needs to be organised.

- Comparison with related problems. As we have already pointed out, very few problems are totally new. Looking at computer systems that solve related problems or the same problem in different ways is useful, e.g. part of the development of Crossword Maker involved looking at potentially competing systems and identifying the weaknesses. Often, a good approach is to ask, "Why is this problem different from that one?" Identifying differences may point to ways in which the ideas in the other system can be adapted.

- The users' own ideas. In many cases, the users of a system already have a good idea of what it should look like. They may already have a manual system, or another automated system, and they have a well-developed model of what their objects look like (although they probably do not call them "objects") and what they do with them, or they want to redevelop a system precisely because it does not give them the model that they want.

One of the most important tools in this process is sketching, whether of formal representations of the system (e.g. data flow diagrams), of aspects of current implementations, or of the context in which the system is to operate. Figures 2.14, 6.4-5, and 6.17 illustrate the level and style of this sketching. As we pointed out in Chapter 2, sketching is not necessarily (or even desirably) a solitary activity. A group of people arguing over a drawing on a whiteboard can be an extremely productive activity.

There is no clear-cut transition between exploration and generation of ideas for solutions. The moment that one begins to feel that one is starting to understand the system

(and this is often almost immediately) ideas for solutions begin to come. Initially, they
will be very vague (although they might be specific on certain features) and may not hang
together very well, but as the process goes on, they begin to flesh out. Sometimes, in difficult situations, formal strategies for creativity (e.g. brainstorming) might need to be em-
ployed, but often the ideas develop as a natural part of the discussion of the problem and
of other potential solutions.

   We also test ideas as we go along, bouncing them off colleagues and the users.
With testing, however, it is often a good idea to become at least semi-formal, particularly
in situations where a user may be tempted to be polite rather than giving their real opinions. At meetings such as walkthroughs, where a designer formally presents their design,
people seem more likely to feel free to comment.

   At this level, we are testing for two things:

   • Does the solution "look right", i.e. is it clear, comprehensible and appealing to
     the user?
   • Does it solve the right problem, i.e. does it look as if it can be used to perform
     the required tasks?

   The end result of the visualisation process is a series of sketches of a possible solution, and of how it might work.

   The visualisation process for the Airline Flight Information system was discussed
in Chapter 2. In order to attempt a visualisation of the club membership system, we need
to concentrate on the two main issues not addressed in the specification:

   • What does the data look like?
   • How would it be used?

Figure 6.3 shows two ways in which the data might appear: a membership application
form; and a team list. We could see these as the basis for the system.

   The maintenance functions could be performed by displaying a form like the application form, containing all the details of a member, and allowing the user (a member of
the office staff) to fill it in (for a new member) or to call it up and change details (where
changes are needed or a subscription payment is to be recorded). It must be remembered,
however, that requests for information or changes will often not be accompanied by the
membership number (the club's unique identifier for a member), so that additional means
of searching may be required. These may often not yield a unique result (e.g. a search for
all people called Smith), so that the user may want to be able to pick the correct person
from a list (Figure 6.3), or possibly to make changes to a number of the records retrieved
(e.g. if all five members of the Smith family have moved house). The user may also want
to obtain lists of members on various criteria (e.g. by suburb). In addition (an issue that

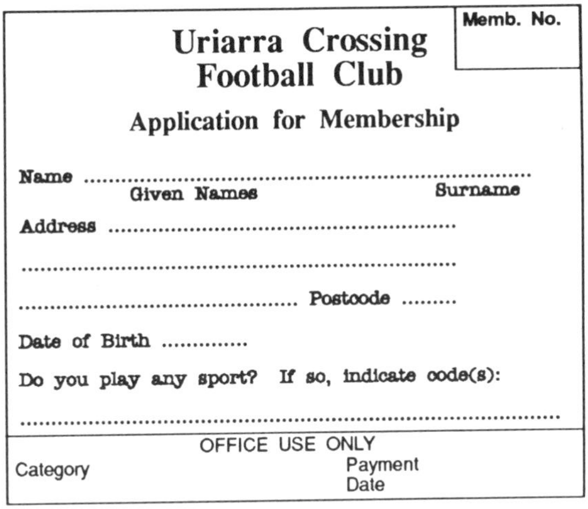

	Memb. No.

Uriarra Crossing Football Club

Application for Membership

Name ....

           Given Names   Surname

Address ....

....

.... Postcode ....

Date of Birth ....

Do you play any sport?   If so, indicate code(s):

....

OFFICE USE ONLY

Category   Payment
                             Date

(a)
Membership Application Form

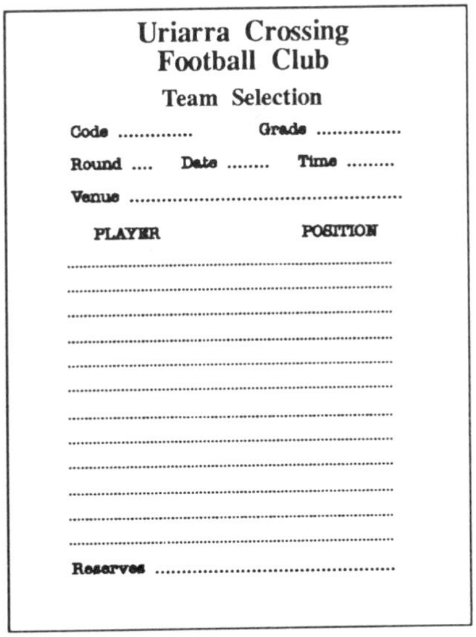

Uriarra Crossing Football Club

Team Selection

Code ....   Grade ....

Round ....   Date ....   Time ....

Venue ....

   PLAYER   **POSITION**

....

....

....

....

....

....

....

....

....

....

....

....

Reserves ....

(b)
Team Selection Sheet

Figure 6.3 Real world objects in the club.
membership system

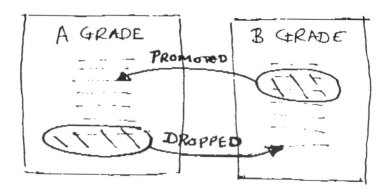

Figure 6.4 Selecting a team.

will not be addressed further), a more streamlined mechanism for recording subscription payments may be needed.

Selection of teams is done by a selection committee, or by a coach. The usual way of doing this is to take last week's teams and make changes, e.g. by leaving out injured or unavailable players, including players who have returned from injury or holidays, dropping out of form players to a lower grade and promoting good players from a lower grade. Notice that this requires being able to see a number of teams at once, as well as lists of injured and unavailable players. Normally, most members of each team remain where they are. The teams are posted on a notice board, and prospective players are expected to look at the board to discover when and where they are playing. In computing terms, this facility can be supplied by allowing the users to display multiple team lists on the screen (Figure 6.4), edit them and then print them out. It could also be useful to be able to extract lists of interested or eligible members from the main membership file, e.g. at the beginning of the season. It might also be necessary to be able to look up contact details for players (e.g. a telephone number).

The testing process at this stage consists of talking through these ideas with the users, in order to find out whether they think that they would like to be able to perform their tasks in the way described.

6.1.3   Abstraction

The second stage of the development process is to formalise our model by expressing our visualisation in terms of a set of objects and actions. We do this because:

- We need to use some sort of framework if we are to get any further.
- We have already argued that the appropriate framework in this context is the object/action model.

There are two main sources of ideas to help in this abstraction process:

- The terminology used in the application itself, e.g. in the vehicle pool system, *vehicles* make *trips* and are driven by *drivers*, all of which appear on a *schedule*.
- Our toolkit of common objects and actions, e.g. in the vehicle pool system, we have two collection objects: the *lists* of drivers and vehicles.

There are two main pitfalls in identifying objects:

- There are, if anything, too many potential objects. A written description in the requirements specification may contain nouns that we can select out as candidates; a data flow diagram will have data flows and data stores whose names will yield ideas; the user may show the designer forms, documents, tables and charts that could be treated as objects. If we included them all and treated them with equal prominence, we would finish up with a system that was an incomprehensible, unusable mess.
- The identifiable (or identified) objects may all be basic physical objects (e.g. *vehicle* and *driver*) or relationships between them (e.g. *trip*), which do not give an overview. This problem is exacerbated if formal system descriptions, particularly data models, are used as a basis for identifying objects.

This is the reason that we draw pictures first. These pictures give an overview, and so direct us towards overview objects, and give an idea of which other candidates for objects are important and which are not.

In this context, it must be stressed that much of design is a process of simplification, of seeing a simple pattern in an apparently complex morass, extracting that pattern, and building on it. Knowing about collections, and appreciating the need for overviews, is one of the tools that we use in recognising such patterns.

From our visualisation, we can identify three objects in the Club Membership system: *Member, Member List* and *Team*. We could, if we like, regard the first two of these as different ways of viewing the same object (*Member*). Team, however, is distinct, since although it is a list of members, it is generated for a specific purpose and is stored as a separate object (at least for the duration of the season).

Member is a sub-class of *Person*, with additional attributes such as *Membership No., Membership Category, Last Subscription Date* and *Interests* (which can have multiple values). Although *Interest* appears as a separate entity in the data model, it is really part of *Member*.

The actions on *Member* are essentially the standard actions outlined in Chapter 4. *New* includes allocation of a membership number. Although computers are good at allocating numbers, there may need to be a manual component in this system, because low numbers carry status and unused low numbers (particularly 1) are often allocated to long-standing members or influential patrons. For the same reason, *Change Value* must be applicable to the membership number (a key change which most computing professionals would automatically forbid in their design of the system). *Find* must be able to search not just on membership no., but on a range of other attributes; precisely which ones will be thrashed out with the user at the detailing or the prototyping stage. The list actions (e.g. *Next, Previous*) will be needed to move through sets of retrieved records, whether they are displayed singly or as a list.

Team is also a list, so the list actions are also applicable here. Editing facilities, e.g. *move*, are required, so that a player can be shifted from one team to another. It may be necessary to *insert* new players, which is effectively a *copy* from *Member*, and to *delete* players that have become permanently unavailable. The operation of *delete* highlights the difference between the team and the member list: *delete* on the member list would delete the member object, on team it merely removes it from the team, leaving the member object unchanged.

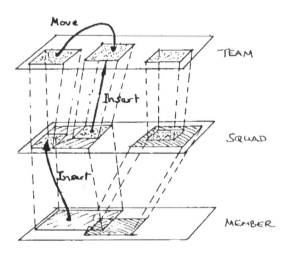

Figure 6.5 The idea of a squad.

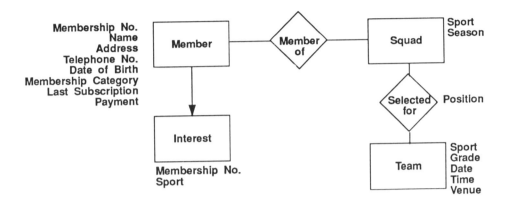

Figure 6.6 Data model modified to include
squad.

It is very rare that one's first attempt at a solution to a problem is perfect. There
are often features that are ignored (or simply not seen) in the early stages of a design, but
which emerge on a second or later look. Often, as a designer, if you are confused or uncomfortable about how something should work, it is because of such a problem.

In thinking about the Club Membership system, such a problem arose. It emerged
during an attempt to detail the dialogue syntax during the prototyping stage, but since it
involved changes to our conceptual model, it required a return to this stage (and, in a
sense, to the visualisation stage) for some rethinking, and so we shall discuss it here. This
kind of "looping back" is an essential part of the design process.

The conceptual model for the Club Membership system has so far been built about
the idea of a number of teams, but this hides the problem of what to do with people who
are not playing in the current round of matches, e.g. because they are injured, unavailable
or simply not required? An obvious ploy would be to invent an "unattached" team, in to
which they could be placed. This is not a good solution because it is a "fix" – forcing
something (a team) to be what it is not (everybody else) – and so is conceptually awkward. The solution comes from looking closer at the real world, and realising that the
teams are drawn from a *squad* containing all the registered players for that sport (Figure
6.5). If a sport has a number of squads (e.g. because it has age-related teams), the concept is still applicable, because the memberships do not (in general) overlap.

The *squad* object acts as an intervening layer between *member* and *team*. The *insert* action on a team object copies a person from the squad. *Insert* on the squad copies

from *Member*. *Delete* from a team affects only the team. *Delete* from the squad should affect any teams containing that player which have games still to play.

Conceptual changes of this type often impact back on the formal requirements specifications, since they reflect changes in the understanding of the problem. Conversely, the ongoing use of formal tools such as data flow diagrams and data models is often useful in helping to crystallise problems that seem to be difficult to grasp. In Figure 6.6, the data model has been updated to include the idea of a squad.

The Flight Information system has a much more complex set of objects than the Club Membership system. The objects are:

- *Map:* Map of area covered by services.
- *Port:* An airport with an air service.
- *Sector:* A direct link between two ports.
- *Flight :* An aeroplane flying on a sector at a specified time.
- *Itinerary:* A list of flights, commencing at the port of origin on a specified date which will get the traveller to the destination port.

Note that *aeroplane* is not an object. We are not interested in which particular aeroplane flies a service (although we might be interested in the aircraft type), only that the service exists. There are two collection objects: *Map*, which contains both *ports* and *sectors* (effectively as the nodes and links of a network), and *Itinerary*, which contains a number of flights, commencing on a particular day. *Sector* is a slot object, in that it contains a number of flights. The main attributes of these objects are:

- *Map*:   Coastline
                      {Port}
                      {Sector}
- *Port*:   Port Name
                      Position
- *Sector*:   Port of Origin
                      Port of Destination
- *Flight*:   Flight No
                      Date
                      Sector
                      Departure Time
                      Arrival Time
- *Itinerary:*   Origin
                      Destination
                      {Intermediate Port}
                      Date Commenced
                      Flight}

Coastline is an unspecified representation of the Australian coastline that can be plotted on the screen. *Position* is the location of the port using a co-ordinate system compatible with the coastline representation.

We also have to begin to think about the actions on these objects. There are two ways in which this can be approached:

- From the direction of the object, where we ask what actions could we perform on this object.
- From the direction of the application, where we ask what actions do we require in order to perform the specified tasks.

The obvious approach is the second one, because in our visualisation we have already attempted to imagine how a user would perform certain key tasks, and have recorded it in some way (e.g. on a storyboard). We should be able to identify our objects on the picture, and the actions required should become clear. If we apply this approach to the Flight Information system, we obtain the following set of actions:

- *Map:*   Display
- *Port:*   Select
                Deselect
- *Sector:*   Select
                Show Flights
- *Flight:*   Select
- *Itinerary:* Set Origin
                Set Destination
                Set Intermediate Ports
                Set Date Commenced
                Next Day
                Previous Day
                Select
                Select "Best"

Note that the action of selecting a flight or a sector is, in fact, to select an appropriate itinerary. However, since the action performed by the user is to select a flight or a sector, these must be provided as specific actions. Note also that deselection of flights, sectors and itineraries is not required. This is because we need only to provide for one itinerary to be selected at one time, and so selection of one automatically deselects the previous one. This is different from ports, where there must be at least two selected (the origin and the destination) and so deselection must be explicit.

In some situations, it is more productive to approach the selection of actions from the direction of the object. There are two reasons for this:

- We have already come from the task direction during the visualisation process, and so approaching from the other direction gives us a fresh look.
- Objects are really very simple things, and most objects have only a limited range of possible actions over and above the "standard" list for objects of the particular type, so that it is relatively easy to write down the actions, particularly since we are not concerned with complex display options at this stage.
- If this approach is adopted, it requires that the tasks are then analysed to weed out unwanted actions.

Since we have now formalised our model, our testing can become more formalised. We need to look at three things:

- Is the set of objects complete, i.e. are there features of our visualisation not included in an object?
- Are all the attributes included, i.e. are there pieces of data that we know about (e.g. from documents or a data model, or that we know we need to keep track of what is happening) that are not attributes of any object?
- Can the actions be used to perform the functions of the system?

The last of these may seem to be a repeat of what we have already done in determining the actions, but in part this is the point of the exercise. We can develop explicit scenarios, with actual data, and work through the steps required to perform the task, using the actions provided. A detailed example of such a scenario for the Club Membership system is given in the section on Prototyping. Not only will this approach usually detect flaws in the process, but the user will often identify points at which the task might need to be performed differently, and so introduce additional requirements which may or may not be met by the tasks provided, e.g. with the Flight Information system, the user might ask if they could build up an itinerary consisting of a number of "legs" each containing one or more sectors, possibly spread over days or weeks? This is possible at the moment only as totally separate itineraries for each leg, because of the way that *select* works for flights and sectors, so that the question would arise as to how to change this.

6.1.4 Detailing

The detailing process takes the objects and actions and fills in the details. Although specification of the precise dialogue syntax is not required, this process takes us through a series of refinements of the representation of the objects and more detailed specification of the actions. The end result is often a series of sketches of screens accompanied by descriptions of how the various actions should be performed.

The background to the detailing process was discussed in Chapter 4, where we looked at the representations of different kinds of objects and the ways in which actions can be performed, the formal specification of actions, and the ways in which appropriate sets of displays must be put together in order to have the necessary information available at the right time. The aspects of the guide-lines and standards discussed in Chapter 5 concerning dialogue structure and object representations are also relevant at this stage.

The membership record side of the Club Membership system is a relatively straightforward database application, the main requirements being to add, modify and delete records, and to find individual records or sets of records. These raise some interesting questions of dialogue syntax, which will be discussed in the next section. The main issue in the detailing of the Club Membership system is to work out how we should display and manipulate the squads and teams.

Figure 6.7 shows the type of screen display needed when picking teams. At any one time, the user will be picking a number of teams based on the one squad, so that squad must be on display. The most useful order in which the squad can be displayed is by level (e.g. all current A-grade players, followed by all current B-grade, etc.), and possibly alphabetically within that level, so that the appropriate members of the squad are on display for the team being selected. This requires an appropriate data item in the squad member entries, which will be discussed below.

The normal approach to team selection would be to start from the highest grade team and work down. Since players would not normally be moved more than one grade, it is sufficient to be able to show two teams at a time. The team currently being selected is on the left, the team for the next grade down (which may also be changed, since it is a source for promoted players and a recipient for dropped players) is on the right. The remaining teams are stacked behind these: those for which selection is complete on the left, those still to be selected on the right. Note that this implies some form of numbering system for grades which permits them to be ordered, or simply an ability to "remember" which order they were in last time and to retain that order.

The procedure for selecting teams for a particular round would work as follows (Figure 6.7):

- The selector must first open a *Squad* window and load the required squad. Squads would be stored as named files, so an *Open* command would be used which would give them a list of file names for the squads for which they have access. The names would (preferably) be meaningful, e.g. Cricket - U19s (or CRICU19 under a system such as DOS where long filenames are not supported).
- The selector then opens a *Team* window. A *New* option would be used to create a new team, but what is usually required is to take the teams from the last round and select new teams based on these. To do this, copies have to be made, so that the team records are not destroyed. For this, an *Import* action is

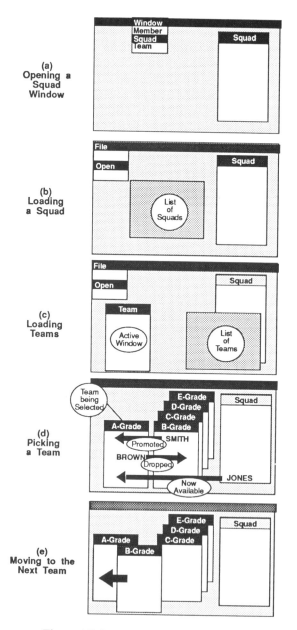

Figure 6.7 Storyboard for picking a team.

needed. (*Open* would also be available, to update already selected teams). *Import* works like *Open* (Figure 4.18), in that a list of file names (the team names) is displayed. These would be for the specified squad only. It is also arguable (an issue which would be resolved when dialogue syntax is being detailed at the prototyping stage) whether all teams for all rounds should be listed, whether a mechanism for listing only teams for a specified round should be included, or whether an *Import All* action (with the round specified or defaulting to the last round) should be implemented which simply loads all teams.

- The teams are then displayed. The selector uses *Move* commands (either *Cut* and *Paste* or dragging) to move players between the displayed teams, and *Copy* commands (*Copy* and *Paste* or dragging) to move players from the squad to the team. The *Delete* command on a player in a team removes them from a team but leaves them in the squad.

- When selection of a team is complete, a *Save* command saves the team to disk. (There may also be a provision for a *Save All* on the same lines as *Import All*, to be used at the end of the process, to save all the teams.)

- The window for the next team (on the right) is then dragged across to the left. The user would also have to scroll the squad window, so that the players at the appropriate level are displayed. In a more sophisticated implementation, a paging mechanism (using *Next* and *Previous* commands on teams) could be implemented, in which case the list in the squad window could also be made to scroll, so that players of the right level (see below) are displayed.

This process continues until all teams are selected.

If so desired, some of the setting-up process could be streamlined, e.g. the selector's initial display could already include both squad and team windows, either with a de-

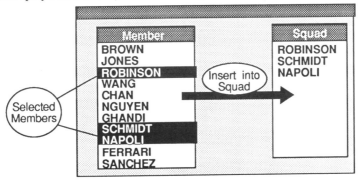

Figure 6.8 Adding members to a squad.

fault squad and last week's teams already loaded, or a single command available which would load both squad and teams. This, again, would be discussed during the prototyping stage.

The issue of adding members to a squad must also be addressed. Members of a squad must be members of the club, so this involves locating and selecting the appropriate member records and then copying them, either by dragging them, by using *copy* and *paste*, or by using an *insert* command on the *squad* object that automatically copies any selected *member* objects. This is illustrated in Figure 6.8. The precise syntax would, again, be decided at the prototyping stage.

It is also necessary to look in detail at the objects in the Club Membership system. Our concept of a team is of a list of members, represented by their names. In a given sport, however, a team has a set number of members (with a set number of reserves also permitted). Players are usually assigned to set positions, which are often determined when the team is chosen. Should we include these features, to develop a more structured concept of a team, or should we simply rely on people's ability to count up to eleven (or thirteen, fifteen or eighteen)? Enforcing a fixed number of team members might be a nuisance, because the user might want to "pencil in" a new member, and then decide who to drop. The fixed number would force them to drop somebody first. Use of fixed positions might also be awkward if it prevented the user from picking a team and then deciding positions. A compromise might be to allow the user to build any length of list, but to supply

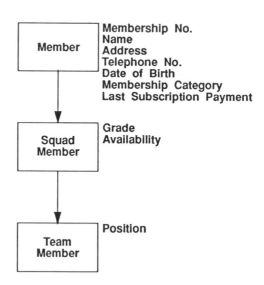

Figure 6.9 Member's class hierarchy.

a count at the bottom, and to allow them to annotate the names in the list with, e.g. a position.

In a similar way, it would be useful to know, for squad members not currently in a
team, why they are unavailable (if they are), when they are likely to be available again,
and at what level (grade) they played last. The first two of these are best handled by a
comment (e.g. "Holiday - 1/6/97 - 27/6/97"), while the third probably warrants a field on
its own, which could be automatically updated each time they are selected for a team.

This discussion crystallises a problem that was implicit in our discussion of the actions in the last section, where we said that the effect of a *Delete* on a member of a team
or a squad was different to the effect on a member in the *Member List*. It is now clear,
from the fact that they have different attributes, that we are dealing with three different
classes of objects: a *Member*, a *Squad Member* and a *Team Member*. These form a class
hierarchy, with *Member* at the top (Figure 6.9). This does not mean that a display of a
squad member or a team member has to contain all the attributes of *Member*, nor does it
mean that all the actions available on *Member* are necessarily available to a team selector:
they may be permitted to display member information but not to change it, and some attributes may remain hidden. Which attributes are to be displayed, and how, and which
actions are to be made available to which users is up to the designer. We will discuss the
second of these problems in Chapter 9.

One feature of the discussion on the Club Membership system is worth specific
comment. It is very easy to over-complicate a solution to a problem by building in large
numbers of features that are highly specific to the application, when a much simpler
solution would be just as effective. In our discussion of the attributes required for a team
member, and in our approach to the display of squads and teams, we have attempted to
use simple, general features which are already available or easily provided (e.g. free-text
fields and management facilities for lists and windows) rather than complex
custom-written facilities. This does not lessen the power of the system (and may, in fact,
increase it), but does make it easier to understand and easier to implement.

The testing of our detailed design is also more detailed, since we are closer to the
way that the final system will perform. We need to check:

- Do the representations "look right", i.e. do they agree with the user's ideas of
  what they should look like, do they show objects in the right relationships?
- Do they contain enough information, i.e. at any point in a task, is all the
  information relevant to a required decision visible?
- Are they usable to perform the functions of the system, i.e. not only are the
  appropriate actions provided, but they are easy to use and their method of use
  fits naturally into the task.
- Do they conform to guide-lines and standards, e.g. criteria such as consistency
  of presentation, clarity of layout and of language; modeless interaction?

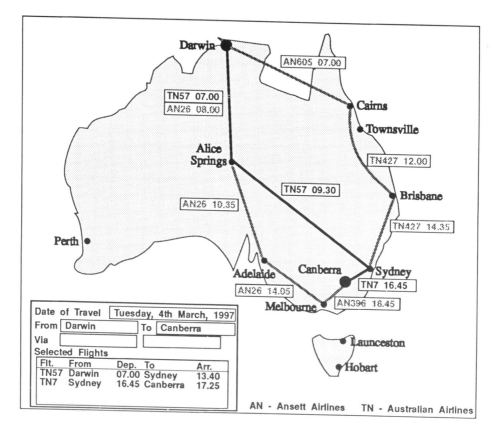

Figure 6.10 Screen for flight information
system.

Tests on the Club Membership system could be carried out using scenarios of the type described in the next section.

The proposed screen layout for the Flight Information system is shown in Figure 6.10. To test our design, we could start out by testing similar situations to the one that we talked about in the design, e.g. Perth to Sydney, Hobart to Brisbane. However, we also need to look at other situations, e.g. Melbourne to Sydney: they are both jammed into the bottom corner of the map, and there are about thirty flights a day, all of which take an hour and ten minutes. How do we display them? What happens to our selection of the "quickest"? There is another problem, too. We have neglected to provide any mechanism for specifying the date of travel, or for the Next Day, Previous Day actions. How are we going to do this?

By the end of this process, we have developed a solution that we are sufficiently confident about to want to prototype. We have confidence because it looks as if it should work, it feels right and the user likes it.

Considerations of ease of implementation may come into our thoughts, but they should not dominate.

6.2 Prototyping

6.2.1 What is a Prototype?

We build prototypes so that the users can see, in a concrete form, what the system will look like and how it will behave. Because a prototype is more realistic than sketches on a piece of paper, the user finds it easier to imagine how they will use the system, and so can provide a more detailed critique of the proposed system than they were able to in earlier stages of testing. It is important, however, that the prototype should be quick and cheap to build and to modify, since the object of building it is to find out what problems there are with the design and what changes are needed. These changes must then be incorporated into the prototype for further testing with the users, thus initiating further cycles of change.

The simplest form of prototype is a storyboard displayed on a screen. It consists of mock-ups of screens, and is operated like a slide show, in which the presenter performing an action actually moves on to the next slide, which shows the effect of that action.

A more sophisticated form of prototype allows the user to enter data on to screens (although it is either not stored, or stored on to sequential files without any internal processing) and to navigate around the system. It contains no underlying functionality, but behaves reasonably realistically from the user's point of view. This means that the user can sit at the machine (or a terminal to it) and attempt to perform the sorts of tasks that they expect the system to perform, thus being able to identify potential problem areas.

It is quite common to build a "prototype" containing large amounts of underlying codes, representing a significant proportion of the functionality of the system. The code may be in the same language that is to be used to implement the final system, or it may be in a "higher-level" language (e.g. a fourth-generation language). This approach is both unnecessary and counter-productive. The purpose of a prototype is to test the *user-interface*. Only when a reasonable level of agreement has been reached on this can detailed program design and implementation begin. The inclusion of this additional code (even 4GL code) makes the user-interface more difficult to change, because of the need to rewrite much of the code, and so interferes with the testing of the user-interface by increasing the time required for change, reducing the scope of the changes possible, and reducing the number of testing cycles possible.

6.2.2   Prototyping Tools

The tools used to produce a prototype are not necessarily those needed to produce the final system. If the prototype is to be a "slide show", then any suitable presentation graphics tools can be used. These can include both vector and bit-map graphics software (e.g.
Corel Draw, MacDraw, PC Paintbrush, MacPaint), business graphics (e.g. *Harvard
Graphics*) or the graphics facilities of a spreadsheet such as *Lotus 1-2-3* or *Excel*, or software designed more specifically for presentations (e.g. *Storyboard, Powerpoint*). Dan
Bricklin's *Demo II* is designed specifically for demonstration of computer interfaces, but
generates character-based displays only.

There is currently very little software available that allows rapid generation of a
prototype that the user can actually sit at and use. This is described as one of the features
that will be possessed by User-Interface Management Systems when they become commercially available. Some CASE (Computer-Aided Software Engineering) tools contain
application generators, but these produce modal dialogue structures with deep menu hierarchies, and so are unsuitable. The currently available windows-based application generators (e.g. *ObjectVision*) are insufficiently powerful to prototype a system of any
complexity.

Fourth-Generation Languages (4GLs) are widely touted as providing rapid prototyping facilities, but this is not really the case. These languages normally contain a reasonably powerful screen-painting facility which allows the generation and display of
forms. In some cases links can be defined which allow a number of forms to be arranged
into a hierarchy or a transaction sequence, but these facilities are of little use in prototyping a modeless dialogue. Some windows-based 4GLs (e.g. *Ingres Windows 4GL*) are becoming available, which allow interactive definition of screens with the standard GUI
dialogue components (see, e.g. Figure 5.11). Any additional development requires coding
in the language itself, which is usually procedural and no simpler than coding in Cobol or
C. The commonly presented idea of developing a "fully functional" prototype in a 4GL,
and then redeveloping it in a language such as Cobol or C, is usually impractical because
of the time needed to develop the 4GL prototype, as well as being unnecessary.

A more satisfactory approach is to accept that the development of a working prototype will involve significant coding effort, and to design the prototype to present a limited
range of features which will be representative of the system as a whole, and which will
elicit the kind of feedback that is useful in determining whether those features being
tested (in particular the type of interaction incorporated in the dialogue) can be incorporated in the final implementation of the system. The fact that other features, such as the
overall conceptual model, are not being tested should not matter, since these should have
been tested already. In any case, the prototype should be supplemented by "mock-up"
prototypes of the remainder of the system.

The Personal Timetable system, which we are using as an example in this book, represents this kind of thinking. It is seen as being one component of a much larger time-tabling system. However, for the purposes of presentation, a relatively small subsystem has been selected and worked through in detail, in order to give a potential user a "feel" as to how the complete system would look and behave. In doing so, we have neglected issues concerning the functionality of the remainder of the system (which would have to be explored), but will have succeeded in giving the user sufficient information for them to make an informed decision as to whether they want further development to take place.

6.2.3 Detailing the Dialogue Syntax

A key element in developing the prototype is the precise specification of the dialogue syntax, i.e. not just the actions which are applicable to the given objects, but what their names are, where they appear on menus, accelerator keys to be assigned, how they are to be performed. During the testing of the prototype, some of the choices made will turn out to be inappropriate, or more effective ways of performing the action will be discovered, but by attempting a specification at this stage, we give ourselves time to discover problems and to correct them, as well as giving the user a clear indication of what the software will be like to use.

We discussed dialogue guide-lines in the previous chapter. There are a number of common problems encountered in applying these guide-lines, e.g.

- Choice of appropriate names for actions, and in particular the applicability or otherwise of the standard (CUA) set of names.
- Movement between different views of an object, and the effect of various actions on these views.

These will be discussed in the examples below.

Figure 6.11 shows the screen layouts for the *Member* object, the *Member List*, and the *Squad* and *Team* objects in the Club Membership system. They are relatively straightforward realisations of the forms and sketches shown in Figures 6.3-5. The layout of the Member screen is similar to that of the application form. The alignment of fields ensures that the personal information (name, address, date of birth, interests) appear as one group, and the status information (membership category and payment information) as another. On initial display, the cursor would be on *Surname*, and would move downwards. *Postcode* would be entered after the last line of *Address*, the cursor then moving to *Date of Birth*. Since *Membership No.* is not normally changed, it is treated as the last field of the screen, being entered after *Last Subscription Payment*.

The acceptable content of the different fields requires serious consideration. It is tempting to put edit checks on fields such as *Surname*, to restrict it to alphabetic charac-

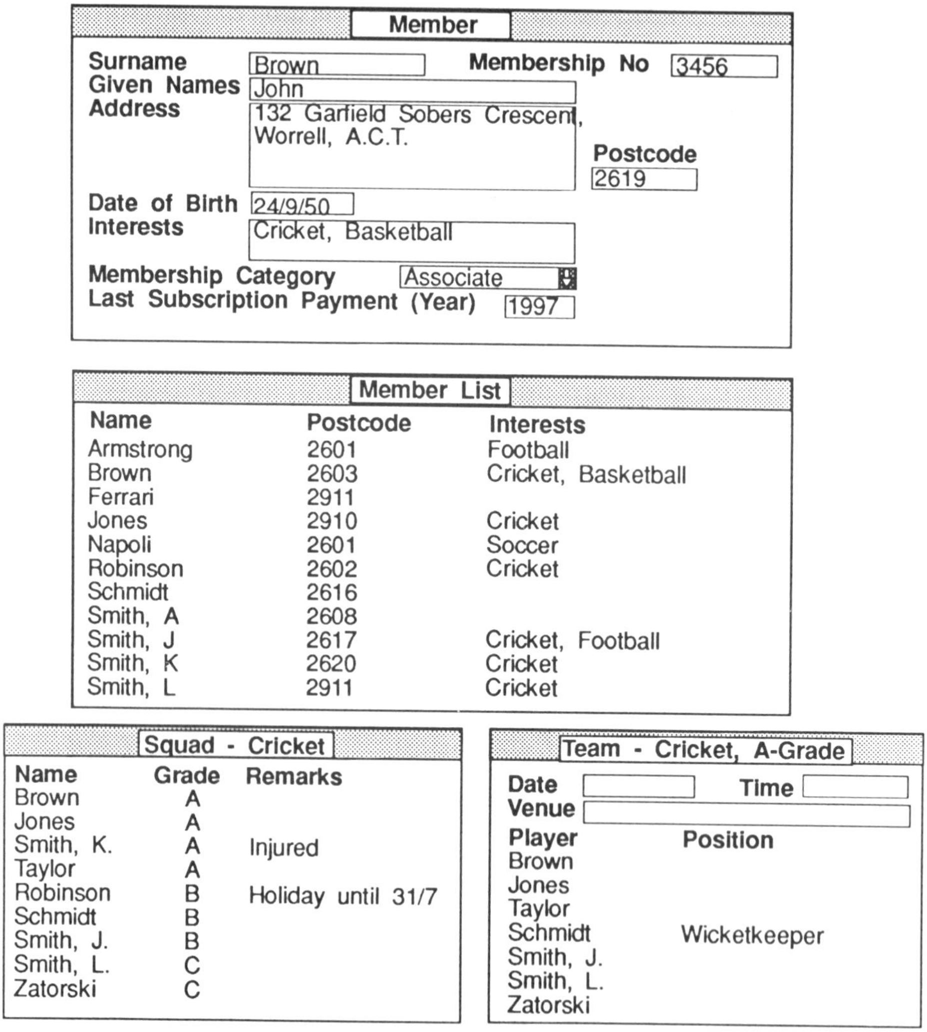

```
┌──────────────────────────────────────────────────────────────┐
│                         Member                                 │
│ Surname        [Brown          ]   Membership No [3456      ]   │
│ Given Names    [John                           ]               │
│ Address        [132 Garfield Sobers Crescent,                  │
│                 Worrell, A.C.T.                                 │
│                                             Postcode           │
│                                             [2619      ]       │
│ Date of Birth  [24/9/50    ]                                   │
│ Interests      [Cricket, Basketball            ]               │
│                                                                │
│ Membership Category      [Associate      ▼]                    │
│ Last Subscription Payment (Year)  [1997 ]                      │
└──────────────────────────────────────────────────────────────┘
```

```
┌──────────────────────────────────────────────────────────────┐
│                       Member List                              │
│ Name              Postcode        Interests                    │
│ Armstrong         2601            Football                     │
│ Brown             2603            Cricket, Basketball           │
│ Ferrari           2911                                         │
│ Jones             2910            Cricket                      │
│ Napoli            2601            Soccer                       │
│ Robinson          2602            Cricket                      │
│ Schmidt           2616                                         │
│ Smith, A          2608                                         │
│ Smith, J          2617            Cricket, Football            │
│ Smith, K          2620            Cricket                      │
│ Smith, L          2911            Cricket                      │
└──────────────────────────────────────────────────────────────┘
```

```
┌────────────────────────────┐  ┌──────────────────────────────┐
│      Squad - Cricket       │  │    Team - Cricket, A-Grade     │
│ Name      Grade  Remarks   │  │ Date [          ]  Time [    ] │
│ Brown       A              │  │ Venue [                      ] │
│ Jones       A              │  │ Player            Position     │
│ Smith, K.   A    Injured   │  │ Brown                          │
│ Taylor      A              │  │ Jones                          │
│ Robinson    B  Holiday until 31/7 │ Taylor                     │
│ Schmidt     B              │  │ Schmidt         Wicketkeeper   │
│ Smith, J.   B              │  │ Smith, J.                      │
│ Smith, L.   C              │  │ Smith, L.                      │
│ Zatorski    C              │  │ Zatorski                       │
└────────────────────────────┘  └──────────────────────────────┘
```

Figure 6.11 Screen for club membership
system.

ters only (which excludes *O'Neill*), to eliminate embedded spaces (wiping out *von Stal-hein*) or to restrict them to one only (eliminating *van der Smut*), and to put the name into a "standard" form with the initial letter capitalised and all others lower case to assist in searching (which gets *McLeod* and *ffoulkes* wrong). The search parameters in the *Find* command should not be case-sensitive (e.g. *MCLEOD, mcleod, Mcleod, McLeod* and any other variation should find *McLeod*), but at the time of entry, it is up to the user how they want to present the data, and, as far as possible, it should be stored as entered. The need to support a range of formats for date fields, e.g. *Date of Birth*, was discussed in Chapter 5. For *Membership Category*, where there is a limited range of choices, we have used a combination box, which allows the user to choose from a pick-list of values.

It is also tempting to make fields *mandatory*, i.e. to force the user to supply a value. A good example is *Date of Birth*, because everybody has one. The club, however, may want to record them only in specific circumstances, e.g. if a member is playing in a team for which there is an age qualification (e.g. the under-19s or the veterans). Even if a field (e.g. *Given Names*) is supplied 99.99 per cent of the time, making it mandatory causes disproportionate problems in the remaining 0.01 per cent. Some people do only have one name, whether by birth or for professional reasons, which would go into *Surname*, thus leaving *Given Names* empty. In this case, the only mandatory fields should be *Membership Number*, because it is the identifier for the record, and *Surname*, because it is the main link to our identification of the person in the real world.

Related to this is the behaviour of the system if the user makes an error, e.g. keys in an invalid date (e.g. 31st April). The system should warn the user, by highlighting the error and displaying an error message, but must not make them correct it before moving on to another field. In many cases, the user will be able to make a correction, but sometimes they will not, and if the system is demanding a correction that they cannot make, it becomes very frustrating. If they do move on without making a correction, the field simply returns to the value that it was before the user attempted to enter the invalid value.

The naming of commands often creates problems. The most usual problem is an uncertainty as to whether a standard name is applicable because of some perceived difference, either from the standard itself or between two potential applications of it. The rule is that an action always applies to the currently selected object, and that the same action, applied to different objects, should have the same name. To be the "same", two actions should have the same effect from the user's point of view, even if their underlying mechanisms are totally different.

The *File Save* command is a case in point. The purpose of this action is to save the currently selected object to disk. However, the Club Membership system has two kinds of objects: a *member*, which is a record on a data file; and *squad* and *team*, each of which is a file in its own right. Because the *Save* action is performed internally in a different way for the two objects (one is adding or updating a record on an existing file, the other is creating or overwriting an entire file), it is tempting to give them different names (e.g. *Add* and/or *Update* for the file record, and *File Save* for the list, the latter being used be-

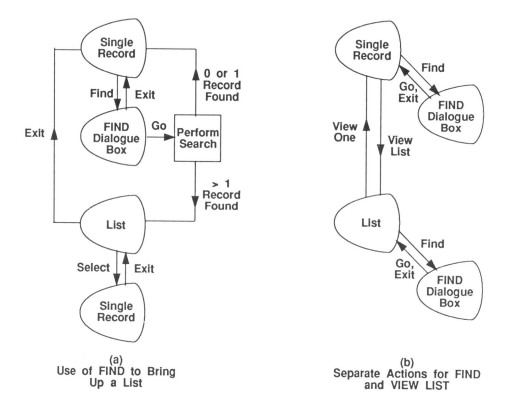

Figure 6.12 Movement to and from list
objects.

cause it is the same as for a document and is an entire file). However, this implies that the user knows about and should be concerned with the differences in the underlying storage structures of the objects, and so adds unnecessary complexity to the system. The same command name (*File Save*) should be used for both actions.

The relationship between the *Member* object and the *Member List* also presents difficulties of a type that are encountered in many systems. These are:

- How do we move between them?
- What is the effect of an action on one or the other?

The basic requirements are that:

- The user can "page" through the records in the list one at a time using the *next* and *previous* actions.
- The user may perform any of the available actions on a given record (including adding new records and changing and deleting existing ones).
- The user can move freely between the list representation of the data and individual records (with any changes being made on one being represented or the other).

Many older systems require the user to perform a search in order to obtain a list [Figure 6.12(a)]. Search parameters are filled in either on the main screen or using a dialogue box (Figure 6.13). The list is then automatically displayed if more than one record is retrieved. The user can then select an item from the list and the individual record will be displayed. An *exit* command returns them to the list. This kind of dialogue is highly modal, since the behaviour of the individual record display depends on whether it was the original display (at the top of the diagram) or that reached from the list. It is also complicated. It is common to require that the user perform a search to see any records at all: the default is a blank screen.

Figure 6.12(b) separates the idea of the list from that of the search. Instead, the *View* menu contains a *One* option that causes a single record to be displayed, and a *List* option that causes a list to be displayed. The default is that the list contains *all* records unless a search is performed. *Find* appears on the *View* menu as the *Some...* option. This displays a dialogue box to obtain search parameters. Once the search has been carried out, the selected record(s) are displayed in the same format as before, but the displayed list or the set of records accessible using *next* and *previous* are limited to those retrieved by the search. If nothing is found, an empty list or blank record will be displayed. To return to the full set of records, *View All* is used.

The dialogue box in Figure 6.13 is different from the representation of the *Member* object because search parameters often take a different form to the data fields that they refer to. In particular:

- It may be necessary to specify ranges (e.g. with Date of Birth).
- More than one value of a field with a limited set of choices may be required (e.g. with Membership Category, where multiple values may be chosen from a pick list).
- It may be necessary to specify *wildcards* in some fields (e.g. using the format *..Richmond..* means that any address containing the word *Richmond* will be selected).

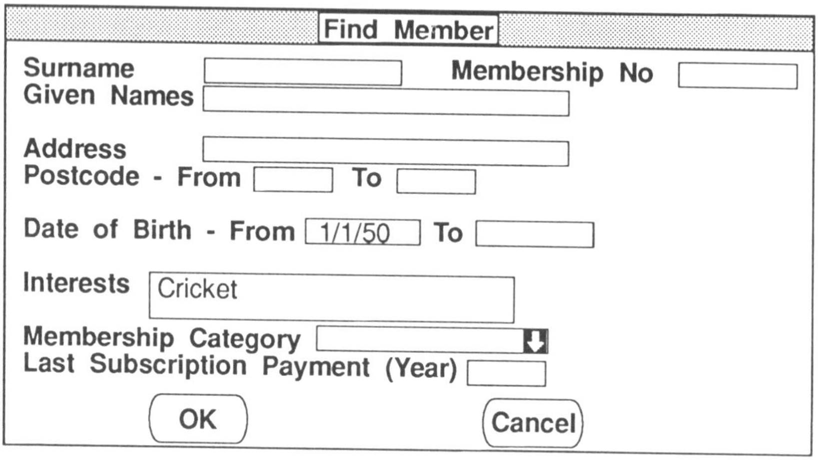

Figure 6.13 The FIND dialogue box.

Unless there is a good reason not to (e.g. a very large database on which only some fields are indexed), the user should be able to search on any field, and on any combination of fields. Dialogues which contain separate commands for searches on different fields (e.g. *Search on Surname, Search on Address, Search on DOB, ...*) are very restrictive. Historically the only reason for their use was ease of programming. They should be avoided.

The effect of further actions on the retrieved list also creates problems for many designers. If we regard the member list as a throw-away (i.e. we perform a *Find* action and get a list of records, but once we perform any other action that list is lost) there is no problem. This is effectively the model adopted in Figure 6.12(a). However, we often want to perform a quite complex series of actions on records from that list, e.g. updating addresses on a number (but not all) of the retrieved records.

Although changed and deleted records must come from the list, a change may well take the record outside the selection criteria (e.g. by changing an interest of CRICKET to FOOTBALL), while an added record may not be relevant to the set at all (e.g. it may refer to an eighteen-year old whose only interest is DARTS). Although these actions will always be reflected in changes to the file, it is not so clear what effect they should have on the list of selected records: e.g. do we always add new records to the list, do we never add them, do we add them only if they satisfy the original search criteria, or do we assume that by doing an add that we have finished with the search and throw away the list?

The problem with any of these solutions is that they involve an arbitrary decision which will inevitably be wrong some of the time, e.g. if we were adding extra cricketers we might want to retain the set, but if we were just adding a random batch of new members (even if some of them play cricket) we would want to throw it away. This is the type of decision best left to the user.

If we look at the problem in an object-oriented manner, this conclusion becomes clearer. We have two dialogue objects here: the individual record, and the list. Our working rule is that actions always work on the currently selected object. Here, we have two objects selected simultaneously, the current list and the current record, so any action should apply to both. (The other way of saying this is that we have a single object, *Member*, which we are viewing in two different ways. This is the reason why the *View* menu is used both to find records and to switch between the single record and list representations.) *Find* creates the list and displays the first record, *Next* and *Previous* (which would appear on the *View* menu but would normally be performed with the *PgDn* and *PgUp* function keys) display other records in the list. *Delete* should delete the current record from the list and the file (and display the next record), *Save* on an existing record should rewrite the changed record to the file (leaving it in the list) and *Save* on a new record (created with *New*) should add a record to the file and the list. *New, Save* and *Delete* appear on the *File* menu, for the reasons discussed above. This gives a consistent behaviour, in which all commands work on the list and the file in the same way.

We need one more action (*Clear*), to get rid of list entries set up by previous actions, making the current list empty. The effect of this could be obtained by performing a search with "impossible" parameters, thus giving an empty list, but it would be more desirable to have a specific command. Under CUA, *Clear* appears on the *Edit* menu and is used to remove part of a displayed object (e.g. blanking out a field), and so is not particularly suitable. We cannot use *New*, because we have already used this to mean "create a new record". The solution that we will adopt is to include an option *None* on the *View* menu in the group including *All* and *Some*....

The combination of the *Clear* action with the *New/Save* combination used to add records now gives the user a range of options:

- *New/Save* on its own will add records to the existing list, so that, e.g. additional cricketers can be added.
- *Clear* followed by a series of *New/Save* actions will create a list containing all the records just added, which can then be reviewed and corrections made.
- The *Clear* plus *New/Save* combination, used repeatedly, leaves only the current record selected.

This gives the user far more flexibility than an arbitrary decision to impose one of these options made by the designer.

Many information retrieval systems (e.g. bibliographic systems) require more sophisticated use of lists or sets of retrieved records, since the user may want to:

- Refine a search by imposing additional criteria.
- Combine the results of two or more searches.
- "Page" through the results of a search, either marking the records that they want to keep or removing records that they do not want.

These actions differ from those discussed above because they work only on the set of selected records, and not on the file. From a dialogue point of view, these have a number of consequences:

- If there is a currently selected set of records, *Find* operates on this set, and not on the file. *Clear* deletes the set (rather than creating an empty set) so that *Find* operates on the file to create a new set. This means that the default is to refine an existing search.
- The results of a search can be *Saved* (and given a name or number for later reference). A *Retrieve (Open)* action allows the search to be retrieved, while a *Merge* action combines the results of the saved search with the current search set. A series of independent searches (i.e. *Clear* followed by *Find*) can be saved and later merged to give a single combined search set.
- *Include* and *Exclude* actions can also be provided. *Include* includes the current record in a new (refined) search set. *Exclude* removes the current record from the search set. These permit the user to refine a search set by paging through (using *Next* or *Previous*) and either selecting required records or removing unwanted ones from the search set.

A *Sort* action, to sort the final search set into some user-specified order, is also useful. This appears as the *By..* option on the *View* menu.

6.2.4   Testing a Prototype

As we mentioned above, a prototype may be simply a slide show which explains to the user what the system will look like, or it may be a piece of software (albeit of limited functionality) which they can actually use.

With a slide show, the presenter is in control of what the user sees. One of the most important aspects of such a demonstration is to pitch it at the level of the user's tasks, and not at the system's features. Displaying a series of screens gives little indication of how they can be used, while going through CUA-compliant menus gives no information at all, because they all say *New, Open, Save, Save As ..., Delete, Print,* etc. Instead, the presenter must devise a set of scenarios which are directly related to the tasks that the user wants to perform. They must include actual data, and show how it will be used, and how it will change. They should cover all the main features of the system, but as a necessary consequence of performing the tasks.

To develop a demonstration for the Club Membership system, it would be necessary to devise data for about twenty to thirty members (enough to display a coherent list), with characteristics which support the kind of scenarios listed below, i.e. at least five Smiths, three of whom live at 33 Rotten Row, about fifteen people over 50 who are interested in cricket, and an A-grade cricket team list, at least two members of which are on the "main" data set (so their details can be displayed). The demonstration would then involve the following activities:

- Add a new member (Melissa Chan, 34 Napoleon Bonaparte Drive, Petain, 3456).
- Find the Smith family (33 Rotten Row) and change their address to (88 The Tan, Hyde Park, 3333).
- Create a new cricket squad (Veterans) based on all cricketers over 50, and use it to select a team. Unavailable players who might be available at a later date should be retained in the squad. The team may be "stiffened" if required by the inclusion of not more than two A-grade players. The selector can be assumed to have knowledge about the ability and availability of most of the squad members, but may have to check on availability, which may mean that they cannot complete the task in one session.

Even in devising this scenario, it has revealed a potential problem. Where is the selector going to obtain the telephone numbers? Should they be held on the membership system, or is the local telephone directory sufficient?

If the user is to test the prototype himself, it is still important to devise data in advance, so that, e.g. relevant codes and other parameters are set up, and an attempt to find data will find appropriate data (even if it is read straight off a file).

6.3 Designing for Flexibility

6.3.1 Introduction

One of the criteria for a good tool is flexibility. This means that the tool can be used for a variety of purposes, some of them unforeseen by the designer. This need arises from three sources:

- Different users will want to use the tool in different ways.
- The requirements for its use will change over time.
- Someone will want to apply it to a related problem for which no specific tool exists.

We have already discussed the first of these points in some detail, in particular the use of modeless dialogues in order to allow people to perform tasks in their own way. The second and third of these involve changes in the requirements for the system, without necessarily negating the original requirements. The aim is to build a system that can meet these new requirements without requiring redesign or reprogramming.

There are three strategies for making systems more flexible:

- Identification and elimination of unnecessary assumptions and rigid rules.
- Providing "tailoring" facilities.
- Constructing the system from discrete, reusable components.

These are discussed in the following sections.

6.3.2   Rules and Assumptions

The cause of a good deal of inflexibility is the making of arbitrary assumptions about how the user wants the system to look and behave, e.g.

- Display of a ruler on a word processor.
- Clearing of a screen after a *Save* action.
- Display of a selection of attributes from an object (there being insufficient room to display them all).

These are cases where there is no "right" answer, e.g. some users like a ruler, others think it gets in the way. The approach here is to avoid making the decision by throwing it back on the user. The mechanism here is to supply a *Preferences* menu. This typically displays a dialogue box with a range of features that can be set by the user, e.g. displaying a ruler. A variant on the *Preferences* menu is the *Options* menu. The purpose of this is to tailor objects so that only selected parts of that object are displayed, e.g. a subset of the available fields (Figure 6.14).

Many computer systems are designed for use in a specific organisation at a specific time. They often incorporate features which are specific to that organisation, which prevent their use in other organisations, or even within the same organisation at a later time. Typical of these features are:

- Classifications and naming conventions.
- Fixed values.
- Size restrictions.
- Procedural rules.

In the Club Membership system, there are three categories of members: Full, Associate and Honorary. Other clubs would have other categories. It might be necessary to include the club name on reports (currently not included in this system). Other clubs will have different names. Even within the club, team sizes vary: Cricket and Soccer are 11, Rugby League 13, Rugby Union 15, Australian Rules Football 18,... Many clubs have a minimum joining age (e.g. 18) that could be checked against date of birth. Other clubs might have a junior membership category for a specific age range, or a "senior citizens' concession" for members over 65.

The way to deal with these features is to make them into data items within the system, so that they can be changed by the user. At times, this means adding additional attributes, e.g. if we add a *Team Size* attribute to *Squad* [Figure 6.15(a)], then the user can define the team size when they create a squad for a sport, and this team size will apply to all teams selected from that squad (e.g. by supplying the appropriate number of lines on the team display). Sometimes we require an additional object class, e.g. to include age-related rules, we need a *Membership Category* object [Figure 6.15(b)] where we can specify them. In addition, the reason why we used a combination box to display the categories, rather than, e.g. radio buttons, is to make it easier for the list to be changed.

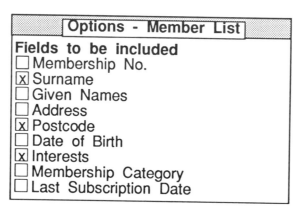

Figure 6.14 An OPTIONS dialogue box.

```
┌─────────────────────────────────────────┐
│░░░░░░░░░░░░│Squad - Cricket│░░░░░░░░░░░░░░│
│ Team Size  11                             │
│                                           │
│ Name        Grade   Remarks               │
│ Brown         A                           │
│ Jones         A                           │
│ Smith, K.     A      Injured              │
│ Taylor        A                           │
│ Robinson      B      Holiday until 31/7   │
│ Schmidt       B                           │
│ Smith, J.     B                           │
│ Smith, L.     C                           │
│ Zatorski      C                           │
│                                           │
└─────────────────────────────────────────┘
```

(a)
Specifying a Size Limit

```
┌─────────────────────────────────────────┐
│░░░░░░░░░░░│Member Categories│░░░░░░░░░░░░░│
│                                           │
│ Category     Min. Age     Max. Age        │
│ Full           18                         │
│ Associate      12            25           │
│ Honorary       55                         │
│                                           │
│                                           │
│                                           │
└─────────────────────────────────────────┘
```

(b)
**Specifying Categories and
Parameters for Rules**

Figure 6.15 Rules and constraints as data
items.

6.3.3   Tailoring

Tailoring can be thought of as making a general system more specific. This commonly involves adapting it for use in a particular organisation, or on a particular machine. Many of the features needed for this tailoring have already been discussed above, under *Rules and Assumptions*. The distinction is that tailoring is often seen as a distinct process (Figure 6.16) which is performed when the system is initially set up, and then later when any major changes are required. For the Club Membership system, the definition of the club name and the membership categories would probably be viewed as a tailoring process, because these are not things that would be changed lightly, or by the majority of users, but features like setting of team sizes would be available to selectors. The set-up (or install) procedures supplied with most personal computer packages tailor the package to the user's hardware.

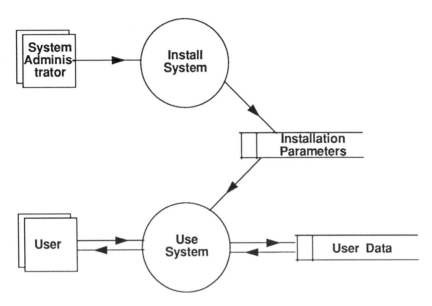

Figure 6.16 Use of a set-up phase to tailor a
system.

Many general-purpose applications, e.g. word processors, have far too many features, and usually expand by adding still more. This creates two problems:

- Novice users are frequently overwhelmed by the number of options.
- Even experienced users may have difficulty in determining what actions are relevant to a particular feature.

A common approach to the first of these problems is to include a *Short Menu/Full Menu* option (e.g. on the *Preferences* menu). The short menus contain only the actions needed for basic operation of the system (i.e. those actions required by a beginner), while the full menus contain all actions. More than two levels can be included, e.g. some systems supply beginners, intermediate and advanced level menus. Deciding on which menu items qualify at a given level is not trivial, because it requires an analysis of the types of task that the particular types of user might want to perform, e.g. it may be decided that a beginner would want to prepare only short documents consisting solely of text, so that the long document features (e.g. outlines, tables of contents and indexes) and graphics features (drawing block diagrams and importing scanned images) can be omitted from the short menus. But will the beginner want to experiment with a range of typefaces, or to draw a box around a paragraph? Sometimes omissions from short menus can be glaring: one electronic mail package will not allow a beginner to print out a copy of a message.

The most difficult part of the tailoring process comes in the specification of new or changed actions. The reason for this is that actions tend to be implemented in terms of procedural code, which is inflexible. Three common areas where this needs to be done are:

- Actions which are a set sequence of already available actions. These are needed when a specific sequence of actions has to be repeated many times. Some systems supply a *keystroke macro* facility which remembers and stores a series of keystrokes. These can then be recalled and executed.
- Report definition. At some time or other, most systems need to produce reports (either in printed form, for display on the screen, or as data files for input into other software). These reports are summaries, rather than individual records, or contain summary information in addition to individual records. The user needs to specify the fields to be included, subtotals, counts and totals, which records are to be included, the order in which they are to appear and the layout of the report. This is a well known and understood problem. Report generators permit the user to define a layout (e.g. by painting it on a screen) and the other features of the report, including any parameters to be supplied at run-time (e.g. date ranges), and to save the definition under a name and then recall and run it.
- More complex actions, which may require input of data and even branching, are incorporated into many systems using the *macro* facility, or by providing *hooks* to which user-written code is attached. This is essentially a programming exercise, which is difficult, slow, error-prone and costly. Where user provision of such actions is needed, it is worth thinking along the lines that were used in developing report generators. This involved identifying the parameters used to define the report (i.e. specifying a very general *Report* object), and writing general procedures to manipulate this object. In this way, the user does not have to write procedures, but merely has to store data describing the particular version of the object that they require. This type of parametrisation is applicable in many situations, but requires very careful design and testing.

6.3.4   Reusable Components

Many systems contain elements that are "similar" to those in other systems. It would be nice if we could use the same components in both systems, and to link them in appropriate ways. Object-oriented approaches assist in doing this as they help us to separate out discrete components based on particular objects.

There are really two distinct issues here:

- Identifying appropriate components to separate out, and generalising them sufficiently so that they are reusable.
- Transferring information between these components.

A good example of a reusable component is the report generator described above. The various objects in the Personal Timetable system, and in particular the timetable grid, should be reusable in other parts of the full system, to handle such things as staff time-tabling, room allocation and scheduling of units.

Systems such as Microsoft Windows and the Apple Macintosh already contain a powerful method for transferring data between different applications: the *clipboard*. We have already discussed the use of the clipboard to perform *move* actions within the same application, but since the clipboard is of the Windows (or Finder) system, which is global to all applications, the *cut* (and *copy*) and *paste* actions can copy data between applications as well as within the application. The only requirement is that the different applications communicate with the clipboard (which requires programming).

In many cases, it is possible to perform a task by using different software packages at different stages, e.g. this version of the book was put together using:

- A word processor.
- Two distinct vector graphics packages.
- A paint graphics package.
- A scanner.
- A desktop publishing package that could read the files produced by the other packages.
- A laser printer.

Personal Timetable System

In Chapter 2, we gave an initial requirements specification for a personal timetable system, including a data flow diagram (with some elaboration of the processing requirements) and a data model. This specification provides a starting point for our design of the system.

Our task now is to develop a conceptual model of the timetabling problem to which the user (who is a student who uses the system infrequently, e.g. once a semester) can relate, and which they can readily manipulate.

Step 1 – Visualisation

Our first move is to think around the problem a little, to find out what we have to do. There are three (complementary) lines of attack:

- Sorting out the scope of the system.
- Thinking about how one would do it manually.
- Comparing it with related problems, and identifying the differences.

Figure 6.17 is an attempt to sketch the context in which the timetable decision is made. The university has already produced its official timetable, and the student is doing a course with set rules that limit their choice of units. In addition, however, they have their own preferences (because a unit looks interesting, or that they have heard that another one has a lousy lecturer), and outside constraints (like a Thursday morning game of golf).

    The implication of this is that the system cannot and must not attempt to make decisions for the student, because it does not have all the information. It is limited to assisting with information within the domain of the university's competence, i.e. in-

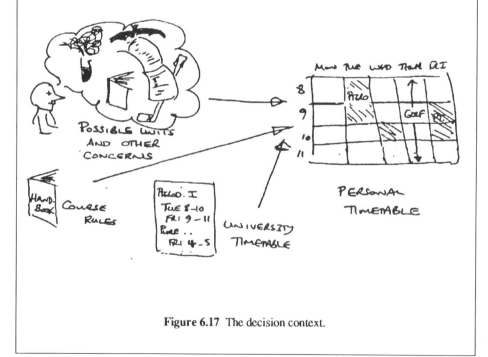

Figure 6.17 The decision context.

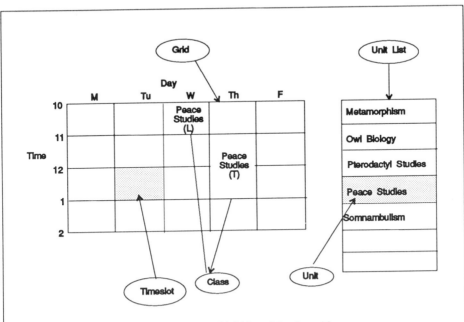

Figure 6.18 An initial idea of the timetable.

formation from the university timetable and course rule information. Note, however, that it cannot attempt to enforce course rules (e.g. by not allowing the student to time-table a unit that violates them), since they are legal documents subject to human inter-pretation and are commonly bent or broken. For the purpose of this example, we will assume that the student has access to and is aware of the course rules. This limits us to supplying university timetable information.

The manual approach involves making some sort of short-list of possible sub-jects (based on the course rules and on interests) and checking to see if they are on of-fer. The actual order is not critical, e.g. a student who already has a good idea of what subjects are allowable may actually use a list of subjects on offer (e.g. the university timetable) to make up the short-list. The short-list is usually ranked in some way, i.e. there may be one or two units that the student particularly wants to do, others that they would not mind doing, and yet others that they will only do if they have to. This last set may be omitted from the first listing, and only included later if the first list is exhausted before a satisfactory timetable is obtained.

The student will then work through the list, looking up the times of the units on the university timetable, and attempting to build a timetable. The usual, but not invariable, approach is to start with the most favoured units and with classes for which only one time is available, e.g. lectures. The almost universal way of recording these is on a grid, with days in one direction, and time of day in the other (Figure 6.17). The timetable is built up by a process of trial and error. Possible times for alternative classes are pencilled in, but with a knowledge that they may have to be changed. Different units are looked at as possibilities. Obvious clashes (e.g. units whose lectures clash) are usually rapidly eliminated (although they may be allowed to stand), but then more subtle clashes appear: a lecture clashing with the only remaining tutorial time of a more favoured unit, forcing the selection of an alternative tutorial time. Eventually, the student will end up with a timetable that they regard as the best possible in the circumstances.

We have been talking about a related problem for much of this book: the vehicle pool system. Both are scheduling problems, and so many of the ideas about how one tackles the problem are similar. We cannot use quite the same representation, since a Gantt chart is not readily recognised as a timetable, but the same sort of approach should be applicable: the building of lists (in this case of units or classes instead of trucks and drivers) from which to choose, and the ability to place objects from these lists on a picture which gives a clear view of the timetable as a whole. In this case, the kind of grid used in the manual timetabling system seems the obvious choice. Although there are other alternatives, the obvious choice seems to be something like that in Figure 6.18.

Step 2 – Abstraction

We now need to express our visualisation in terms of a set of objects and actions.
There are two main sources of ideas to help in this abstraction:

- The terminology used in the application itself, e.g. the student attends classes offered as part of a unit.
- Our toolkit of common objects and actions, e.g. we have two collection objects: the grid and a list of units. The grid is made up of timeslots, each corresponding to a set time period (an hour here) on a given day.

Thus there are five object types: *unit* and *class* are fairly conventional data objects; *timeslot* is a means of representing a time; and *unit list* and *grid* are collections of the more basic objects. The unit object could be regarded as containing the class objects for that unit.

Attributes for the objects are listed in Figure 6.19. The most critical are probably those chosen for unit, since these will determine how the user can select units to make up the unit list. Those chosen (besides *unit name*) are *discipline* and *level*, e.g. Philosophy, 3rd year. The implication of this will be discussed below.

The timetabling problem consists of the selection of *classes* and their placement in the grid, i.e. the allocation of one or more timeslots to a class. Any attempt to allocate more than one class to a timeslot constitutes a *clash*, but it is up to the student (and not to the system) to decide whether or not to accept a timetable containing clashes. The strategy used is the same as that for the manual system, as outlined above, and so is a trial and error operation in which the student will want to choose their own order in handling the data, to go back over the data, to tentatively add classes to the timetable and later remove them.

In order to achieve this, we need to design a set of actions.

Firstly, it is necessary to *create* a unit list. It could be the entire list of units available at the institution, but it would be more convenient to let the user create a set more closely attuned to their needs. This could be built via a search mechanism of some sort, or could be one of a predefined set of lists. We will discuss this in more detail below. It is also necessary to move about the list, so, e.g. *next unit* and *previous unit* actions will be needed.

At the unit level it is necessary to be able to *select* a unit (either by the *next unit* and *previous unit* commands or by other means, e.g. with a mouse), to locate (*select*) one or more classes in the unit and to *schedule* them, i.e. to place them in the grid. It will also be necessary to *unschedule* a class or all scheduled classes for a unit, i.e. to remove them from the grid.

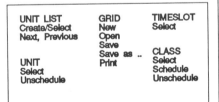

UNIT LIST	GRID	TIMESLOT
Create/Select	New	Select
Next, Previous	Open	
	Save	
	Save as ..	CLASS
UNIT	Print	Select
Select		Schedule
Unschedule		Unschedule

TIMESLOT	UNIT
Day	Unit Name
Start Time	Discipline
Length	Level
	{Class}
GRID	
Start Day	
End Day	CLASS
Start Time	Class Type
End Time	Class Start Time
{Timeslot}	Class End Time
	Location
UNIT LIST	Staff Name
{Unit}	

Note: Braces {} indicate repetition

Figure 6.19 Attributes of objects.   **Figure 6.20** Actions.

A particular grid represents the timetable for a particular student, and so we must be able to perform the standard set of actions on that timetable, i.e. create a new timetable (*new*), retrieve an existing one (*open*), save a completed one under a default name (*save*) or a new one (*save as ..*), and print it (*print*). In this system, there are no specific actions on the timeslot object, except possibly a select to be used in conjunction with unschedule.

These actions are summarised in Figure 6.20.

Unit Name	Class Times	
Metamorphism	F 1-2	
Owl Biology	M 11-1	F 2-4
Pterodactyl Studies	Th10-12	
Peace Studies	W 10-1	Th 11-1
Sonambulism	F 3-4	

(a)

Include Class Times in Unit List

Unit Name
Metamorphism
Owl Biology
Pterodactyl Studies
Peace Studies
Sonambulism

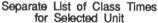

(b)

Separate List of Class Times for Selected Unit

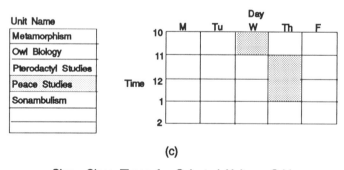

(c)

Show Class Times for Selected Unit on Grid

Figure 6.21 Possible representations of information on class times.

Step 3 – Detailing

The detailing process involves filling out the skeleton that we have developed above by determining the attributes for the various objects, detailing the actions, and developing the representations for both the objects and the actions.

The grid and the unit list need to be on the screen together, because to schedule units one has to see both what is available and where they will fit, so that our main screen would be similar to Figure 6.18. However, our initial concept omitted some key details, for example the problem of displaying information about class times before the class is scheduled (a rather crucial point, since otherwise the user will not know whether classes in a unit are at suitable times or not). Some of the possibilities (Figure 6.21) are to include class times in the unit list, in a separate list (possibly only for the currently selected unit) or to highlight the times for the currently selected unit in the grid. These are all fairly "standard" approaches to solving this particular type of problem, and again should be part of a designer's "toolkit" of ideas. For clarity, we have omitted the class type, but this should probably be included (along with the location and possibly the staff member's name).

The first of these options gives the best overview of available classes, but is likely to be cramped for space when it comes to displaying any substantial information about classes, and inflexible if a unit has a large number of classes. The second is more flexible in this regard. The third is the most direct: it actually *shows* the user what the various choices look like on their timetable, and so is intuitively the most pleasing. The class type would probably be coded using different colours or patterns for lectures and tutorials. This is the option that we will use.

We need now to look more closely at the actions, in order to see within what parameters they need to operate, and also to check whether they do provide an adequate set of tools to solve the problem. There are two main areas to be considered here:

- How do we go about building the unit list?
- How do we schedule units?

The unit list is intended to be a list of units that the student regards as "possible". It is usually relatively short, and can often be set up by letting the user key in the unit names or identifiers (e.g. in blank spaces in the list, possibly created via an Insert command). If the unit cannot be found or is not on offer that semester, the insert is rejected (with an appropriate message). Another way is to list the units required (and offered in this semester) for a specified course or in a specified discipline. The latter works best for compulsory units and electives in the discipline area of the course, the second where students can select units or sequences from a wide variety of disciplines. What is required here is a *Find* action, based on course and/or discipline and (optionally) on unit level. There is a need to be able to edit this list through a delete action.

The user is likely to use a combination of these actions to build up a list, so we will use the approach outlined earlier in the chapter (Section 6.2.3), where actions such as *Insert* and *Find* add to the list rather than creating a new list. A *clear* action deletes all the units in the list. Ordering of lists is usually done through a *sort* action, but it is difficult to imagine here what fields would be appropriate, since the ranking of units is highly subjective. Instead, we will supply a *move* action, which will allow the user to rearrange the order of the list, e.g. by moving the most important units to the head of the list. This means that our original *Create Unit List* action has become five actions: *Clear, Find, Insert, Delete* and *Move*. This is typical of the way in

COMMAND	MEANING
NEW grid	Display a blank timetable grid
OPEN grid	Retrieve a timetable from the disk file FILENAME
SAVE grid	Store the timetable on disk under its existing filename
SAVE grid AS filename	Store the timetable on disk in the file FILENAME
PRINT grid	Print the timetable
CLEAR unitlist	Delete all units from unit list
FIND unitlist FOR (COURSE = course name OR DEPARTMENT = department name) AND LEVEL = level	Set up a unit list containing units satisfying the stated criteria
INSERT unit INTO unitlist	Insert unit into unit list at current position
DELETE unit FROM unitlist	Delete unit from unit list
MOVE unit TO position IN unitlist	Move unit to specified position in unit list
NEXT unitlist	Select the next unit on the unit list
PREVIOUS unitlist	Select the previous unit on the unit list
SELECT unit	Select a unit, display class times on grid
UNSCHEDULE ALL unit	Unschedule all classes for the unit
SELECT timeslot	Select a timeslot
SELECT class	Select a class
SCHEDULE class	Schedule the selected class
UNSCHEDULE class	Unschedule the selected class

Figure 6.22 Command language representation
of actions.

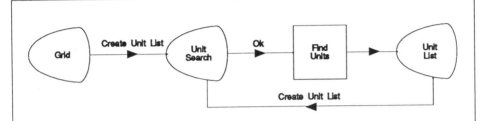

Figure 6.23 State diagram for FIND UNITLIST
dialogue.

which a design evolves as more detailed investigation and consideration of the problem takes place.

Scheduling is then performed by moving through the unit list. For the currently selected unit, the class times are displayed on the grid. A specific class can be
selected (e.g. by clicking on it) and then scheduled using the *schedule* action. Classes
can be removed from the grid by selecting them and using *unschedule*. *Unschedule
All* will remove all classes for a unit, but we will need to consider (when designing
the actual dialogue syntax) the mechanism for this, e.g. will selecting a class automatically select the unit?

Figure 6.22 gives a command language representation of the main actions, plus
a brief description of their effect. As has already been pointed out, the command language does not strictly represent the way in which the system would actually work,
since an object is selected and then the command executed on that object. However,
by including the object in the command, we make sure that we do not forget it.

Find Unitlist will need to invoke a sub-dialogue in order to obtain the search
parameters. This is shown in Figure 6.23 using state diagrams. This action can be initiated either from the window containing the timetable grid or from that containing
the unit list. A window (a *dialogue box*) is then opened which allows the user to
specify the search parameters. If the user issues an OK command, the system performs a search (indicated by the square box) and adds the units found to the unit list,
which becomes the active window. If the user issues a CANCEL command, they are
returned to the window from which they initiated the action. CANCEL is not shown
on the state diagram because it is part of a general UNDO command which has a
common meaning throughout the dialogue.

Actions such as *Open, Save As ..* and *Print* also invoke sub-dialogues, to specify file names and printer parameters. However, these sub-dialogues have a standard
form for all applications and so do not need to be specified here.

We are now in a position to test whether the actions that we have provided are adequate to perform the functions of the system. These functions are given in the data flow diagram in Figure 2.26.

Identify Possible Units: The unit list manipulation actions are intended to facilitate the performance of this function. The system does not contain any information about course rules as such, but through use of the Find action, the student can build up a list of relevant units which are on offer in this semester, e.g. a student in third year of a Computing Studies course with an Accountancy major can do a Find on the Computing Studies course (at level 3) and a Find on the Accountancy discipline (also at level 3) to obtain a list of relevant computing and accounting subjects. They can then edit this by deleting units that they are not interested in and by moving the ones that they are most interested in doing to the head of the list.

Find Class Times: Class times for a particular unit are found by selecting that unit on the unit list. The times for the classes are then displayed in the grid. If a class is full, it is displayed in a distinctive way and cannot be selected. Units not on offer are eliminated because they do not appear in the unit list.

Choose Units and Classes: The student moves through the unit list, displaying class times. Classes can be scheduled by selecting them and performing the schedule action. The order of scheduling is up to the user, but compulsory classes would normally be scheduled first, in order of importance (to the student) of the unit, and classes with alternative times second. Hence, times for a given unit may be viewed more than once. Changes can be made by selecting a class on the grid, using unschedule, and then scheduling an alternative class. Unschedule All will unschedule all of the classes for a unit, if a change in the unit is needed. This process does not make any decisions for the student, so that they can bring whatever criteria they like to bear.

Enrol in Classes: The schedule action automatically puts the student's name on the list for that class. Unschedule removes it. Enrolment for the unit must be done separately.

Another function not performed by this system is the printing off of the class enrolments. Although this is obviously necessary, it is not included in the functional specification. Obvious anomalies of this kind need to be checked with whoever is responsible for the specification of requirements. In this case, the response is that it is part of a separate reporting system.

Step 4 - Detailing

The dialogue for the student timetabling system has a single main screen, which is shown diagramatically in Figure 6.24. This is fairly characteristic of mode-less systems, since we want the user to be able to see all the relevant information at once. It also makes the system easier to use, because there is a consistent presentation of data.

The screen contains two windows, one containing the grid, the other the unit list. This is the default display, but can be rearranged by the user if they so desire. The menu bar has grouped the actions as a set of pull-down menus. There has been some renaming, e.g. the File menu contains the actions on the grid (New, Open, Save, Save as .., Print) since File is the conventional heading for these actions, Search contains the Find option on the unit list (plus Clear, Insert, Delete and Move), and Schedule contains Schedule, Unschedule and Unschedule All. The features normally incorporated in window borders (e.g. scroll bars and resizing boxes) have been omitted for clarity.

Units are selected from the unit list by moving the highlight up and down using the mouse or the cursor keys. (This is the implementation of the Next and Previous actions.) Scroll bars (operated by the mouse) and function keys (PgUp and PgDn) allow larger movements if the list is long. When a unit is selected, its class times appear on the grid, suitably labelled (e.g. L means Lecture, T means Tutorial). Where there is a clash, the class is shown in a different colour (e.g. red).

The unit list is initially empty. The menu options under search are used to build the unit list. Insert, Delete and Move are the standard list operations imple-

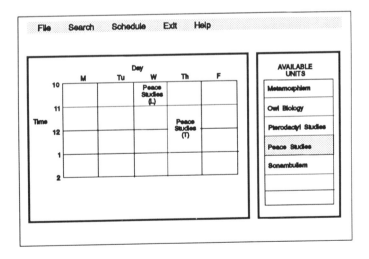

Figure 6.24 The main timetable screen.

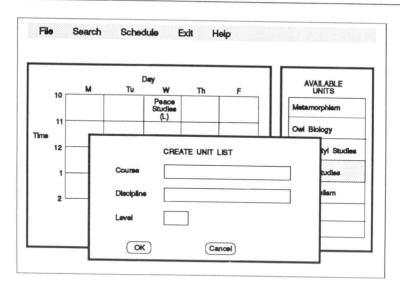

Figure 6.25 The FIND UNITLIST box.

mented in a standard manner. Find displays a dialogue box (Figure 6.25) which allows the user to enter search parameters (Course and/or Discipline and Level). If a field is left blank, all values are retrieved. The units found are added to the unit list. Clear empties the unit list, Undo reverses the last operation on the list. In theory, Insert needs to distinguish between a non-existent unit and a unit not on offer. If, however, we offer a list of possible choices, the absence of the required unit from the list should be sufficient, and is consistent with Find which also treats units not on offer as if they did not exist.

A class is selected by clicking on it (in the grid) with the mouse. To include the class in the timetable, the schedule menu option is used. Double-clicking the mouse will have the same effect. To remove an already scheduled class from the timetable, it is selected and the unschedule menu option used. Again, double-clicking will have the same effect. To remove all classes in a unit from the timetable, any class in the unit can be selected and the Unschedule All menu option used.

This dialogue must now be tested by building a prototype and exposing potential users to it. As mentioned before, this system is interesting because the people most closely involved in specifying it are unlikely to be the eventual users. Although these people must, of course, see the prototype and approve it, it must also be tried out on some students. The number need not be large (e.g. three to five people), but they must be selected to represent a cross-section of the computing skills available, as well as from a variety of courses and levels. They should be told that their opinions are needed on both what the system does and on how easy it is to use.

They should be shown any draft overview documentation which describes the functions of the system, and given a draft user manual for reference. The task allocated should be a realistic one, e.g. to develop their own timetable for the following semester. They should be observed in their operation of the system, and areas where they have difficulty or make significant mistakes noted. Any spontaneous comments should be recorded.

Afterwards, they should be asked their opinion of the system, and in particular to identify areas where it did not actually do what was needed (e.g. the method for building the unit list or the facilities for resolving clashes might be totally useless) as well as areas in which it was simply awkward to use, since otherwise they are likely to accept the scope of the system and its built-in functionality "as read" and concentrate on the detail.

Making the System More Flexible

A version of the personal Timetable system, usable only in a specific institution, might contain the following features:

- Three types of classes are available – lectures, tutorials and practicals.
- Room numbers are of the format BXNN, where B is the building number, X is the floor (A,B,C or D) and NN is the room (a number from 1 to 99).
- Classes start on the half hour and last an integral number of hours.
- The earliest class starts at 8.30 a.m. and the last finishes at 9.30 p.m. (Monday to Thursday) and 5.30 p.m. (Friday). There are no Saturday or Sunday classes.
- The maximum enrolment in a tutorial is 15, in a practical it is 12.
- Full-time students cannot enrol in evening classes; part-time students cannot enrol in day classes.

None of these restrictions is unreasonable in the context of a single institution at a single time, but all are likely to render it unusable at another institution, e.g.

- Classes may start on the hour.
- There is a different room numbering system.
- The only classes available are workshops and seminars.

Even within the same institution there are likely to be problems, e.g.

- Building 10 is constructed, and room 7D25 is split into 7D25A and 7D25B.
- Class sizes are increased to eighteen for tutorials and fifteen for practicals, and the length of some is reduced from 2 to 1 1/2 hours.
- Saturday morning classes are introduced.

The way to deal with these problems is to make these rules into data items that can be modified by the university timetabler (but not by the student user), e.g.

- The day and time range for classes, and the slot length on the grid can be set using an *options* menu.
- A list of rooms is stored on a file which can be updated as required and this list is used to display lists of rooms and to check room numbers.
- A list of class types and their maximum sizes is stored in the same way.

The class types, the timetable grid parameters and the room list would be defined during the set-up stage.

Crossword Designer

In Chapter 2 we outlined the requirements for Crossword Designer. In this section we show how we designed the user-interface for the program. We first looked at different ways we might represent the problem, determined the overall approach, worked out our objects, determined the actions, and detailed the screen.

Ideas for Displaying the Crossword

You could represent a crossword on a computer in ways other than the traditional pattern. Figure 6.26 shows the partially solved crossword shown in Figure 6.27 but displayed as a list. The computer knows the underlying connections and as the words are entered the corresponding letters appear in the other words. This method has a certain attraction to it but you cannot see the final relationship of words and for some crosswords that might be important. However, making the crossword as a list of places to fit words suggests the importance of the *slot* as a crucial object in the user-interface.

Certainly, this method would be easiest to program. (We might include it as a View option in a later release.)

Another way of representing the crossword is Figure 6.26 and this is the way we chose. We started with a simple crossword pattern and it developed into the final screen.

We wanted a user-interface that satisfied the following:

- You *start* with a pattern and fit words into it.
- The *pattern* is an important part of the idea of a crossword and it should be shown on the screen.
- The crossword compiler likes to see the juxtaposition of words in the slots.
- The crossword compiler needs to *know* the words that will fit into a slot and if they are likely to connect to other words.
- The crossword compiler finds the *words first*, then finds the clues.

We arrived at Figure 6.26 after several iterations, but the solution was driven by the above points and by imagining how we would manipulate the *objects* that make up our crossword. Our initial sketch of the solution was a crossword on the screen into which we typed words. When we wanted a word we bought up a list of words that might fit into the slot. However, this did not seem to satisfy all our needs and so we started to think about the structure of the problem. We did this by specifying our objects and actions.

Objects and Actions

In this case we defined the objects as *words, word lists, clues, clue lists* and *slots* into which we put words, and a collection of slots to make a *grid*.

We now looked at manipulating these objects to help us make up a crossword. Although the clues are important, we kept them *hidden* in the first pass as we first wanted to get the words without worrying about clues. When we create a crossword we want to work our way through the *slots* and fill in words. A good heuristic is to start with the slot that is going to be the *hardest* to fill and to find a word for it. We would like to put in a *good* word that would fit many other words going in the opposite direction. Thinking this way suggested that the important objects to display are the slots and the information about them. The crossword pattern shows the slots, by making a highlight we could show the current slot, and by showing information about that slot the crossword designer could choose words to fit into the slot. We wanted the

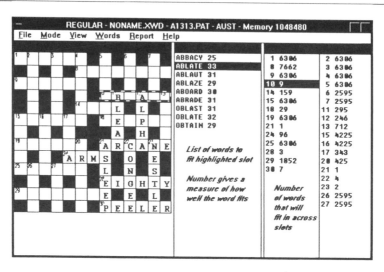

Figure 6.26 Crossword Designer screen
display.

user to have control and so, although we suggest slots into which to put words, the user can move through the slot list and choose any they like.

Our user-interface thus became a way of moving through slots and doing things to them. The actions we wanted to do on the slots are, *put* in a word, *delete* a word, *show* a list of words to fit in the slot, *move* to a different slot, *attach* a clue to the slot, *sort* the words that will fit into the slot inthe best order, get the computer to *select* a word at random. Notice the perspective we have when we think of manipulating the slot objects. Other crossword programs manipulate words. You type in a word and then find other words to fit around that word. The idea of a slot does not appear in their dialogue at all. This style of user-interface is shown in the *Build your own* mode in Crossword Designer. It is hard to over-emphasize this aspect of the dialogue design. If you choose appropriate objects and now think how to manipulate them to achieve the user's goals the dialogue details often suggest themselves.

Command Language

We made up a simple command language to summarize the different actions. The commands for the slots are:

select SLOT

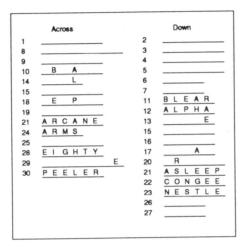

Figure 6.27 Crossword solutions as a list.

attach WORD
remove WORD
sort WORD LIST
automatic select WORD from WORD LIST
attach CLUE
find hardest SLOT
show WORD LIST

Detailing

The actions we do on the slots are put in the action menu labelled *Words*. We used the word *Words* instead of the word *Slots* as we thought people would be unhappy with the word *slot* and not know what it meant. The underlying structure of the slots is visually apparent and so it was appropriate to use *Words* as people would be thinking of words when they did the actions.

   The double-click action is used to delete words already in the crossword and to select a word from the word-list. These are the most common actions. The user can move through the crossword slots with the mouse or with the cursor keys. Most of the time the user only uses the mouse and it is possible to fill a crossword solely with mouse operations.

We put a lot of thought into how to display the slot cursor (Figure 3.7). We considered a normal flashing cursor, but it was too obtrusive if made large and if made small it did not show the slot. We tried putting a pattern into the slot but that hid the words. We tried colour, but that would not work well on a monochrome scheme. We finally decided on a *moving* border as the movement made the persons focus on the slot, but it was less irritating than a flashing cursor. This does not work well when the slots become too small and some users still think the movement is too intrusive. Another solution is not to decide at all, but to allow different styles of cursors and let the user choose.

Summary of Design Process

This abbreviated description of the design for this computer application shows how the needs of the person who was going to use the program drove the design. If you consider what is the *easiest* for the programmer, or if you have a different model from the way we think a human designs crosswords you will come up with a different solution.

Other parts of the program, such as word-lists, the algorithms for finding the best words for a slot, the algorithm for finding the hardest slot to fill, the way of creating a grid and the printing all came after the initial structure. The way in which the human compiler thought about making a crossword was the imperative that dominated the design. The next development of the program will be driven by the needs that arise from program use.

Summary

In this chapter we have discussed in detail the first four steps in the dialogue design process: *visualisation, abstraction, detailing* and *prototyping.* These steps form a guide to the processes involved in the development of the dialogue, and are not a rigid sequence of activity.

In the visualisation stage, an overall picture of what the system will look like, and how it will work, in the form of a series of sketches, is developed.

The visualisation begins with an exploration process, which is concerned with coming to terms with the requirements for the system. Even if there is a formal requirements specification, this is at best a guide to some features of the system, and must be discussed further with the users before any real understanding is obtained. One of the most important tools in this process is sketching, whether of formal representations of the system (e.g. data flow diagrams), of aspects of current implementations, or of the context in which the system is to operate. The exploration process becomes one of generation of ideas as understanding of the problem begins to come.

Ideas for solutions can be tested to see if they are clear, comprehensible and appealing to the user, and to check whether they can be used to perform the required tasks.

The second stage of the development process is to formalise the model by expressing the visualisation in terms of a set of objects and actions. There are two main sources of ideas to help in this abstraction process: the terminology used in the application itself, and our toolkit of common objects and actions. Potential problems can arise because there are too many possible objects, or because all identifiable objects are low-level physical objects, and there is no overview.

Testing of this model needs to establish whether the set of objects is complete, whether all the attributes are included, and whether the actions can be used to perform the functions of the system.

The detailing process takes the objects and actions and fills in the detail. Although specification of the precise dialogue syntax is not required, this process takes the designer through a series of refinements of the representation of the objects and a more detailed specification of the actions. The end result is often a series of sketches of screens accompanied by descriptions of how the various actions should be performed.

The testing of the detailed design is correspondingly detailed, since it is closer to the way that the final system will perform. The representations of the various objects need to agree with the user's ideas of what they should look like, the objects should be shown in the right relationships, contain enough information, be able to perform the functions of the system, and conform to guide-lines and standards.

The purpose of a prototype is to show users, in a concrete form, what the system will look like and how it will behave. It is important that the prototype should be quick and cheap to build and to modify, since the object of building it is to find out what problems there are with the design and what changes are needed. These changes must then be incorporated into the prototype for further testing with the users, thus initiating further cycles of change.

The simplest form of prototype is a storyboard displayed on a screen. A more sophisticated form of prototype allows the user to enter data on to screens and to navigate around the system, but contains no underlying functionality. Prototypes should not be "fully functional" systems.

The tools used for developing prototypes should be those most convenient for the purpose at hand and are usually not the same as those used to develop the final system.

A key element in developing the prototype is the precise specification of the dialogue syntax, i.e. not just the actions which are applicable to the given objects, but what their names are, where they appear on menus, accelerator keys to be assigned, how they are to be performed. These should conform to guide-lines (e.g. Common User Access). Care should be taken not to make distinctions which are based on the underlying implementation of the system rather than on the user-interface, not to impose unnecessary restrictions on the user, and not to build features into the system that make it inflexible when it comes to future change or use in another environment.

The testing of a prototype system should be based on a set of scenarios which are directly related to the tasks that the user wants to perform. They must include actual data, and show how it will be used, and how it will change. They should cover all the main features of the system, but as a necessary consequence of performing the tasks.

One of the criteria for a good tool is flexibility. This means that the tool can be used for a variety of purposes, some of them unforeseen by the designer. This need arises because: different users will want to use the tool in different ways; the requirements for its use will change over time; and someone will want to apply it to a related problem for which no specific tool exists.

In addition to the use of modeless dialogues, there are three strategies for making systems more flexible: identification and elimination of unnecessary assumptions and rigid rules; providing "tailoring" facilities; and constructing the system from discrete, reusable components.

Exercises

1. In our testing of the airline flight information dialogue we found a number of issues that required attention:
    *   Entry of dates.
    *   Display of information on busy sectors (e.g. Melbourne-Sydney).
    *   Some mechanism for building up on the machine an itinerary spanning a number of days or weeks (e.g. with stopovers).
    See if you can refine the design developed to date to incorporate these requirements.

2. Design a user-interface for a computer program to help new home buyers plan their gardens. When people buy a new house they often have a block of land with a house and nothing else on it. They have to decide where to plant trees and shrubs, where to put garages, where to have utility areas, how much lawn, where the paths should go, where to put the barbecue etc. They may want to plan for the future and leave space to be later converted to a swimming pool, or a place to put a granny flat in twenty-years time. They need to have help in choosing trees, shrubs, ground covers and other plants. They need to see the effect of plants on their house. For example, they want to know the effect on heating and cooling of wind break trees and trees that shade. These effects will vary during the day, during the seasons, and over the years. They have little knowledge of houses, gardens, computers and of the problem they are trying to solve.

3. A selection committee conducts a regular series of rounds of appointments to positions. In a typical round there may be 50 positions and 100 applicants. Although there are a range of different positions, with different (but often overlapping) skill requirements, most of the applicants apply for and are eligible for appointment to more than one position.

    There are two parts to the selection process: applicants are ranked for each position, independently of other positions (which can, of course, mean that a person gets top ranking for more than one); and decisions are made to appoint a person to a particular position rather than to another one. These processes go on simultaneously, so that a person may be "pencilled in" to one position, and then moved. This can create a chain reaction, since the next ranked person in the now vacant position may have been pencilled in elsewhere, and so on.

    Devise a dialogue to assist the committee in keeping track of the current state of positions and applicants, and to explore the consequences of moving applicants between positions, while not preempting the committee's decision-making role.

4. The store clerk in a small organisation is responsible for stocking and issuing consumable items within the organisation. The manual system involves the use of stock cards. A typical stock card is shown below. There is also a card file of suppliers, but as the bulk of supplies come from six suppliers, their telephone numbers are also written up on the whiteboard in the store.

    The clerk currently performs the following tasks:

    *   **Issue of stores:** Stores are issued over the counter. The name of the requesting person's section, the date of issue, and the quantity are recorded. The clerk supplies the accounts section with a weekly summary of this information.
    *   **Ordering of stores:** Stores are usually reordered when the quantity of that item falls below a specified reorder level. This is set by the stores clerk on the basis of past experience, and may be changed by them. If the clerk decides to reorder an item, they must decide on an appropriate quantity. For fast-moving items, this is a week's supply, for slower-moving items, a month's supply. The store clerk estimates this from past orders for the same item, particularly the previous order. Other possible actions are: to postpone reordering, e.g. because the item is moving more slowly than expected (which may also, but not necessarily, include reduction of the reorder level); a decision not to reorder; an attempt to find an alternative supplier (by ringing other suppliers of these items and getting quotes); and the ordering of items not previously stocked. Orders are made over the telephone. Most suppliers supply a range of items. All items required from a supplier are included on the one order.

- **Recording deliveries:** When a delivery is received, the date and quantities received are recorded. The stores clerk initials the delivery docket or invoice accompanying the goods and passes it on to accounts, who arrange payment.

The system uses the following coding systems:

- Stock items have an item code (e.g. 323-444671), in which the first three digits are a classification and the remainder a serial number.
- Suppliers are given a six-character code made up from the company name (e.g. PENSPL).

Design the user-interface for a computer system to assist the stores clerk in the performance of these tasks. The solution should be presented as a series of sketches of screens, and storyboards showing how one or more of the above tasks would be performed. The dialogue should be based around suitable representations of the Stock Item and Supplier objects.

Item Code: 323-444671			Supplier: PENSPL		
Description: Pencil, HB (2 doz box)					
Unit Price: $3.25			Reorder Level: 5		
Date	Section/Supplier	In	Out	On Hand	Inits
	Forward			15	
24/6	ADP		5	10	
28/6	Personnel		3	7	
13/7	ADP		4	3	
14/7	Reordered 15				
18/7	PENSPL	13		16	K
19/7	ADP		6	10	K

		Supplier Code: PENSPL
Company Name:	Pens Pty Ltd	
Company Address:	32 Calligraphy Crescent,	
	Scrawl,	
	A.C.T. 2600	
Telephone:	(06) 277 7717	
Contact Name:	Jane Word	

Figure 6.28 A typical stock card.

Chapter 7

User Documentation

A central theme of this book is to judge computer systems on their usability. This means users must understand them and know how to operate them. For this to happen we need a good keyboard, mouse and screen user-interface, but we also often require user documentation to make the application intelligible. The point of view taken here is that documentation should be considered as part of the overall user-interface. In this chapter we define user documentation and discuss how to integrate it into the application development. The ideas are illustrated by describing the Crossword Designer documentation. Chapter 8 contains details of different documentation components.

We call any form of explanation of an application *user documentation*. It may be a user manual, or it may be a film about the application, a brochure to give its salient points, an on-line tutorial to teach, a training course to instruct or on-line help to assist. These all help the users understand the application and help establish an appropriate conceptual model.

7.1 A Strategy for Documentation

Planning documentation as part of the overall interface design means we should start with the reason for doing it. If we have no reason for producing it, it is a waste of resources to create it. All documentation should have a purpose and the purpose drives the documentation form and content. Once we are clear on the reasons for producing it then we should plan its construction.

Figure 7.1 gives the points covered in a documentation plan. Planning for documentation is similar to planning program construction. The method is not only similar but we can use many of the tools and techniques of software engineering for documentation

Statement of purposes
Control
Attitude
Identification of users
Ongoing documentation
Standards
Document reuse
Usability testing

Figure 7.1 Documentation strategy.

Original Sentence:
If your product is not used then it is a failure.
Message:
Passive voice: is used.
Consider revising using active voice.
Author's revised sentence:
An unused product is a failure.

Figure 7.2 Messages from a style analyser.

production. There is even merit in thinking of it as another form of programming. We must plan it, write it, test it and maintain it. It is *soft* and we use word processors and editors to build it. We can even analyse it by passing it through spelling and grammar checkers. (Figure 7.2 shows the output from an English usage checker.) The following sections expand on the stages in the plan.

7.1.1   Statement of Purposes

The reasons for producing documentation will vary depending on the product and the environment. Figure 7.3 gives a common set of reasons which cover many projects. From these and other reasons we decide what we want the documentation to achieve and then we decide how to do it. If the purpose is to teach new users, then Figure 7.4 gives some ways you could do this. If the purpose is to advertise the product then we might write internal company memoranda, or put notices on the electronic mail system.

Having defined the purpose of our documentation, we now plan our work. The plan tells how we will achieve our objectives and details techniques, costs and effort. A typical overall plan will contain:

- An executive summary of the plan.
- A statement of purposes or reasons for doing the documentation.
- The proposed forms of documentation to realise the purposes.
- The method of construction.
- How the documentation will be tested.
- Time and cost estimates.

Teach new users the package mechanics.	Give immediate help on package use.
Teach users about the application domain.	Describe the package functionality.
	Give an overview.
Show how the package helps the application area.	Show installation on different computers.
Re-introduce old users to the package.	Show the limitations of the package.
Advertise the existence of the product.	

Figure 7.3 Reasons for documentation.

On-line tutorial.	On-the-job training.
Tutorial actions in book form.	Interactive video training material.
Face-to-face classroom instruction.	Film of program operation.
Individual tutoring.	

Figure 7.4 Teaching users.

After approval, plan each documentation component separately. The next chapter outlines plans for different documentation such as user manuals and brochures. Planning for documentation is similar to planning for any other development activity. Typically organisations have planning methods which should be used. If not then adapt the ideas here.

7.1.2 Control

The production of documentation is a subsystem of the total development effort. Control is typically done through standard project management techniques such as:

- A schedule showing all the tasks to do.
- The assignment of people and other resources to the tasks.
- Specification of milestones.
- Formation of a budget.

The documentation should be tested, maintained and revised. When it is delivered it is necessary to establish change control procedures. Software for version control of computer systems can help maintain change control.

7.1.3   Attitude

The reasons and motivation for doing documentation are important determinants in producing successful documentation. If designers want to explain and show people their products, and if they want others to use them, then their explanations will reflect this. If they think users are stupid and a nuisance, then their explanations will reflect this attitude. They will skimp on explanation, patronise their readers and fail to test documentation.

To make it easy for people to understand computer systems it is best to design and construct explainable products. Most people find that producing documentation helps them discover if the product is explainable. The earlier it is started the earlier problems of explanation appear. For this reason, if designers have this attitude then user documentation will interweave with product development.

With this approach the task of producing documentation becomes simpler; sometimes it might even disappear. If the product is intuitive, obvious and has all explanations built into the user-interface then there may be no need for further documentation. In practice this is unlikely and the system will need other explanations. As well as explaining how the computer product works it is important to explain how the product applies to the user's environment. For example, as well as telling people the mechanics of using a database tell them where a database might help and how to apply it to user information retrieval problems.

7.1.4   Identification of Users

Producing documentation requires a knowledge of the target audience. Explanations for programmers might differ from explanations for managers, which might differ from explanations for first-time users. If the users know nothing about a computer's operating system it may be necessary to explain how the operating system affects programs. If the users know about the application area, then there is no need to describe subject matter ideas. Documentation for accountants can assume they know double-entry book keeping. Documentation for a home accounts package should describe accounting principles, as the users may not understand the basis of your package.

One technique, to use when creating documentation, is to write for particular people who represent most users. Think of real persons and imagine whether they would have the background to understand the documentation, or whether the material is unnecessary. There is a balance to how much documentation to produce; too little and too much documentation are both faults.

7.1.5   Ongoing Documentation

With a plan in place the creation can start. In most projects this should proceed in parallel with the development of the application. As previously mentioned, explaining an application helps formulate the design. The earlier we find changes the cheaper it is to include them. Make the overall documentation plan at the start of the project. Try to have the first version of the documentation finished before starting programming.

Modern production techniques make it easy to change documentation. One argument used by people who leave documentation until later in the project development is that they do not know what it is they are documenting until the programming is finished! If this happens they will then have to redo masses of documentation. The argument given here is the reverse. If it cannot be documented then it should not be programmed because the program specifications are inadequate. This means it is inevitable that the programs will change. However, it is easier to change documentation than to change programs, hence the documentation should be part of the program specification as it helps reduce program changes. In general we should write the programs to fit the explanations rather than the explanations to fit the program.

7.1.6   Standards

It is widely recognised that standards within organisations help control quality, reduce the work for individual projects, help maintenance, preserve an organisation's memory, and make it easier to manage projects. All organisations should have standards and they should be applied. However, *bad* standards can be worse than no standards. If the standards are flawed then all the products will be flawed. Unfortunately, organisations typically have difficulty constructing good standards and standards for documentation are often the worst of all.

There is a solution for documentation standards. This is to use existing documentation as the standard, rather than trying to abstract the elements of good documentation and embody them in a set of rules. Luckily good examples of documentation exist. These may not come from the organisation; they might be a commercial product. When planning documentation for a new product, say that it will follow the existing examples, but will vary in certain ways. Organisations will soon build up sets of good documentation as each new product builds on the previous. There will soon be good standards from which to copy. The standards will also be observed because using existing documentation as a model is a common practise and appeals to most developers.

This strategy applies to all phases of systems development, including programming and user-interface. Traditional standards manuals have their place, but they will contain examples and explanations of the examples. An example of the format of standards is this chapter and Chapter 5 guide-lines. In both cases there is a general description, then some specific examples from real applications.

7.1.7   Document Reuse

Adopting the above standards approach and the strategy of early documentation means much of the documenting effort only requires changing existing work. Previous documents form the foundation of a new project. This increases productivity and is the chief mechanism for improving the efficiency of documentation production. Not only will it increase the efficiency for production, but it produces a mechanism for documentation maintenance. The approach to initial construction is much the same as later maintenance.

Luckily, in the computing business, we already have the tools to make this approach possible. It is called software and is soft because we can easily change it. We will use the term *softdoc* to mean this idea. Use the same tools and techniques used to produce programs to produce documentation. Use word processors, desk-top publishing, drawing packages, and save all the documentation electronically. Paper manuals can be printed, but produce them from an electronic soft medium. Foster an ethos of reuse within organisations.

7.1.8   Usability Testing

We would never write a program and give it to people to use without testing it. Software goes through rigorous testing and quality assurance; treat documentation the same way. Develop testing strategies and test it with the same rigour and thoroughness of other software components. The major difference with testing documentation is that it is more difficult than testing programs. It is relatively easy to find and recognise most computer program errors, but it is not possible to find all the documentation errors because of the human side of the equation. Every new reader will have different expectations and background and may misunderstand what previous users understood. Even though the task is difficult it should be done. Chapter 3 outlined how to do usability testing and the principles and procedures given there apply to documentation.

Documentation testing is driven by the purposes established for producing it. If we designed the user manual to be a reference guide for experienced users we can test to see if that objective is achieved. If it is meant to teach inexperienced new users we can test that objective. We can also apply mechanical style checking on whether it conforms to the organisations standards.

Crossword Designer Documentation

This section describes Crossword Designer documentation as a case study. It illustrates the points raised in the previous sections and introduces documentation components described in Chapter 8. During construction we made many compromises for economic and technical reasons. This will always be the case and it means the final products have room for improvement. However, choices and compromises are essential parts of any engineering project.

For this product the capital and time available for development was limited, and it was the first Microsoft Windows application we had produced. This meant that there were few documentation tools to assist and there were few resources to construct new ones. The next Windows application and the next version of this application will have better documentation because more *softdoc* tools will be available.

The documentation was planned and created in parallel with the application. We knew what we wanted, even if we had to compromise on the final products. Although we compromised on documentation, we also compromised on program functionality. There are many ideas to improve the product that we would like to implement. We stopped both documentation and program development well short of our ideals.

We spent most of our documentation time on the user manual. In total, all documentation consumed about one third of the development effort. Parts of it were finished before the application. With products for sale it is essential to explain the application, otherwise it will be a commercial failure. While this is obvious for products for sale, it is also important for in-house applications. People must be told about the product, otherwise few people will ever know about it and hence few will use it even in in-house applications.

Purpose and Users

Crossword Designer helps people construct crosswords. What is needed to construct a crossword? First a person needs some idea of why they want to construct a crossword and what it is they want it to achieve. Helping people with understanding reasons for constructing crosswords took much of our effort. Millions of people solve crosswords every day, but only a handful compile them and there must be a reason. We believe the major reason is the difficulty of construction, but part is having a reason to construct a crossword.

As well as this, people need help with making patterns, choosing words, putting the words into a pattern, developing clues, associating clues with words and finally printing and publishing the crossword.

Typical users are articulate and literate with little computing knowledge or background. They are likely to be teachers in English or History, editors of magazines or freelance journalists. Most have little experience with creating crosswords.

With this view of users, the documentation has to show people the package and help them with the task of creating and designing a crossword. The complete package must address not only the mechanics of using the package but give ideas on crossword use and on the general techniques of crossword construction.

The computing part of the package has to be intuitive, it must be obvious what to do and easy to use. Users will not spend much time learning to use it.

It is a new package with only one or two competing products in the marketplace. The package as constructed, has no known competitors. This means that the documentation has to inform people about this new application. This is different from documenting common, known applications such as word processing. People know what word processors are and there are plenty of other books around to describe the idea and principles behind word processing. Even the task of creating crosswords by hand is not a well known skill. A search of the literature gave few supporting books for hand designers of crosswords. For these reasons, it requires material to explain and describe ideas to help people create crosswords, both by hand and with the computer.

As well as information about the application, the documentation must explain the mechanics of package use. As many of the users have little knowledge of computers it needs some teaching and training material. When people use the package they need a quick memory reminder of the scope of the package and some explanation of complex operations. If people come back to the application after a period away, they need some way of quickly getting an overview of the package and the way to use it.

The package will need some explanation of its internal workings to try to remove any mystery about how it works. It also needs an explanation of all the functions it performs. When people first get the package they need to know how to set it up. Users need to know what to do if it does not work the way they expect or if error messages appear.

The Documentation Plan

Most applications have similar needs to those outlined above. How much documentation and what to produce depends not only on the purposes for the documentation but on the complexity of the application and the knowledge of the user community and the resources available.

The user-interface should be the basis of the best product explanation. Sometimes this may be the only form of documentation. Although we have separated the dialogue design from other forms of documentation they all help explain the application. We kept the dialogue uncluttered and used documentation to explain ideas about crossword creation. We went through the identified purposes and showed how the dialogue or other documentation satisfies those needs. These were:

- Background to crosswords and their uses.
- An explanation of other ways of doing the same task.
- How the program helps create a crossword.
- How to tell people about the package (advertising).
- Details of some functions.
- Quick reminders of operations.
- Teaching people how to use the product.
- An overview of the product.
- Initial installation.
- Problems and what to do if they arise.

We now expand on each of these points and discuss both what we did and what we would have liked to do.

Background to Crosswords and Their Uses

Most people know about crosswords and the way they work, but few consider them in any depth. For example, we know people who have done the daily newspaper crossword for years and never realised the black squares made a pattern. Few people have thought of them as a teaching tool or as a communication medium and few have ever thought of creating one themselves.

One of the tasks of the documentation is to show the possibilities of crosswords. It is to convince people that it is worth their while to create crosswords. To do this people need some information about crosswords. The obvious way to do this is to give many examples, to show the development of crosswords and to give ideas on crossword use. A book of crosswords in various forms and created with Crossword Designer is a good way of doing this.

This book could be stand-alone or be part of the user manual. We should try to interest a publisher in such a book and get it distributed by the publisher's network. The book would tell people about crosswords and how to use them. It would give an address from where people could buy the product. Ideally this should be written by an independent person.

Another way of telling about crosswords is to write articles for the popular press or for educational journals with the same information. Reprints of the articles could be distributed with the package.

One of the best ways of telling people about programs is to teach them in a class. It is probably impractical to teach all the people who may wish to use this product, and it is unlikely they would pay to go to a specially designed course. However, it is possible to use existing educational institutions to help with training. Do this by offering the package cheaply to training institutions, in the hope they will use it in their courses, or set up an educational package for people who train teachers. Distribute the package along with instructions on use in teaching packages to teaching institutions. Instructors in those institutions could show people about crosswords and their uses.

With a commercial product like this we must tell people about the product and advertise it in various ways. However, we should do the same with in-house applications. Many organisations have under-used excellent programs and systems that people do not know about. This is particularly the case with large organisations who often lack the culture and methods to tell people about internal products.

Explanation of Other Ways of Doing the Same Task

An effective explanation technique is to relate a task to something people may already know or may more easily understand. While most users of Crossword Designer have never made a crossword by hand they can still understand how to do it by hand if it is explained. For this product this is an effective way as the program operation is similar to doing crosswords by hand.

The most obvious way of doing this description is to do it on paper as part of a user manual. However, we could do it as a class exercise or as a video instruction tape.

How the Program Helps Create Crosswords

We can show the operation of a program with on-line demonstrations, self-teaching tutorials both manual and interactive, user manuals, courses of instruction, or video tapes. For this product we could use an on-line demonstration or do it in the user manual. Which method to use depends on your budget, your intended audience and the way you plan to distribute your application.

As well as showing how the package works, on-line demonstrations may satisfy some of the following documentation purposes. The demonstration disk is an important advertising and promotional tool. It helps teach people about the package and gives an overview of the package.

For economic reasons we created a demonstration disk as a restricted version of the full program. It allows people all the functionality of the full program except they cannot print or save crosswords. This is a second-best alternative to a proper demonstration disk, but it is cheap and easy to do.

Advertising

With this package the chief advertising documentation is the promotional brochure. This is a simple, inexpensive way to respond to information requests and as a way of soliciting business. Other promotional techniques which bring the existence of the package to the notice of prospective clients are:

- Writing articles about the product.
- Getting the product reviewed.
- Sending press releases to newspapers and magazines.
- Newspaper and magazine advertising.
- Incorporation in product catalogues.
- Writing articles and books that mention the product.
- Trade display promotions.
- Using the product as the basis for competitions.

Detailing Functions

The function details are put into a traditional user manual. Although this could be put on-line, the technology and techniques of on-line documentation was too expensive at the time of writing.

This is an example of where previously created on-line documentation would assist. Crossword Designer was our first Windows application and supplementary tools for such purposes were unavailable. Because of economic and technical reasons we detailed functions in a traditional user manual. This also served other purposes, besides giving people information about the product. With this product it acts as a vehicle for promotion. If it contains useful information people like to get it with the product when they buy them, and the manual can help with store displays of a product for impulse sales.

Quick Reminders of Operations

The traditional and most effective way of helping people use software packages is through on-line help. Crossword Designer had on-line help designed, but not initially implemented.

Again this was caused by lack of suitable *softdoc* tools. Windows 3 was the first Windows product to provide a standard help mechanism. The decision was made not to implement help with the Windows 2 on the basis of cost and of standardisation. We decided it was better to wait for a common Windows help tool and use a form of help available on other Windows applications. We intend to implement help when we produce a Windows 3 version.

Teaching People to Use the Product

The user-interface to the product is intuitive. An important factor in teaching package use, is teaching crossword design. Previous sections discuss ways of doing this. However, it still takes some time to learn the mechanics of the package and some things may not be obvious to all users.

We intend to produce an on-line demonstration to give people an overview of the product and show them how to use the program. This was not done initially because the Windows programs to help were unavailable. This purpose was achieved through the user manual.

An Overview

One of the important pieces of documentation is the system overview. On-line help can give an overview and summary of the application. It provides a shorthand description to remind people of the functions and to summarise the application operation. We intend to create a quick reference overview "mouse-pad" to distribute with the product. Other ways of presenting a product overview are:

- Context level dataflow diagram to give a technical overview.
- Summary quick reference cards.
- Wall posters showing the program functions and structures.
- Mouse-pads with a concise description similar to on-line help.
- An on-line help summary.

Internal Workings

Many of the design decisions for this program are scattered throughout this book. Thus the crossword sections of this book are part of Crossword Designer documentation. We can recommend this narrative form of systems documentation as it is a good way of describing the rationale behind many of the decisions made during package construction. The section in this book describing the data abstractions for the application are particularly important. This was translated almost directly into application code. The other main form of internal documentation for this program are the program comments and personal diary of the developers.

We keep a diary of changes and the reasons for the changes. With most computing products we lose the history of development decisions and the reasons for the decisions. A diary that records what happened with a product is an invaluable maintenance tool. When you maintain a product you often wonder why people did things in particular ways and you often think of changes that the designers tried and rejected. A good diary may help you understand the product history as well as being an excellent educational tool.

Installation

Crossword Designer has installation instructions in the manual and some other information is put on a README file on the distribution disk. It is best not to include installation instructions in the user manual as this information changes with different machines and different media. Keeping it separate from other documentation makes it easy and cheap to change. However, we put it in the first edition of the user manual for economic reasons and because we expect to change the user manual significantly with the next version of the program.

Problems and What to Do

We should minimise the impact of error conditions and try to correct or prevent them within the application. Unfortunately we cannot always keep problems from users.

In this program we have difficulties because of Windows software running on machines with limited memory. This can cause the program to stop under some conditions. When this does occur we have to tell people what to do. The important things should be given in the on-line dialogue but we may need further explanation. We do this in the User Manual.

The Documentation Plan

Having decided on the different components to the documentation we now list the components we wish to produce and make an estimate of size and effort required.

- User manual including description of crosswords, how to make crosswords by hand, and details of crossword operation (100 pages taking 200 hours of work).
- On-line demonstration of the package (20 minutes for a person to view and 40 hours of work).
- On-line help documentation (40 different screens of information taking 40 hours).
- Promotional brochure (2 A4 pages taking 8 hours of work).
- Installation sheet (1 A4 page taking 4 hours).
- Magazine articles and promotional literature (each article requires about 20 hours).
- Internal documentation (most is included in the construction, but the information in this book is estimated at 40 hours).

It is interesting to compare the documentation effort with the effort to create the application. Using the above estimates the documentation effort is about 400 hours. The total programming and testing time for the application was about 800 hours.

Not all the documentation was completed with the first version of the program, but it was all planned and most designed. The reasons some things were not being constructed are explained above. The manual took much longer than we planned because of problems with new documentation tools and we spent a lot longer playing with the package and making our own crosswords for "fun".

How to Create It

It is important to organise the mechanics of creating documentation and to reuse documentation components wherever possible. The computer is the chief tool to help automate documentation. All people creating documentation should have access to word processors, drawing programs, desktop publishing systems, on-line help utilities, screen-saving utilities and presentation tools. We detail how to create different forms of documentation in the next chapter.

It is preferable for persons other than the program authors to help with user documentation. Authors are so familiar with applications that they have difficulty recognizing what they have to explain. The act of explaining to a documenter often clarifies explanations and can make an impact on the design of the package. However, the designer must explain to someone, either to a documenter, or by writing the first version of any documentation.

Testing Documentation

We must test documentation. The best way to test is to use it and to monitor the people using it. The way we did it with this product was to:

- Give sample programs to people on condition that they try the application and comment on the documentation.
- Give the application and documentation to reviewers and ask for their comments.
- Ask people to use the package and do a co-operative evaluation.

The last suggested method is the best and cheapest way of testing documentation and all user-interfaces.

Summary

Documentation should be planned and controlled in a similar way to other software. Some informal rules for documentation development to help consolidate ideas are:

- Documentation is explanation.
- Start documentation early.
- Specify who will use the documentation.
- Define the purpose of documentation.
- Write documentation before writing programs.
- Make standards from existing documentation.
- Test documentation and measure its quality and success.
- Use the softdoc approach to documentation.

Exercises

1. Prepare a documentation plan to explain how to use a motor car.

2. Take a commercial software package and list all the documentation components. For each component list out its purpose. Evaluate whether they fulfil their purpose. Is all the documentation necessary?

3. Take an in-house application and prepare a retrospective documentation plan for the product. Compare your plan and documentation products with the existing documentation.

4. Find three pieces of documentation written for different users. For example, find some documentation for systems programmers, some for subject area specialists and some for an average suburban person. Compare the writing style and the content.

5. Find all the softdoc tools available in your organisation. Make a list of them and summarise the functions they perform and the way they work.

6. Take a text on managing and controlling software program development. See how many of the techniques apply to documentation.

Chapter 8

Forms of Documentation

This chapter describes different forms of documentation. A given system may have all or none of these forms. Go through the steps suggested in Chapter 7 and decide on what is required for the application. At a superficial level, most documentation is unnecessary for a computing product, as the program will operate without it. Only when we try to use the program does it become an issue, as documentation is for people.

There are many similarities between documentation and dialogue design. Both are concerned with the way people understand systems and both have a strong visual compo-

	User Manual	Brochures	Courses	Demos	Help	Quick Ref.	Tutes
Reference	XXX				X	X	
Installation	X					X	
Overview	XX	X	X	X	X		X
Trouble shooting	X				X		
Memory aid	X			X	XXX	XX	
Learning	X		XX	XX			XXX
Promotion	X	XX	X	XXX		X	
Review	XX			X	XX		
Integration with environment	X						

Figure 8.1 Documentation types and reasons.

nent. The layout of screens has many parallels with the layout of paper forms, the use of colour on screens is similar to the use of colour in a user manual, and a demonstration dialogue uses the same principles for user-interface design as an application. There are many ways in which knowledge of documentation will help dialogue design and vice versa.

Figure 8.1 summarises the different forms of documentation discussed in this chapter. The more Xs the more the reason applies. Many of the ideas apply to different forms of documentation; to prevent too much overlap we have detailed most of the general points in the user manual section and referenced them elsewhere.

8.1   User Manuals

People often equate a *User Manual* with computer documentation. They believe that documentation starts and ends with the production of the paper User Manual. While it is important, it is only one of the many ways to explain computer systems. However, in many projects it will be the most time consuming and expensive piece of documentation and we need to carefully consider its design and production.

In this section we describe how to plan, write and produce a User Manual. Much of this material is covered from a different perspective in Chapter 6. Here we are more concerned with techniques, while in Chapter 6 we were more concerned with purpose and planning. We illustrate the ideas with the Crossword Designer user manual, while discussing different options and approaches. The approach applies to other paper manuals such as a Program Maintenance Guide; the details may vary, but the strategy remains the same.

8.1.1   The User Manual Plan

In Chapter 7 we discussed the production of a documentation plan. When deciding the overall structure of the documentation we specified the purpose, audience, and the audience needs for the different documentation components. Figure 8.2 is a check-list of items to include in a plan.

Phase	Tasks
Set Objectives	Purpose, Audience Needs
Production	Contents Writing Illustrating Layout, Editing Indexing
Management	Estimating Costing Controlling

Figure 8.2 Steps in planning.

8.1.2 User Manual Objectives

Each application will have its own objectives for its user manual. These vary with different systems, but they all concentrate on tasks for which the user manual is best suited. These tasks relate to starting up, the overall view of the package and how it fits into a wider context. These topics are difficult to cover with other forms of documentation. For the purposes of this book, the particular details of what to include in a manual is less important than the approach. Chapter 7 gave the objectives in the Crossword Designer user manual plan. Any other manual will vary from this, but the same strategy can be used to design it.

The plan tells us why we are doing the documentation, what we will do and how we will do it. For economic reasons it is often best to keep all functions within the one manual, although with larger systems they may be separated into different volumes.

8.1.3 Audience

A critical decision in all documentation is to define the likely users of the documentation. Who are they? What do they need to know? What level of knowledge do they have? What documentation are they used to? How do they best understand? This is discussed in Chapter 7.

Write in "Plain English".

Introduce and explain technical terms.

Use a personal style in which you "talk" to the reader.

Use the Minimal Manual approach (Carroll 1990) for instructional material.

Use extensive indexing and referencing to make it easy to find information.

Use many figures and tables to focus attention and as illustration.

Use examples.

Figure 8.3 Guide-lines for manual
construction.

8.1.4   Guide-lines for Manual Construction

For all manuals use the principles shown in Figure 8.3. This book and the Crossword Designer manual use many of these principles.

Plain English

There is a strong movement in English-speaking countries to use Plain English for instructional, administrative and legal documents. Plain English uses the active form, common words, and shorter sentences. There is a wealth of literature on the topic. Williams
(1981) and Strunk and White (1959) are typical books. We suggest using this style for
much of the prose in documentation. Like all guide-lines, use them with discretion. Do
not blindly change all passive forms of sentences to the active form; use appropriate
words for the audience; use longer sentences if they are easily understood.

- This sentence would be changed if you follow the suggestions of a Plain
  English text.
- A Plain English text will suggest you change the previous sentence.

Technical Terms

The definition of technical terms depends on the reader. What is technical to some is normal to others. Where possible use common words with common meanings rather than
specialised words. Try to reduce the use of acronyms, but if they are used, make sure people know what they mean.

However, sometimes precise words are required for a precise meaning. To distinguish between eight bits and a text character use the word byte for eight bits and character
for text. If people are unlikely to know the meaning of words in the text, and it is important that they know, then include a glossary of terms. In the Crossword Designer manual
we included a glossary of crossword terms as they are important and need to be understood.

Personal Style

One of the techniques to make manuals friendlier is to write as though you were talking
to someone, rather than writing as though the reader did not exist. The impersonal style is
used in many scientific journals, in much government and administrative writing, and in
places where writers wish to remove themselves from the prose and appear objective. For
example, writing in the so-called impersonal or objective style may create:

If the reader follows these guide-lines, he or she will improve their manuals.

Allow users to start doing things quickly.

Rely on people to reason and improvise.

Embed information in real tasks.

Take advantage of what people already know.

Support error recognition and recovery.

Figure 8.4 Minimal manual instruction
guide-lines.

instead of:

If you follow these guide-lines your manuals will improve.

Using a personal style is particularly important for user manuals. It makes for fewer words, is direct and helps the writer communicate with the reader. You care about them and you want them to understand. You do not want to remove yourself from your prose.

Minimal Manual

Carroll and Rosson (1990) describe some important experiments and give guide-lines for the construction of instructional material. Many manuals contain instructional material. Figure 8.4 summarises the guide-lines to help create such material. We used the guide-lines in the construction of the Crossword Designer manual and we will now use examples from it to illustrate the guide-lines.

Allow Users to Start Quickly
When the user first uses Crossword Designer the program starts with a grid pattern and they are ready to enter the first word. There is a short description telling them how to enter a word and a short description of what Crossword Designer is doing. The instructions get the new user entering words immediately and do not initially discuss algorithms, variations and so on. Until a person has tried to use the package many points in the manual make little sense.

Rely on Reason and Improvisation
Rather than give a detailed blow by blow description of all tasks, suggest things for people to try. Introduce ideas, but allow the user to discover the variations. For example, we

tell people they can use the cursor keys to move the cursor around, but do not give detailed instructions and illustrate each cursor movement. In the manual we do not give a prescribed set of steps to go through to create a crossword. We show people the basic idea and encourage them to create their own crosswords in whatever way they can.

A common alternative is to make our instructional material follow a systematic prescribed set of steps. For example, rather than encourage people to think about and create their own crossword we could have given them an existing crossword and asked them to carry out a set of prescribed mouse and cursor movements to create the given crossword. That approach presents material as a hierarchical set of learning objectives, followed by an orderly sequence of sets to achieve those objectives. The reason that this approach often fails is that people are not interested in the user dialogue and do not want to learn it. They want to create crosswords. Instead of teaching the dialogue we suggest people concentrate on the overall goal of creating a crossword and learn by reasoning and improvising their way through the dialogue.

Embed Information in Real Tasks

People do not like exercises to which they see little purpose. It is possible to invent or give good examples to which users can relate, but the easiest and best way is to use real examples of the *normal* work people might do with the package. In our examples the task is the real one of creating a crossword. There are no small independent exercises. All explanation revolves around doing the task for which the package was created.

Take Advantage of What People Already Know

We build our knowledge on our background. As an explainer take explicit advantage of that knowledge and do not assume people are empty vessels ready to be filled with knowledge. People already know how to fill in crossword answers in a completed crossword. The dialogue is structured so that making a crossword is similar to solving it. Placing words into slots and the slot worked on is immediately recognizable from the moving cursor.

Support Error Recognition and Recovery

The dialogue does not allow "mistakes" in the sense of people getting error messages. Mistakes are indications that the system cannot find any more words. This is easily recognized and users can easily recover by removing words or by finding words themselves to fit the difficult slots. The program is not prescriptive in the sense of requiring things to be done. It gives visual feedback and allows them to decide how to change the crossword. For example, if a word is entered twice into the same crossword the user is alerted, but they can enter the word as many times as they wish.

Tables	Who writes the manual?
Photographs	What is in it?
Drawings	When is it done?
Graphs	How is it done?
Diagrams	What style?
Cartoons	How is it manufactured?
Maps	How is it edited?
	How is it indexed?

Figure 8.5 Illustration techniques.   **Figure 8.6** Questions.

Indexing

Users read reference manuals randomly. They rarely start at the beginning and work their way through the manual. Even if they do this once, the next time they look at the manual they will access it randomly. Figure 8.13 lists techniques to help random access reading. See the section later in this chapter for details on how to do this.

Illustrating

It is difficult to read solid pages of text in a reference manual. This book has many tables, sub-points, diagrams and pictures to break up the text. This is done deliberately to make reading and information assimilation easier. The book may be entered at different places when wishing to do a particular task. Previous chapters or sections may or may not have been read. This means we must sometimes repeat or cross-reference material. People who are scanning for pieces of information look at illustrations and different forms of high-lighting such as bullets. We have done this throughout this book to help you scan for information and we have used different forms of illustration through the book. This makes the text more interesting and more easily understood.

The same techniques can be used with user manuals. Crossword Designer has many illustrations and where it does not have illustrations it has examples. The main blocks of solid text are in the preface and introduction where we expect readers to read sequentially.

Examples

Manuals and reference texts should be full of examples. We illustrate this idea with the way we have structured this book. Within this book an idea is described and then there is an illustration. We may then illustrate the idea in a larger example and, lastly, we often summarise the idea. Flower and Hayes (1983) investigated how readers made sense of abstract ideas. They found people made concrete examples to explain the ideas. To make a manual usable, supply readers with examples instead of requiring them to invent their own examples.

A rapid check for an unusable manual is to look for examples. If there are no examples, no pictures of screens, no scenarios, then it will almost certainly be unusable. The reverse, unfortunately, is not true; having examples does not guarantee a usable manual.

8.1.5   Production Plan

The mechanics of production influence the style and contents of the manual. Decide on how to do the manual early in the planning. We have to decide the items shown in Figure 8.6.

Who Writes the Manual?

The person who writes the manual should be in a position to influence the package development. Knuth (1989) found that writing the Te(X) manual caused him to make major revisions to the product. He suggests that the designer write the first user manual. We agree with him, but the practicalities are that a single person cannot do everything. However, it is important for the documentation people to have good links to and be able to influence designers. Explaining a product is a quick way to find its deficiencies.

What is in It?

The purposes of the manual determine the overall content. However, the writing level and the amount of detail is determined by

Table of Contents

Preface

About this manual

Background to the package

Getting started

Minimalist instruction for
   package use

Detailed application task
   reference

Technical details to help
   understanding

Index

Figure 8.7 Suggested generic table of contents.

how much time is available. It is easily possible for the documentation to cost more than programming. A decision has to be made on how much of the total budget is to be devoted to documentation.

One way to specify the manual contents is to produce an outline or provisional Table of Contents. This becomes the planning and estimating basis and gives a structure to the document. Figure 8.7 is a suggested Table of Contents for a user manual. See the later section on alternative structures and ideas on how to organise a manual.

The suggested manual contents should produce a manual that emphasises the application of the package. It gives instruction on how to use the package and provides supplementary information that may help understanding. Not all readers are expected to read the whole manual, but most users will read the preface, getting started and the first section of instruction. They will read other parts of the manual when the need arises.

When is it Done?

Start work on the manual at the beginning of the project and work on it in parallel with other parts of the project. The details of the text might remain until towards the end of the project, but map out the overall structure and start work as soon as possible. Word processing and desktop publishing technology has made this incremental approach possible. Make the parts in whatever order is convenient, whenever time is available, and fill in details as soon as possible.

The first draft of this chapter in this book was written before most of the preceding chapters. It was substantially rewritten three times, but the first drafts helped form the preceding chapters. This chapter in many ways is an easier chapter than the first two chapters as the subject matter is concrete. This is the same with manuals. Some parts are *easier* as they are more concrete. It is often best to start with those areas and to write the more abstract, summary and overview material later.

The worst time to start on the manual is when the product is finished. Trying to explain the application will suggest improvements and if you leave the explanation too late it becomes difficult to include them in the package.

How is it Done?

Use desktop publishing tools. See Chapter 7 for a discussion of the softdoc approach. If possible use tools that permit capturing information from the application. Explaining a computer application will almost certainly require screen images and output from the application.

Prose style
Page size and layout
Font types for different parts
Figure and table styles
Referencing and Indexing
Use of colour

Figure 8.8 Stylistic points to decide.

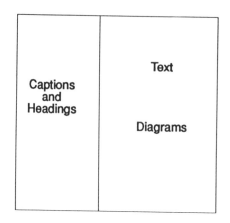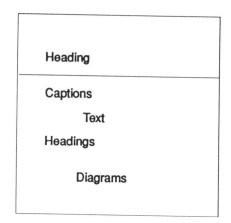

Figure 8.9 Simple layout variations.

The documenter requires tools that allow the entry and editing of text, diagrams and pictures. The tools help structure the information and format the document. Ideally the manual production software should work in the same environment as the application. The less transferring of information the more efficient will be the construction.

Both the Crossword Designer manual and the software was produced on the same machine under the Windows environment. This made the mechanics of the production of the manual much easier. There was little trouble in moving screen images and it was easy to check if the package worked the way it was described.

An organisation should have a house style for manuals as part of its internal standards. As discussed in the previous chapter, make the standards dynamic and use the best manual as the standard. Desktop publishing systems give a simple way of specifying layout standards through the use of style sheets. Crossword Designer was produced with Word for Windows. If we wanted it to be a standard for our organisation we would make the template sheet used to produce it the basis for the standard. Figure 8.8 is a list of some important stylistic decisions. Figure 8.9 shows two possibilities for page layouts.

8.1.6 How is it Manufactured?

An organisation should have an approach to the physical production of manuals. This depends on the technology available. The number produced and the final cost influence the decisions and the manual style. The manufacturing techniques used make radical differences to the construction of text and diagrams. The size of the paper changes the positioning of diagrams and the related text. With A4 paper there may be enough space to fit both diagrams and related text on the one page. A5-sized pages may require diagrams on the left page and text on the right. With B5-sized paper there may be enough space to allow substantial margins.

With Crossword Designer the manual was designed for small printruns of 100 using photocopying techniques. The size of the page and hence the layout was determined from the economics of printing. The size is A5 which is exactly half the size of A4 and which allows cheap photocopying techniques. The manual was bound with spiral binding to permit flat opening of pages. To keep costs down it has no structural aids to referencing (such as plastic section separators). This meant that all referencing had to be printed. The manual has no colour except for the cover.

If the manual had glossy paper, colour diagrams, saddle stitching, B5-sized paper and offset printing then the cost of producing 100 copies would give a unit cost about an order of magnitude greater than the current method. To produce economic, high physical quality manuals requires large printruns as the incremental cost is relatively low. The cost of producing 500 copies of the first edition of this book was only twice the cost of producing 100 copies.

Producing half a dozen manuals may best be done with different production techniques. Perhaps use ring binders and A4-sized paper as these are readily available and no special handling is necessary. This also gives an easy method of incrementally updating the information.

Most modern software packages use a permanent binding technique. Some older packages come with ring binders and updates are sent out. While this might seem an attractive idea that might save many trees, it becomes impractical to control and many people never update their manuals. A more practical approach is to use permanent binding, to put changes in a "softer" form such as a README file on disk and to periodically issue an updated manual.

8.1.7 How is it Edited?

Plan for editing. Editing is not only correction of prose but editing in a wide context. Editing is analogous to the testing and debugging of programs. As with testing it should be done by people other than the authors. It should be done with users and it should be planned and structured. The chapter on usability testing discusses how to test the user-interface; similar usability tests should be carried out on all documentation. As well as usability editing we should do technical editing. Van Buren and Buehler (1980) discuss technical editing and the different levels at which it can be done. Figure 8.10 summarises the levels.

Co-ordination

Co-ordination editing covers the material in this section of this book. Has the manual been planned, costed, production decided, editing arranged, and so on?

Policy

Policy editing ensures that the manual fits in with the host organization's policy. Is there a house style and does the manual fit; have the legal requirements been covered; have all the appropriate acknowledgements been made; has the manual been submitted to the National Library?

Co-ordination
Policy
Integrity
Screening
Copy clarification
Format
Mechanical style
Language
Substantive

Figure 8.10 Levels of edit.

Integrity

The integrity check sees if all the documents are internally consistent. Are all figures referenced correctly, are indexes correct, do all references exist, and are cross-references correct?

Screening

Screening checks to see if the prose and illustrations make sense. For example, if sections of text are missing, everything else might appear alright, but the thread of the argument may be lost. Screening should check if the document needs an extra illustration to explain a point or if the illustrations are in the appropriate part of the document.

Copy Clarification

This covers what most people mean by editing. It checks for correct syntax, grammar and punctuation. "This sentence are wrong" would hopefully be corrected with a copy clarification edit.

Format

The format edit checks the application of the organisation's standards on typography, layout and illustrations? Does the manual use the appropriate fonts for headings and for illustrations. In this book the font for text is Times Roman and the font for illustrations and diagrams is Helvetica.

Mechanical Style

This edit checks for capitalisation, spelling, hyphenation, use of symbols, bibliographic reference format, use of italics and use of bold. References such as the Australian Government Style Guide (1988) gives a complete reference for mechanical editing of style in Australian Public Service documents.

Language

Language edits check for usability of the prose. As discussed previously, write manuals in Plain English. This edit checks observance of the guide-lines.

Substantive

The substantive edit checks to see if the manual works as a whole. It will draw on the usability evaluation, but also looks for coherence, completeness, and non-essential material.

8.1.8 How is it Indexed?

Manuals are reference documents. Because of this people need to have ways of accessing the information in the document. A good table of contents is crucial; a good index is important for any manual over fifty pages; tables of figures, page referencing and sections on using the manual can all help the user find information. This topic is discussed in the indexing section.

8.1.9 Ways to Organise a Manual

When constructing a manual decide how to structure it. Having a logical structure to the order of the document helps readers find information. People do not want to get lost; they prefer if things are "where they expect them to be". Standard styles and an internal logic help.

Figure 8.11 gives different ways to organise contents. Different techniques may be used within the same manual. We suggest using a chronological order for the overall structure and to use other techniques such as

Chronological order

Alphabetical order

Program structure order

Order of importance

Order of difficulty

Most common task order

Question/answer

Spatial (screen)

Figure 8.11 Ways of organising manuals.

Spatial or Alphabetic for sub-sections of the manual.

Sometimes manuals are organised alphabetically, for ease of access, and then other sections are written that repeat the information, but in different groupings. A simpler way to achieve the same purpose is to group the information, then produce good indexes to help access by name.

Chronological Order

This is the most common and normally the best method for standard applications. It presents the information in the order that the user is likely to need them. Thus a person with this style of manual can often work through the manual as though it were a tutorial. Most of the Crossword Manual has this structure. The first part of the manual gives an overview of the problem, then the installation, then creating a regular crossword followed by more information about crosswords and finally infrequently used items. We could have organised the manual alphabetically on actions. The manual structure might be as in Figure 8.12. This is a typical organisation of a programming manual. It might work where the access is always alphabetical and the book is supplemented with other texts on how to create crosswords. However, the functional grouping works best for Crossword Designer and alphabetical access is provided with an index.

Preface

Introduction

Add to Wordlist

Automatic

Build your own

Clue Add

Clear Grid

etc....

Figure 8.12 Possible alphabetical order for a Crossword Designer manual.

Alphabetical Order

Computer programming language or other command language reference manuals are often organised alphabetically. With these manuals there is no chronological sequence and the manual is normally looked at via the command name. In contrast, it is unlikely that a word processing manual is best organised alphabetically because access is often on overall function and so it is best to have all aspects of a function in one place. An alphabetic approach often splits functions and spreads them throughout the manual.

Program Structure Order

This is the lazy way of writing a manual and is typically done by programmers. They take the functions done by the program and work their way through the functions. Only rarely will this correspond to the way in which people use the package. Be suspicious of any manual with a table of contents order the same as the first menu on the screen.

Order of Importance, Difficulty or Most Common Task

This can be a good method if the order of importance corresponds to the order of importance for the normal reader. However, the difficulty is in determining the order of importance and then making sure the reader is aware of it. The same applies to order of difficulty or most common task.

Question/Answer

Here we base the structure on a set of questions that a typical user might ask. This is often used as a sub-order within another framework.

Spatial (Screen)

This technique works well when describing the function of particular screens. Within the Crossword Designer's overall chronological structure we describe different crossword modes by describing the meaning of the screens. This method does not work with highly modal dialogues where there are many screens of menus. People soon become totally confused as to where they are.

8.1.10 Table of Contents and Indexing

Indexing in its various forms is crucial to the success of a manual. Indexing and access is the most important advantage of on-line

Table of Contents

Glossary

Back-of-book index

Top-of-page headings

Figure index

Orientation paragraphs

Numbered headings

Tabs on pages

Figure 8.13 Ways of indexing.

Do not use a term (or a variation) to define itself.

Do not define procedures in a glossary.

Use examples.

Use many explanations and diagrams.

Figure 8.14 Rules for glossaries.

documentation (see the section on on-line help), but there are many things we can do to make the information in a manual accessible.

Have multiple ways of accessing the document (Figure 8.13). Use tables of figures and diagrams, use indexing headers as on the top of this page, use back-of-the-book indexing, have orientation paragraphs telling people where things are and where they can find related information in the book. Use a good word processor to help make these tasks easier.

Table of Contents

The first and most important reference aid is a good Table of Contents. Use a word processing system that allows text outlining and use the outlining features to help structure and compose the document. Use the automatic Table of Contents feature of word processors to produce the Table of Contents. This saves time and helps ensure the Table of Contents is correct.

Glossary

A glossary is a small dictionary within the manual. If there are software or application terms that readers might not know then use a glossary combined with a back-of-the-book index. The glossary entry defines the meaning, and the index shows where else it occurs. When constructing glossary definitions use rules that apply to all dictionaries (Figure 8.14).

Back-of-the-Book Index

Indexing is difficult and time consuming. However, a good index is important for readers. When indexing try to imagine why people will use the index and what they are looking for. People who use indexes normally know what they want to look up or know the function (but not the name of the function) they wish to perform. They want to find where it is in the manual so they can get a reference to it or they may have found it and want to know where else it might appear. With short manuals it might be sufficient to have a very good Table of Contents and let people browse through it. However, once the manual has fifty or more pages it probably requires an index.

When creating an index there are conflicting goals. How many words should go into an index versus precision? Too many words make it difficult to find any particular word. Too much culling of unnecessary words or entries will make you miss important words. The technical terms for these ideas are Exhaustiveness and Precision.

One of the other purposes of an index is as a thesaurus for index entries. Thus the word keyboarding may be used within the manual, whereas others might use the word typing. Typing could appear in the index and refer to keyboarding, or there could be a separate thesaurus.

Top-of-Page Headings (Running Heads)

Putting chapter or section names on the top (or bottom) of a page is a quick, simple, inexpensive, yet effective way of indexing. Many desktop publishing packages do this automatically. This book has this feature. Skim through looking at the top of the page and you will soon get an idea on where different things are in the book.

Figure Index

Make a simple list of all figures. This is useful in the same way a Table of Contents is useful. It helps readers find figures, but also gives them an overview of the illustrations.

Orientation Paragraphs

As people access manuals randomly it sometimes help to put orientation paragraphs at the beginning of sections. People may not have read the previous sections and a few words to set the scene, although it may appear repetitious, will help many readers.

Numbered Headings

Headings are crucial in manuals. Use them for the same reason we use paragraphs; to divide text into coherent junks. However, they are much more than a useful dividing mechanism. People often only read the headings and the captions of diagrams until they find what they want. Headings also summarise ideas and keep the user oriented.

Many people number headings so they can cross-reference material. It is preferable to cross-reference with page numbers, but it is easier for the author to cross-reference with numbered headings, unless the word processor supports page cross-references. Numbers on headings clutter up the heading and it is easier for the reader to find a page number than to find a heading number. This book uses numbered headings to fit the house style of the publisher.

Understand the problem.

Plan the manual.

Write the text.

Create diagrams.

Make first draft.

Edit the document.

Revise.

Usability testing.

Revision.

Setting up for the printer.

Printing.

Binding.

Figure 8.15 Tasks in manual creation.

Tabs on Pages

There are various physical formatting devices to help index a document. The simplest is the extended tab put onto the page. However, other ways are the indented thumb mark, paper or plastic or cardboard dividers, different shaped pages or "staggered" tabs as in a telephone reminder device. This is normally not a good approach as it makes production expensive, and is relatively limited in indexing functionality.

8.1.11 Layout of Text and Diagrams

The layout of text and diagrams deserves a book on its own. In fact there are many such books (White 1988). Decide on a standard layout format. Will it have one or two columns, will the headings be in a separate column, will the diagrams be on pages on their own? The style used will depend, amongst other things, on the house style, the size of the page and the purpose of your document.

8.1.12 How Long to Construct

McKilliam (1984) estimates it takes one and a half to two and a half months to complete an average 100 page manual. Brockmann (1986) refers to one organisation taking ten hours per page for documentation, and another taking an average of two pages per employee per day.

The length of time will vary depending on the quality required, the skill of the workers, the type of project, the size of the manual, the method used, the tools available, and the frequency of document production. Figure 8.15 is a list of common tasks to produce a manual. Even this abbreviated list shows there are many things to producing a manual. However it is done, it will take a lot of effort and much time. Invent strategies, as suggested in the previous chapter, to streamline document creation.

Estimating how long to create a manual is a similar exercise to estimating how long it takes to write the computer system. The best estimators build upon experience and on estimating then measuring each project.

The Crossword Designer user manual took 300 hours to design, write, edit, and produce. In the plan we had estimated 200 hours, but there were difficulties with the technology, and it took longer than expected to create the examples.

Cost is related to time. If we use the figure of two pages per day per employee, and a daily cost of $240 for an employee, a 100 page manual will cost $12,000 before printing. Whatever numbers are used, and whatever the cost figures, document production is expensive.

8.1.13 Evaluating a Manual

Evaluate a manual by comparing it to the ideas in this section. Other ideas on evaluating manuals come from reading reviews of texts and computer products. Field testing manuals is difficult and expensive. Co-operative evaluation usability testing is perhaps the simplest most effective method. Figure 8.16 has a brief summary of the important points to consider.

Is the purpose and audience clear?	Is it illustrated with tables, screens and diagrams?
Does the manual explain how it is meant to be used?	Is the prose appropriate?
Is the production pleasing and is it easy to read?	Does it contain all that is needed?
Can you find information?	Does it have too much in it?
Does it use a minimalist approach to instruction?	Is it consistent in layout?
Are there many examples?	Does it have appropriate format conventions?
	Does it help you understand the computer system?

Figure 8.16 Evaluation check list.

8.2 Brochures or Flyers

This section describes how to produce an information brochure or flyer for a product. If the product is for sale it requires a shorthand description to give to people who enquire about the product. Computer systems produced in-house should also have an information sheet, to tell people about the product, and to form part of an index to applications.

If all internal applications had brochures or information sheets, and they were collected in one place, then it would form an excellent quick reference for the organisation's applications. Many organisations do not advertise their computer packages internally and so the applications are often under-utilised. New people come into organisations, and old applications might be useful in other parts of the organisation. An information sheet is a good way of telling people about such systems.

As with all forms of documentation build a library of example brochures. Look for ideas in commercial products, both computing and non-computing.

8.2.1   Brochure Contents

A brochure should have a concise description of crucial information about the product. Information sells computer program products more than smart presentation. A brochure has different contents compared to a quick reference. Brochures have a concise description that tells people about the product. A quick reference tells people about product use.

It is important that people know what the product does. Include part of or the whole quick reference guide in the brochure or make a short one or two paragraph summary of the product. People will often scan a brochure (before throwing it away), looking for the crucial information. They want to find whether this product will be of use to them. Extravagant claims and flowery prose are ignored. However, information-rich testimonials and quotes can add impact.

There will be other competing ways of doing a user task than with this product. Tell people about the features that make it different and why to use it - instead of using something else. If the product is yet another spreadsheet program it needs to have some new twist to make it worthwhile. Perhaps it is one-tenth the price of a similar product, perhaps it requires half the number of keystrokes to do similar operations, perhaps it takes half the time to learn or perhaps it has 100 extra functions. Highlight those features that make the product distinctive.

If people are interested then they must know what to do to find further information. This must be clear and easy to follow and must give the correct information. If selling the product, give a list of all distributors and their addresses. If people have to enquire in writing, provide an easy, simple way for people to enquire further. Some suggestions follow in the layout design section.

Selling price is often a most crucial piece of information. Say something about price, but do not necessarily give the price unless it is the major selling-point; in which case you should include it.

What the product does.

Any special features.

How to get more information.

How to get the product.

What hardware and software you need to use the package.

Information on pricing (not necessarily the price) for items for sale.

What purchasers get when they obtain the product.

Figure 8.17 Things to put in a brochure.

If people need a special piece of hardware or software to run the package then tell them in the brochure. Equally if it runs on all known machines with all configurations then tell them that. The hardware and software to run the package is often the crucial piece of information for prospective users.

A software package is not just a program. There will possibly be other items supplied to help people understand the package. The package may include a one month in-house training course, or it may have a training video or a 200 page instructional manual, or internal hotline support. Tell people about these extra elements in the brochure.

8.2.2   Layout

Keep brochures and information sheets concise. Try to fit the information onto, at most, one A4 sheet. Use a standard format within an organisation to make the information sheets or brochures easy to file and easily recognized. This also reduces the time spent in producing new sheets.

People who prepare brochures want others to act on reading the brochure. Make the effort to get further information simple and easy. A telephone enquiry number to a toll-free number is excellent, but make sure there is someone knowledgeable at the other end and that the phone is rarely engaged. Design the brochure so that people can write their name and address and send it, or part of it, to a prepaid mail address. Include a preaddressed sticky label to help people mail for information.

A significant part of any product is the name. All commercial products have to have a name. Internal packages should also have a name, or abbreviation, rather than some long title that people will inevitably shorten. A name is important to a program package in the same way a title of a film or a title of a book is often crucial to the success of the product.

A LOGO for the product and for the organisation are important features of all documentation and particularly brochures. They help make the products and the organisation easily recognized. Again this is important for in-house applications as well as products for sale. They tell people in a quick, simple way the origin of packages. They become, in effect, the brand name for your applications.

8.3   Courses

This section describes how to design and run a course to teach people how to use a computer package. The strategies and techniques described in this chapter come from standard texts on the design of instructional courses for other subjects and from our experiences in designing and running courses for many different computer packages (Cox & Collings 1985).

Few people think of courses as a documentation technique. However, they can be the major way to document a package - particularly for in-house applications. The running of courses to teach people how to use common computer packages is a multi-billion dollar growth industry and the sparsity of published work is surprising. We need more information and experiments to help devise the best ways of teaching computing packages. We hope this section will prompt people to work in this important area and to think of courses as a documentation tool.

Courses for computer packages are relatively easy to design and construct. This is because we can state many course objectives in concrete terms and measure how well people achieve those objectives. The packages are often well structured and help the instructor construct an appropriate course. To construct a course, work out the course objectives and how to meet those objectives. Determine the instruction strategy, write the course, test it and modify it with experience.

8.3.1   The Objectives of a Course

People learn to use computer packages so they can do a particular task. We learn to use a word processor because we wish to write letters, or to write a book. We rarely learn a package unless we have some operational objective. Few people learn packages for the

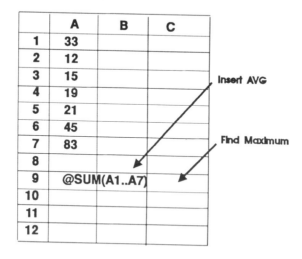

Figure 8.18 Teaching a spreadsheet.

sake of learning. Working out why people want to use a package provides the basis for course objectives.

For example, if we only wish to use word processors to produce class assignments then we may need a different course from one in which the participants wish to produce standard departmental letters. The major problem with teaching packages is helping participants relate the package to their work tasks. It is relatively easy to teach the mechanics of packages, but teaching the application and appropriate features for the application is difficult. However, if people do understand how to apply the package then it is easier to teach the mechanics of package use.

8.3.2 Instructional Strategy

Use the minimalist approach as described in the user manual section on instructions in manuals. A variation on the approach is the "training wheels" strategy. In this the objective is to teach the minimum features to achieve a goal and to teach people how to build on those features. This approach works well with large packages such as a full featured spreadsheet.

Notwithstanding the desire to teach people an understanding of what the package does it is often easier to teach this understanding by giving a "recipe" to produce a desired effect. However, recipes without understanding only work when the user tasks match the recipes. It is not possible to provide enough recipes to cover all user tasks. When using recipes tell people what it is they are trying to achieve. Tell them why a sequence of actions will achieve the result, then give them the actions to do the task. Reinforce the ideas by giving them a similar task, but which requires a small variation on the sequence of actions. Get them to devise that variation.

If constructing a course for spreadsheets, a key idea to impart is the concept of using functions in cell formula. It is possible to give people a blow by blow description of creating, say @SUM(A1..A7) in LOTUS (Figure 8.18). Get them to put data in cells A1 to A7, move the cursor to cell A9, enter @SUM(move the cell pointer to A1, anchor the cursor, paint in the area to A7, close bracket) and press Enter.

Now ask them to find the average of the cells, put the result into B9. Give a hint that the formula for average is AVG. Next ask people to find a formula that will find the maximum value of the cells and put it into cell C9.

In this sequence of instructions we gave people a detailed set of instructions to do one task, we then gave them a similar problem, but gave them most of the information, finally we gave them a problem where they needed to look up some documentation as well.

8.3.3   Building Courses

Figure 8.19 is a set of guide-lines for building courses.

Task Orientation

A common fault with any course for learning skills, whether it is a short course or a University degree, is an emphasis on content rather than process. Courses that teach a body of knowledge are relatively easy to construct and teach. However, they are likely to be boring and not achieve the real objective of teaching people skills they can USE. We still have to teach facts and people have to learn skills, but we should do it so that people can apply the knowledge outside the course environment.

A course in user-interface design could discuss the principles of design and give many examples of user-interfaces. It could test by asking for discussion on principles and to say what to do in particular circumstances. Alternatively, a course in user-interface design could give principles and examples, but ask people to apply the principles and to create a user-interface. It could test by seeing how well the participant could create an interface to a novel problem. The orientation in the first is knowledge or feature while in the second it is task.

A course to teach Pascal could be organised around the language syntax, or it could be organised around the solution to programming problems and the syntax needed to express solutions to those problems.

When devising courses build your course around tasks, not around features.

When creating courses make sure people get many rewards by being able to produce significant results throughout the course.

Make sure the course material has many examples of completed work and the steps to get to the completed work.

Devise shorthand ways to summarise a package.

Use all the aids and tools that come with the package to help you in your own course.

Make sure people understand how to use the user manual and find out what it contains.

The most important part of any course is teaching people how to teach themselves.

Figure 8.19 Guide-lines for building courses.

Rewards

People want to learn. They want to acquire skills and they want to know how they are doing. Build rewards into courses by giving people achievable goals and organise it so that they know they have achieved the goals. Tell them they have achieved the goals through testing, or give them tasks so that they recognise their own achievements. It is not enough to assume that people can see their achievements. Make it clear that the work they have done is satisfactory.

If designing a word processing course a first objective might be to teach people to write a personal letter and print it out. The next objective might be to print out an addressed envelope in which to send the letter. Then they might put in a picture to print with the letter. Give people meaningful goals and when they achieve those goals remind them of their achievements. Give many rewards continuously through the course.

Examples

People understand through examples. In the previous section the first paragraph discussed the idea of rewards. It talked about tasks and achieving them. The second paragraph gave an example of the meaning of reward. If the second paragraph was not present you might well think rewards were handing out chocolates at the end of each exercise, rather than the reward of people themselves recognising achievement.

Examples make the abstract meaningful. Abstraction means it can explain many different operations while examples focus the meaning. For example, we might say adding two numbers gives a third. Figure 8.20 gives two different ways of interpreting the meaning of "adding" numbers.

2 added to 3 gives 5

2 added to 3 gives 23

Figure 8.20 Two ways to add numbers.

Thinking Aids

As well as examples, think of other ways to help people understand the material. Powerful methods are analogies and visualisations. We have discussed the use of visualisation in designing user interfaces. We can do the same thing with courses. We can give people pictures that summarise a course or part of a course. Figure 8.21 is a picture summarising an introductory word processing course.

We could draw an analogy between people doing a course in user-interface design and a baby learning to walk. The baby learns the idea of walking by watching other people walk; the student learns the idea of user-interface design by "watching" someone else do a user-interface design. The baby learns to walk by getting up and trying. At first it does not succeed, but it knows what it wants to do and keeps trying. It gets rewards from the satisfaction of achieving goals of walking to its mother across the room. Similarly people learn user-interface design by trying it out. They may fall over and not succeed the first time, but they know what it is they wish to achieve, and so they keep trying.

Tools and Materials

When designing a course use appropriate tools. Computer packages often have tools supplied with the package. For example, if the package has a demonstration make sure all students have seen the demonstration before doing the course. If the package has an on-line tutorial make sure everyone has done the on-line tutorial before doing the course.

Plagiarise and copy material from other courses. If the organisation has an evaluation procedure for courses then use it rather than invent another. If a good text already exists for the package use it rather than writing another. We could have paraphrased the material in the Common User Access manual and incorporated it in this book. Instead we refer to the book (IBM 1989).

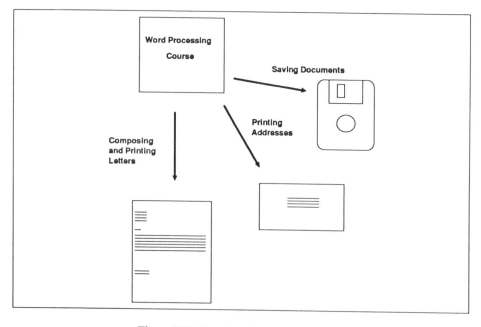

Figure 8.21 Overview of a word processing course.

Reference Material

Have copies of any quick reference material for all students. If there is no quick reference, make one. If possible make sure every student has a user manual for the product. Make sure people know how to use on-line help and use the user manuals. Make sure they know who to ask for more information and for further assistance. Consult with your own organisation's training section before designing your own material.

Remember Objective

The objective of instruction for computer packages is to help people understand the package. They need to have some idea of how it works. Learning by rote works for some limited cases, but learning to understand and applying that learning will last longer and cover more situations.

8.3.4   Testing Courses

Test a course by seeing how much people have learnt. If the course is structured as a set of learning tasks there is a ready measure of the course. Tests of students are as much a test of the instructor as they are of the students. If the students have a high failure on tests then the instructor fails as well as the students.

Test by seeing how long it takes for people to learn to achieve certain tasks. With computer packages test the course by visiting students, in their workplace, one month after they have taken the course. If they are using the package for their work tasks the course probably succeeded. Check to see how many functions in the package people use. See if the tasks they do could be improved by using the package in different ways.

Get people to do evaluations at the end of the course. Make these evaluations optionally anonymous. Try to get feedback from students on where they had difficulty and what they would like to do next.

Get an expert in education to attend the course and get them to evaluate it.

8.4   On-line Demonstrations

The on-line demonstration is an important tool to show the functions and overall structure of an application. It shows the application in a dynamic form. This is an excellent way to explain how an application looks and feels and for this purpose it is superior to static techniques such as user manuals.

Demonstrations differ from on-line tutorials in emphasis and objectives. The final form of an on-line tutorial may be similar to a demonstration, but it has a different purpose and will often differ substantially in presentation and content. It is sometimes tempting to include tutorial functions in a demonstration, but in most cases this results in a poor demonstration and a poor tutorial.

Similarly, demonstrations differ from on-line help although the on-line help may include parts of a demonstration. People who look at on-line help often know what they want to do, but want to know how to do it. People who look at demonstrations often have no idea on what the application does.

8.4.1   Why Make an On-line Demonstration?

A demonstration shows people what the application does. It may show how to use it, but only if it helps show the function of the application. When designing a demonstration list out the main functions of the application and decide how to demonstrate those functions.

An on-line demonstration is similar to giving a demonstration in person and should have the same objectives. Show what the application does; show the features that make the package easy to use; point out differences between using the package and doing things in other ways and finally, and most importantly, show how the package helps people achieve their own task-related goals.

The demonstration of an invoicing package should emphasise invoicing as a user objective. It will concentrate on the final objective and show how to achieve it. It could start with the final output and show how it was derived from input data and calculations. It would show how the data-entry function fitted in with other user tasks, like accepting payment. It would show what the package does and relate it to the work tasks of the user.

8.4.2   Demonstration Content

Stating the objectives and designing the application using the methodology in this book specifies the content of the demonstration. The demonstration will show the user tasks highlighted in the design.

Because a demonstration relates closely to the design objectives, we can use the demonstration as an important design tool. Showing the user tasks in a demonstration rather than simply stating them checks the design goals. Seeing how an application works will almost always lead to refinements and adjustments in the application design and specification.

In the outline of the dialogue design methodology we stated that it is important to prototype the application interface before commencing construction. The style of prototype is the on-line demonstration rather than an on-line tutorial.

8.4.3 Designing a Demonstration

After specifying the objectives and content of a demonstration, now design the demonstration delivery. Because of the similarity between on-line demonstrations and personal demonstrations, giving a personal demonstration is a good way of starting the design. Try to find a naive user who has not seen the application and explain to them what it does.

This helps determine the content of the demonstration and the best way of presenting it. Observe things the person misunderstands and note the questions they ask. Another observer can help see difficulties in presentation and can record the demonstration. It is even possible to videotape the manual demonstration for later analysis.

It is possible to use the demonstration as a design tool even if there is no package to demonstrate. Simulate the package, as discussed previously, by drawing on white boards or paper and show people the concept and structure of the application with a personal demonstration.

Once the purpose, content and idea of how to do the demonstration are fixed, make up an overall structure for the presentation. Story-boarding in advertising and film-making is a similar activity. This outlines the structure of the demonstration and specifies the user-interface for the demonstration.

Demonstrations may start at the beginning and continue through to the end without a break. Although the demonstration may have this capability this structure is too restrictive. Make the demonstration so that people can replay parts, can go to any section, go at their own pace and break the demonstration whenever they wish. This structure simulates the things that happen when giving a personal demonstration. People ask questions, the demonstrator redoes an explanation, they adjust the speed to the comprehension of the audience and stop at any time.

Two common structures for demonstration dialogues are the main menu and the application menu. In the main menu approach the users have a menu showing all the tasks to be demonstrated. During the demonstration people can return to this menu to select operations or they automatically come back at the end of the partial demonstration. This is often the best approach because it lets the demonstration be organised according to complete user tasks.

In the application menu approach the demonstration is divided into sections according to the application menu. For example, if the application uses the SAA pull-down menu action bar it may be a suitable way to divide the demonstration. This structure sometimes works for demonstrations, but is more appropriate for on-line help.

Divide the demonstration into scenes and within scenes divide into frames. Each frame shows an item of information and each scene shows a chunk of information. Allow the user to move through the frames either automatically or by pressing a key or clicking with the mouse. Allocate a standard key to redo the previous demonstration frame. The

How to work this demonstration.

Some ideas on using crosswords.

Some ideas on designing crosswords.

A short tour of Crossword Designer.

Moving around a regular crossword.

Using the word-list and adding words.

Deleting words from a regular crossword.

Loading old patterns.

Saving your work.

Making a new pattern.

Making a free-format crossword.

Deleting words and putting words anywhere.

Printing crosswords.

Changing printers and writing to a file.

Figure 8.22 Main menu for demonstrations.

backspace is a good selection. Allocate a standard key to get back to the main menu such as Esc and any other key moves forward through the demonstration to the next frame.

Within the demonstration, have the application as it appears to the user and have explanations about the application. These two things should be kept separate and distinct. The "talking bubble" used in comics is an appropriate analogy for this idea. Use a distinctive colour and layout for explanations to separate them from the normal application. There should be a way of removing the explanation so the whole user screen is visible. Allocate a standard key (such as the Del key) to this operation.

The objects for the demonstration interface are scenes, frames and explanations. The actions are to choose and show a scene, to move through the frames and show explanations. Use the user-interface methodology to specify a generic demonstration application. Expand on the objects and add other actions such as "animate", "freeze" and "print".

Allocate F1 as the Help key. This should give help for the demonstration rather than show the application help.

8.4.4   A Plan for a Crossword Demonstration

We are planning to make a proper crossword demonstration, but at the moment our demonstration disk is a cut-down version of the whole package. This can be one way of making a demonstration disk, but it is not as satisfactory as a properly composed and constructed demonstration.

The plan for the Crossword Designer demonstration we would like to make follows.

The demonstration will have a main menu of scenes (Figure 8.22), keystroke assignment of Backspace (back one), Esc (to main menu), F1 (to help), Del (remove explanation from current frame). The application also works with the mouse. Each frame has a main menu icon, an explanation icon and a help icon. A single click on the mouse moves to the next frame and a double click moves back a frame. Explanations appear in a distinctive colour or highlight and are framed within a distinctive border. The special icons appear within the explanations. (Note the mouse can be used to drag the explanations to other parts of the screen.)

8.5   Quick Reference Guides

For many systems the quick reference guide is the most used piece of documentation. In this section we describe the reasons for producing quick references, some of the different styles and give an approach to their design.

8.5.1   Reasons for Producing a Quick Reference

Figure 8.23 summarises the reasons for making a quick reference.

Reminder

A quick reference can be a short-hand way of presenting the user with a reminder of common functions or it can be an overall summary of the application. In many applications the 80-20 rule of thumb applies. This rule says that eighty per cent of users only need twenty per cent of the information. A good quick reference will often consist of this most used information presented in a concise form.

Summary

A common quick reference is a summary of the content of the application. This may take many forms such as a list of functions or a set of screens or output reports. It gives a top

level map of the whole application and helps
the user understand the structure and how all
the different elements fit together.

A summary of Crossword Designer
could be pictures of the four main screens.
The Regular, Build, Create and Report
screens with appropriate comments summarising their function.

Reminder
Summary
Help design
Project control
Marketing

Figure 8.23 Reasons for quick references.

Help Design

Like other documentation use the quick reference to help design and build the application. A quick reference overview of the
application can help the design. Alternatively, the quick reference may develop out
of the design sketches.

Project Control

A summary quick reference is a good basis
for project control. The person responsible
for an overall project needs some way of
keeping the whole project in mind. The
quick reference does that. It may list all the
major functions and provide a good check-
list for measuring progress.

ADD {identifier-1} [identifier-2]... TO identifier-m [ROUNDED] [identifier-n [ROUNDED]]...[ON SIZE ERROR imperative-statement]
COMPUTE identifier-1 [ROUNDED] = {identifier-2} [ON SIZE ERROR imperative-statement]

Figure 8.24 Quick reference syntax
summary.

Marketing

A good quick reference can be a helpful marketing device. It is often cheap to produce
and it can be handed out in place of, or with, a brochure on the product.

8.5.2   Styles

Most mass-marketed software has a quick reference guide. Most other mass-produced artefacts from cars to microwave ovens have a summary of how they work. Many ideas on
presentation are found by looking at these products.

The following styles, obtained from common products, represent different styles of
presentation.

The Syntax Summary

Applications with command languages often use this style. Figure 8.24 comes from a COBOL language card. It shows the syntax of the language.

The Menu Summary

A quick reference consisting of a menu summary is an inexpensive, useful, quick reference for applications with hierarchical menus.

Common Operations

The PABX telephone on our desk provided a good example of a quick reference showing common operations. This quick reference comes as a small booklet with common operations listed. Figure 8.25 shows part of the booklet.

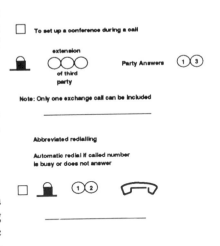

Figure 8.25 Common operations.

The Big Picture

One good way of producing a quick reference is to produce it on a mouse-pad. It is possible to print most quick-reference guide information on material suitable for a mouse-pad. It could be plastic or thick cardboard. One side of the pad could show the application, the other how to obtain help or to order the package.

Hot Keys

Many applications use hot keys as quick ways of performing different operations. The summary of these hot keys is good material for a quick reference. These are often manufactured as a plastic keyboard template that fits over the keyboard.

The Information Guide

A common form of quick reference is the mini user manual. Here, instead of a full-format user manual we combine the quick reference and user manual into a small compact guide of a few pages and we produce it in a note book format.

Procedures as Pictures

The control panel of most photocopiers are good examples of quick references as pictures. They give a picture of the common procedures and print them on and near the command keys. Use this style both for a quick reference and as part of the user-interface.

Moving Devices

Although these are expensive there may be some occasions where it is desirable to highlight combinations. The "slide rule" conversion guides to convert between imperial units and metric units use this approach.

The Wall Picture

Many of the above could be produced as wall posters. Computer terminals are often surrounded with sets of home-made instructions stuck to walls or even on the computer itself. Design a quick reference as a wall poster, add some features to make it more pleasant to look at and it may replace some of the hand-made posters.

8.5.3   Designing a Quick Reference

Designing a quick reference is similar to designing any other documentation (Figure 8.26). Look in the section on user manuals for details on the steps in design and production.

8.6   Interactive Tutorials

On-line demonstrations often include elements of an interactive tutorial. However, it is best to consider these two forms of documentation as separate products. They can be combined, but the presentation of tutorial material often interferes with the demonstration objectives.

    An interactive tutorial teaches a person how to use a package to achieve user task goals. Good interactive tutorials are very difficult to design and construct. It is easy to make a tutorial in which people step through a set of actions by forcing them to press the appropriate key. However, in our discussion on Course

First state the purpose of the quick reference.

Detail the information content to fulfil the purpose.

Choose a syntax and a style of layout.

Produce the first trial attempt.

Refine and adjust it.

Produce the final product.

Test the product.

Figure 8.26 Steps in quick reference design.

design we said that it is best to show people a set of actions to get them started, but it is desirable for learners to experiment and work on real tasks. This exploration and making the tasks meaningful is where the on-line demonstration falls down.

An interactive tutorial is a form of Computer-Aided Instruction. People have been trying to do Computer-Aided Instruction for decades and most attempts at "instruction" have failed. We do not see mass markets of CAI instructional material in the same way we have mass markets for word processors or other forms of software. However, there are successes with computers in education. For example, the use of word processors to help people write, the use of simulators in which students can explore some domain and games where students can discover things. These programs are not the same as the straight forward drill and practice instruction which has had limited success.

If we examine the principles outlined in the section on course design we can soon see why drill and practice instruction is limited as an educational strategy. It will help for simple mechanical tasks like learning to type, but it most often fails when we want people to learn concepts and to understand. The minimalist approach to instruction says that we allow learners to work on real tasks, allow them to reason and improvise and get them started fast. One way of thinking about this form of instruction is to think of it as guided exploration.

This is difficult to do with an on-line interactive tutorial. Most people when they construct such tutorials fall back on the drill and practice model. They show people some actions and then get them to practice the same actions. Showing people is a good idea, but showing is just a demonstration.

Getting people to practice a set of actions is not an effective way to make them understand. It works for some motor skills, but does not help people relate a package to their work tasks. Build exploration and experimentation with real tasks into the tutorial.

8.6.1   Designing a Tutorial

In this section we suggest a strategy for designing on-line tutorials. It is based on the previous ideas for course construction. Figure 8.27 lists the steps. We will illustrate by designing an on-line tutorial to teach people a little about spreadsheets.

Objectives

We have no idea of the real task objectives for the users of an on-line tutorial. They may be doing the tutorial many years later in a different country.

One way of making the tasks we get learners to do in tutorials is to invent a scenario in which the operations have some meaning. We can then relate the material we present to that scenario.

For example, a scenario might be to create a summary of trip expenses and to add the total. This will be our objective. Note our objective is not to teach people the mechan-

ics of adding up a set of numbers. It is to
achieve a sensible user task. As part of
achieving that objective we will learn how to
add up the numbers.

Show People

This part of the tutorial is a demonstration.
We show people how to do the task. We do
this simply, without requiring them to mimic
the keystrokes, but by moving through the
steps.

Decide on objectives.

Show people how to achieve
objective.

Get them to do it with the
real program.

Figure 8.27 Designing a tutorial.

Get Learners to do It

This part of the tutorial should use the real package, or a subset of the package. Students
know what the final goal is, they have seen it done, they now do it themselves.

The important point here is that they can explore, can make mistakes, but they are
learning through understanding not through rote. It should be easy for them to switch
back to the demonstration part of the tutorial and to see again the steps involved.

Note the difference with standard drill and practice tutorials. In those tutorials, if a
student hits the "wrong" key then the machine beeps. With the suggested method students
will hit many wrong keys as they construct the exercise. However, at the end they will
understand the idea of adding up a set of numbers and be able to apply it to other tasks.

8.6.2   Summary

Creating on-line tutorials is difficult. Be wary of simple drill and practice instructions as
they are rarely effective and very boring for learners. A cheap, effective approach is to
combine the ideas of a demonstration with use of the package. Show people some task
and then get them to do it themselves without direct prompting.

8.7   On-line Help

Almost all applications have some form of on-line help. In this section we give reasons
for including help, suggest possible contents and how to create it.

We use the term Help to mean the ability to get on-line explanation while running
an application. This distinguishes it from other explanations that happen as part of the
normal running of the application. It also distinguishes Help from prompts that appear

automatically in a dialogue. Help, as defined here, is a deliberate act on the part of the user who has a problem. Successful Help solves users' immediate problems. This gives us a criterion by which to judge Help systems and forms the basis for the following discussion.

Like all forms of documentation Help can try to achieve different goals. The goals and effort required will vary depending on the package and situation. This ranges from Help being the only documentation through to no Help at all. The tendency with applications, however, is for more and better Help.

Figure 8.28 gives the main reasons why we might provide help. As, with all forms of documentation, state the reasons for producing Help before designing and implementing it; this determines its style and content. It is important to keep in mind the way Help is delivered and the other ways we might achieve the same purpose. In this chapter we take a position on how to use Help based on our own experience. Research into the most appropriate reasons and delivery of Help is difficult and there are no absolute guide-lines. We suggest experimenting with different forms of Help to define the most appropriate form of help within an organisation.

To Show the Mechanics

By mechanics of use we mean showing people how to achieve known objectives with the package. For example, with a word processor we can show people how to input and manipulate text, but we do not show them how to write. We assume the user knows the concepts.

The section on on-line tutorials discusses why we have on-line tutorials and how to design them. If the package has an on-line tutorial then integrate it with the help. Keep the two items independent, but allow access to one from the other.

We do this because:

- Learning the mechanics of use is a task we may wish to do before we start using the application.
- The teaching function may interfere with other Help objectives.
- When learning we often want on-line Help.

As a general rule do not try to include teaching the mechanics of use with Help. Give them examples of how to do things, but do not try to explain any further. Show people

To show the mechanics.

To give a map.

To explain errors.

To give examples.

As a reference tool.

As a reminder.

Figure 8.28 Reasons for help.

how to get more information either
through on-line tutorials or by reading a
user manual.

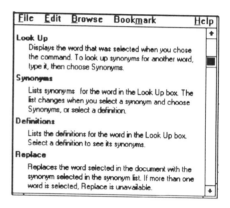

To Give a Map

This can be a useful function of Help.
People sometimes get lost in applications
or want to know how to get to other parts
of the program. Help can serve the same
purpose as some forms of quick references and can show people where different functions are located. A simple on-line
index available with many packages, such
as Microsoft Word, is a powerful method
of summarising a package. It gives the
user a quick way of finding what is available and then reminding them of what to
do.

Figure 8.29 Sample help screen.

To Explain Errors

The space on a screen is limited and precious. Too much information can clog up the dialogue so minimise the text for common well known errors. This works well when people
know about the error condition and they only need to know it has occurred. Help gives us
a way of providing more information in an unobtrusive way - in particular it tells people
how to stop getting the error indication. For example, the application may beep if a user
presses an invalid key. If the user now presses the standard Help key (F1), an explanation
of the reason for the beep, together with an explanation of how to solve the problem, can
appear.

   This principle can apply to all error situations. The F1 key will always give further
explanation if an error has just occurred.

To Give Examples

Simple examples are often a good use of Help. However, there may be too many to show
during normal execution and they take up too much room on the screen.

   Use Help to provide further access. In a spreadsheet package there are dozens,
even hundreds, of available functions. The occasional user of a function has trouble remembering the different parameters for each function. This information may be available

in a reference manual, but it is more convenient if it is on-line under Help. Again a simple method is to type in the function name,
put the cursor on the name, and press F1.

   Other forms of examples are summaries on how to do particular operations. A
word processor Help might give the instructions in Figure 8.29 to explain how to access
the thesaurus.

As a Reference Tool

Help can provide the same functionality as
an index and table of contents in a user manual. Read the section on indexing in the user
manual section and apply the same ideas to
an index for Help. Note that the help index
can refer to other forms of documentation.

   A simple index allows us to use various words to describe the functions of a
package. For example, we could put information on the function of making a word
bold under different headings - highlighting,
bold, marking, text emphasis. This allows us
to assist the user who does not know the exact word we have used in the package.

Function keys	
Press	**To**
F1	Get help on the currently selected command, open dialog box, or message
Shift+F1	Get help on a command, a region of the screen, or a key combination
F2	Move selection to next position you specify; if nothing is selected, moves next selection to current position of insertion point
Ctrl+F2	Make font one size larger
Shift+F2	Copy selection to next position you specify; if nothing is selected, copies next selection to current position of insertion point
Ctrl+Shift+F2	Make font one size smaller
F3	Insert glossary
Ctrl+F3	Copy to Spike
Shift+F3	Change case of letters
Ctrl+Shift+F3	Insert from Spike
F4	Repeat previous command
Ctrl+F4	Close active document window
Alt+F4	Close application window

Figure 8.30 Quick reference for function
keys.

   Many Helps allow us to browse through screens of information. This can be valuable if we know what it is want, but cannot think of the appropriate word to use.

As a Reminder

A common form of Help is the simple reminder. Figure 8.30 shows the help from Microsoft Word giving the meaning of the different function keys. Note that this information
can be provided as a plastic template for your keyboard, in a user manual, or in a tutorial.
However, on-line help can be a useful permanent way of providing such reminders.

8.7.1   Purposes for which Help is Inappropriate

Do not use Help for functions better done in other ways. Provide links from Help to the
other functions, but make sure the Help is uncluttered with inappropriate functionality. If
there are too many things the main purposes of error explanation, quick reminders, refer-

encing will become obscured and difficult to access. Help must be quick and easy to understand.

Do not use Help to instruct, to demonstrate, or to give context and background; use on-line tutorials, demonstrations or user manuals for those functions.

8.7.2   Guide-lines for Creating Help

Figure 8.31 shows a set of guide-lines for constructing on-line help.

Fast and direct.

Easy to use.

Consistent dialogue.

Unobtrusive file structure.

Change and modification.

Simple adaptable indexing.

Figure 8.31 Guide-lines to create help.

Fast and Direct

Help should be available at the press of a single key. It should appear instantaneously and be context sensitive. People who use help want to get it before they loose the thread of their task. They want it to apply to the problem at hand and they do not want to have to battle through a long series of screens to find the information they need. An application should try to anticipate the reason why people might call for Help at different places in the package and should act accordingly. It is infuriating to press a Help key and get several information screens on using Help before seeing the information requested.

Easy to Use / Consistent Dialogue

Help may include short-cut keys and fancy text retrieval methods, but the Help dialogue must be at least as easy as the application being assisted. One way of doing this is to use a standard Help dialogue across all applications and to make the Help dialogue fit in with other guide-lines and standards. Make the Help another standard, simple application. This will make it easy to use. Always use F1 as the quick Help key.

Unobtrusive File Structure

Information for Help will be structured and contained in a file. Make the access to the information straightforward and make it easy for people to navigate around the help. One problem with Hypertext-based help systems is the problem of navigation. Although there are interesting aids to assist the effective access to Hypertext it is probably best to stick to a simpler file structure.

A good strategy is to divide the information into pages or blocks of information and to allow access via simple indexes or by sequential browsing. Thus the file structure is a simple sequential file with multiple access points.

Change and Modification

One of the advantages of computer systems is that we can change them. Very few systems allow people to change and modify the help information, yet we would often like to leave reminders to ourselves, or others, about the application. When providing a help system consider allowing users to add to it, annotate it, and adjust access to it.

Simple Adaptable Indexing

Allow users to search the text with a free-text enquiry. Often people do not know the exact access words to use, but they know other words that might occur in the problem domain. Allow a simple free-text search with wild cards. Complicated Boolean search expressions are unnecessary.

8.7.3   Usability Testing

Monitor the use of on-line help. Log the screens accessed and relate them to the tasks people were doing. Give questionnaires and run experiments to test the usability of help in a similar way to usability of the user dialogue.

Summary

The following condenses the ideas of this chapter as a set of sayings:

- Plan user manuals.
- Usable computer packages need usable manuals.
- Writing a user manual is an excellent usability test.
- The technology of production influences manual structure and layout.
- Make the manual organisation apparent to the readers.
- Manuals are expensive.
- Use brochures for in-house advertising.
- Brochures tell people about products.
- Standardize the layout of information sheets and keep the physical size to A4 or smaller.
- Construct course objectives from the anticipated program use.
- Design courses around achievement rewards.
- Use diagrams and other thinking aids in courses.
- An on-line demonstration is not an on-line tutorial.
- An on-line demonstration shows what an application does.
- Use the demonstration as a specification and design tool.

- Use the personal demonstration as a prototype for an on-line demonstration.
- Design demonstration user-interfaces in the same way as other user-interfaces.
- The quick reference is a summary of the application.
- Build a library of quick reference guides to help choose a syntax and style.

Exercises

We give exercises for each of the different documentation components described in this manual.

Exercises for Manuals

1. Using the check-list (Figure 8.16), evaluate the user manual for some software you own or use.

2. Read a review of a product you know. Compare the comments about the documentation with your experience and with the information in this chapter. Write a review of the review.

3. Find a good and a bad manual and compare the two. Make sure you understand why one is better than the other and write down your reasons.

4. Take one page from a manual and try to construct index entries for that page. Compare your efforts with the efforts of the authors and try to reconcile the differences.

5. Take three manuals from different organisations and see how they organise the text on the pages. Do they have more than one way of layout within a manual?

6. Write a plan for this book.

7. Estimate the time and cost to write this book using four hours per page and an hourly cost of $30. Estimate the cost of photocopying this book (include time as well as photocopies and include $1.50 for binding). Assume the authors receive ten per cent royalty on the wholesale price. Assume the retail markup is thirty per cent. How many copies, and at what price, need to be sold before the authors break even?

8. Devise some usability tests for this book.

9. Try to find a text or manual without concrete examples. Read it and try to understand what it says. Was it necessary for you to invent concrete examples to understand the material?

Exercises for Brochures

1. Take a brochure for a commercial package and turn it into an information sheet for an in-house application. (If you have standard commercial packages used in an organisation this might be a common task.)

2. Take any software package you have used and try to write a brochure for the package.

3. Write a brochure to describe (and sell) a course you are currently taking.

4. Collect five brochures for commercial products. Compare them for information content. Compare them for unnecessary hyperbole. Compare them for presentation. Which ones do you think will sell the best?

5. Think of brochure usability tests. Try to test a commercial product brochure.

Exercises for Courses

1. Take your favourite word processor and work out the minimum course content to teach a person to produce a simple personal letter.

2. Show how a task-oriented course would vary from a feature-oriented course.

3. Show how features such as replacement, searching and changing screen options can be added to the course content from Question 1.

4. Find the course curriculum or brochures for any commercial course for packaged software and evaluate the stated course objectives and method of achieving those objectives.

5. Devise an experiment to test the proposition that people retain how to use packaged software more quickly if the course is based on understanding rather than rote learning.

6. Evaluate a course in which you are currently enrolled. Is it feature-driven or is it task-driven? Categorise the last dozen courses you have taken and rate them on interest, whether they left you with skills and knowledge you can apply, and whether they were feature or task-oriented.

7. Specify the "reward" structure of the course you evaluated in Question 6. Can you think of other ways to let you know you are achieving something?

Exercises for Demonstrations

1. Take a package you know well and demonstrate it to a person who is unfamiliar with it. Write a script for a third person to do the demonstration.

2. Use the script as the basis for an on-line demonstration and create the main menu and one of the demonstration scenes. Use a demonstration tool such as DEMO2 or Presentation Maker or create a set of screens with a text editor and connect the screens together.

3. Take a commercial package with on-line help, on-line tutorial and on-line demonstration and compare the objectives of the three on-line documentation items.

Exercises for Quick Reference Guides

1. Make a quick reference for a learner motor car driver.

2. Take any software package and think of three different styles of quick references you could produce for the package. Sketch out the information content and make a mock-up of the three different quick references.

3. Produce a summary quick reference for a new student at the place you are studying. Produce a most "common operation" quick reference for the same new student.

Exercises for Tutorials

1. Find a tutorial for a common computer package and use it. What strategy does it use? Is it drill and practise or is it show and construct? Will it allow you to make mistakes or do things in different ways? Are the tasks meaningful or are they techniques presented outside any user context?

2. Design part of an on-line tutorial for your favourite word processor. You want to teach people how to move text from one part of a document to another.

Exercises for Help

1. Evaluate a Help system using the ideas in this chapter. How closely does the system fit our suggestions? Are the variations justified and do they help?

2. Next time you use a computer package and you want help jot down the reason you wanted it and what happened when you tried to obtain it.

Chapter 9

Implementation

In previous chapters we have discussed the software life cycle and our concept of iterative design based on usability criteria. To bring these ideas to fruition we sooner or later have to write some programs. How we design and construct those programs, how we use new interface tools, and how we manage a project with seemingly fuzzy boundaries, is the subject of this chapter.

9.1   Software Design and Construction

9.1.1   Hardware and Software Platforms

During our discussion of dialogue design we have deliberately assumed the "best possible" environment, which, at the time of writing, is a windowing system incorporating high-resolution colour graphics. A dedicated processor is available to drive the user-interface, thus guaranteeing rapid response times. Facilities of this type are available on personal computers (e.g. the Apple Macintosh and through Microsoft Windows on IBM-compatible PCs) and Unix workstations (e.g. through Motif). They are normally programmed in a high-level language such as C through an application program interface (API), which is a series of procedure calls to the windowing system, thus providing the programmer with a great deal of control over the presentation of the interface at the cost of considerable programming difficulty. Although more powerful tools (e.g. windowing 4GLs, Microsoft Visual Basic) are becoming available, they are still at a relatively early stage of development.

Mainframe systems, with block-mode or asynchronous text-based terminals, poor response times, and 4GL development tools incorporating modal dialogue paradigms are seen by many people to be another world. In fact, most of the ideas discussed here can be used to develop mainframe systems. Mice and graphics are not essential, and most 4GLs can be used to implement modeless dialogues.

The available software development tools, on both mainframes and personal computers, have a wide variety of capabilities. The types of tools that are often encountered are:

- Text-only windowing systems.
- Displays (text-only or text and graphics) which permit partial-screen pop-ups (which are, in effect, modal dialogue boxes or child windows).
- Full-screen displays (text-only or text and graphics).

There are often limitations imposed by the hardware, e.g. some displays (including many high-resolution graphical workstations) are monochrome, or can handle text only. There may not be a mouse. Pull-down menus may not be available, being replaced by single-line menus or by function keys. Some mainframes have block-mode terminals, in which input is stored within the terminal, and the entire screen transmitted as a unit. This places significant restrictions on the types of feedback possible to the user.

Many fourth-generation languages also contain assumptions about the dialogue style to be used. This is typically a hierarchical, menu-driven structure, the language containing separate provision, for MENU screens, ADD screens, UPDATE screens, ENQUIRY screens and other essentially modal features.

None of these hardware or software limitations negates the approach adopted in this book. A full-screen display can be used to display data for one or more objects; cursor keys can be used to select appropriate items, or entry fields can be provided to mark them as selected; actions can be invoked equally well through function keys as through pull-down menus. Considerable care is often needed in laying out text screens in order to differentiate groupings of data.

In most cases, a 4GL can be used quite readily to implement modeless dialogues simply by ignoring the irrelevant features. An UPDATE screen (which permits data to be entered or changed) can be used to represent the relevant dialogue object, and appropriate actions implemented as menu or function key options on that screen.

The IBM Common User Access guide-lines illustrate the way in which a consistent interface can be presented across a range of hardware. The *Advanced Design Guide* describes a full graphical interface (colour or monochrome) of the type described in Chapter 5. The *Basic Design Guide* describes how this can be adapted to non-programmable terminals (e.g. mainframe terminals) which are text-based and have no mouse. The Basic Design Guide contains two models:

- A *text subset* of the graphical model.
- An *entry* model.

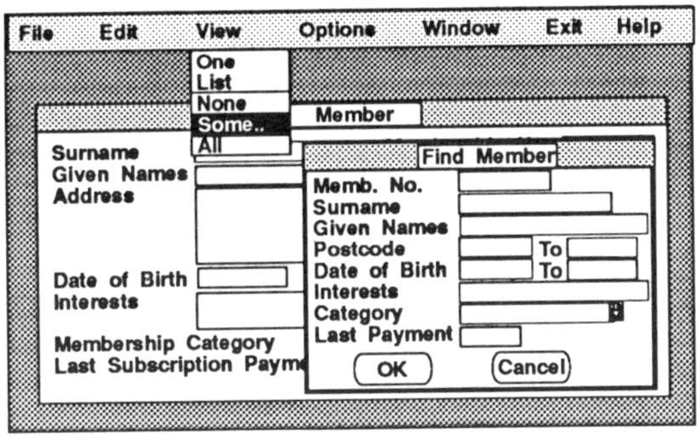

(a)
Graphical User-Interface

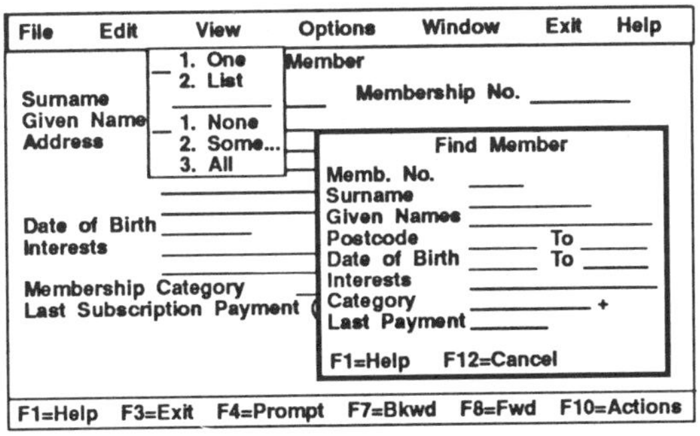

(b)
Text Subset of Graphical User-Interface

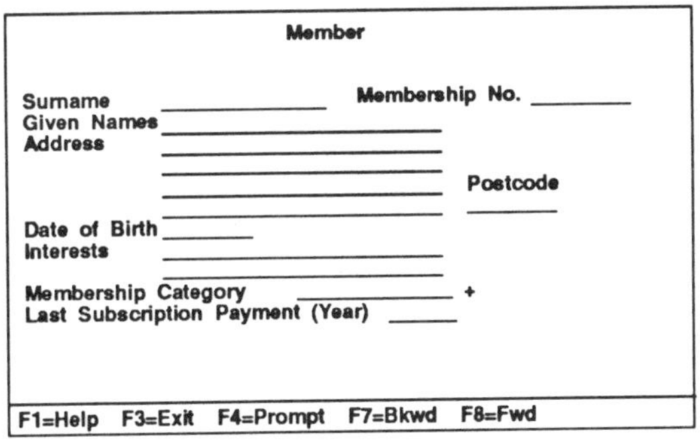

(c)
Entry Model

Figure 9.1 Levels of implementation of the
Club Membership system.

The text subset incorporates an object/action model, and attempts to approximate the way that displays and commands work on a graphical user-interface with the closest possible representation in a more restricted environment, e.g.

- The main window for the application is a full-screen.
- Child windows and dialogue boxes appear as pop-ups (which cannot be moved) over the main screen.
- Options on the action bar are selected by moving the cursor to the action bar (using a function key, F10-Actions), using the tab or cursor keys to move to the required option, using enter to bring up a pop-up menu containing numbered choices, typing in the number of the choice, and pressing enter again to perform the action.
- Function keys are used to initiate the more common actions, and are displayed at the bottom of the screen.
- Function keys are also used (instead of push buttons) to select actions on pop-ups, enter being used for OK and F12 for Cancel.
- Data-entry fields are underlined, not boxed.
- The prompt to indicate the availability of a pick-list (as in a drop-down combination box) is a plus sign at the end of the field, with a function key (F4 - Prompt) used to bring up the list.
- Entries in a list are either numbered and are selected by typing their number in a specified field (as with the pop-up menus), or are selected by typing a specified character (a slash) against them.
- Scroll bars are replaced with the word *More* accompanied by symbols for up, down, left and right arrows, depending on the directions in which scrolling is permitted.
- Messages appear as pop-ups or on the line above the function keys.

The entry model is based on the idea of a data-entry application, where each object only has one action available (*New* or *Save*). There is no action bar, and all displays (including child windows and dialogue boxes) may be full-screen. The conceptual model is not necessarily object/action based. It is essentially a carry-over from traditional mainframe dialogues. Its most useful role is probably as an aid to standardising syntactic components such as selection methods in existing modal dialogues in situations where a total rewrite is not warranted.

Figure 9.1 shows how the Club Membership system might look using the three levels defined in CUA. In the graphical and text subset interfaces, both a pull-down menu and a dialogue box (a simplified version of the *Find* dialogue box) are shown. At entry level, only the main screen is shown, since any action, e.g. a search, will either not be available, or will overlay this screen.

9.1.2   Program Structure

An application can be thought of as having a main window, with each of the dialogue objects occupying a window which is a child of this main window. Whether these child windows are independent or are linked in some way depends on the application. From the programming point of view, this gives us a way of separating out the actions on each object, even if they appear together on the same screen.

A windowing system is driven by user input. The system waits for the user to do something (e.g. to press a key or move the mouse), and then directs the input to the currently active window for processing. Thus the main control structure of any windowing program is an *event loop*:

> open main window
> repeat
>   check for input
>   if input then process command
> until finished.

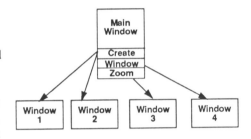

Figure 9.2 Initiating windows from the main application window.

The main application window is opened before the event loop is entered, but the way in which the different object windows are opened depends on the application. There are three possible ways, which are illustrated in Figure 9.2:

- The main application window can contain initialisation code (part of the *Create* action for that window) that opens other windows, and either displays them or their icons.
- The user can use a *windows* menu to open the windows that they require (see, e.g. Figure 6.7).
- Windows can be opened as a direct result of user actions, e.g. double-clicking on an object in an overview (a *Zoom* action) might open a window containing that object (as in Figure 4.40).

A given application can use one, or a mixture, of these methods. If initialisation code is used, it can also be used to tailor the system for individual users, e.g. in the club membership system, office staff may be given a *Members* window, while the selectors may be given *Squad* and *Team* windows.

Each window has associated with it routines for all of the input (e.g. text input, mouse actions and menu choices) that it expects to receive. In object-oriented languages such as Smalltalk or Eiffel, input is referred to as a *message*, and is sent directly to the relevant routines. In languages such as C, a control routine must be coded, which accepts all input for the window and then calls the appropriate routine. Some inputs (e.g. clicking on an inactive window) are interpreted by the windowing system as commands to change the active window, and so are processed by the windowing system itself. The complexity of the development environment is determined largely by the commands that the programmer is expected to handle. In some development environments (e.g. programming in C using Microsoft Windows), the event loop and a control routine for each window have to be coded explicitly, actions are reported at the *mouse up* and *mouse down* level (representing button presses) and actions such as scrolling a window have to be handled explicitly in the program. In other cases (e.g. windowing 4GLs) the development environment sets up the event loop and much of the display handling automatically, the developer being required to generate code only for the actions specified by the user, e.g. as menu commands.

Although the level of complexity is different, the structure is essentially the same (Figure 9.3). Each window contains an object, with which is associated a series of actions. These are implemented as a *data structure*, containing the attributes of the object (and any additional status information), and a number of *procedures* (or *methods*), one for each action.

In an object-oriented language, e.g. C++, Smalltalk or Eiffel, this is implemented as an object with its associated methods. In a language such as Ada, the data structure

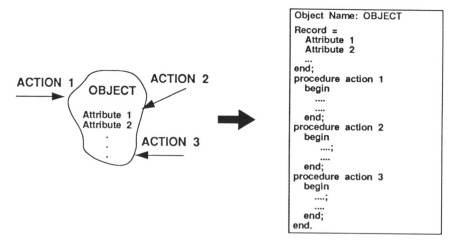

Figure 9.3 Implementation of an object.

and procedures become a *package*. In some implementations of Pascal, this same group-ing is known as a *Unit*. In C, which provides a lower level of encapsulation, the data structure and procedures (functions) can be grouped in a separate source file. With fourth-generation languages, where the code tends to be built around a screen (which here represents the window), blocks of code are attached to the screen to handle actions re-quired on exit from a field, and the menu commands. The only real difference between these implementations is the level of detail required in the procedures, whether a control procedure is needed, and whether or not procedures are needed for low-level interactions with the window.

There is a level of confusion here between the window and the object occupying the window, which is a reflection of the reality of the implementation. In general, the programmer must handle messages to both within the same piece of code. Usually, there is no difficulty in this: it is merely additional work. Sometimes, the terminology is poten-tially ambiguous, e.g. does *New* create a new window, or a new object within the window (e.g. a new member record within the *Member* window)? In some cases, these may be the same action, but in others two distinct actions are needed, e.g. *Create* for the window and *New* for the object.

The program structure for a series of independent windows is effectively a set of independent program objects, one for each window [Figure 9.4(a)], irrespective of how the windows were created. An object may perform actions on another object (including accessing data in that object) by passing it an appropriate message, which calls a proce-dure in that object. If a windowing system is not being used, and the language supports only hierarchical calls, then a structure more like that of Figure 9.4(b) is appropriate, in

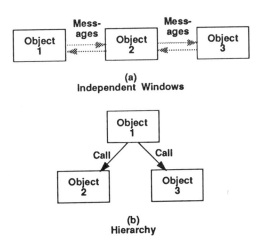

Figure 9.4 Relationship between program
objects.

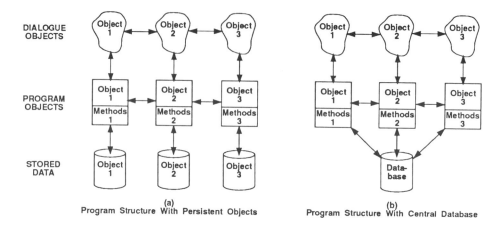

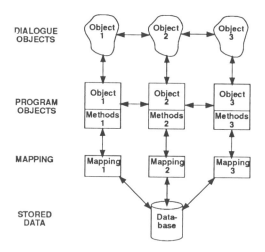

Figure 9.5 Relationship between data storage
and program structure.

which the main window contains the overview object, and child windows are opened by calls from that window, and are closed again on return. Data is passed between procedures as part of the calling sequence. This is quite suitable for many applications (e.g. the vehicle pool dialogue structure in Figure 4.40 already fits this model), but can be restrictive.

The manner in which the data is to be held on secondary storage also affects the program structure. The simplest case is shown in Figure 9.5(a). This approach assumes the use of *persistent objects*, i.e. that the objects can be stored on disk in the same form as they were held in memory. For some systems, where the objects are relatively independent of each other, this is a perfectly satisfactory way of storing our data, e.g. in a word processor we store each document (which is an object) as a unit.

In most cases, however, this is not what we want. As we pointed out in Chapter 4, our dialogue objects are not the same as our database objects, because the criteria for a good dialogue design and for a good database design are very different. In many cases, different dialogue objects contain the same data represented in different ways, so to store the dialogue objects themselves would result in data redundancy, with all its associated problems of potential inconsistency. Instead, we must be able to specify a mapping between the dialogue objects and the database. There are two ways of doing this:

- Include the necessary code in the *Open* and *Save* routines for the object [Figure 9.5(b)].
- Provide a separate level in the program structure that provides the necessary mapping [Figure 9.5(c)].

Inclusion of the mapping within the object is undesirable, since it couples the application too closely to the database so that any changes in the database structure necessarily affect the main part of the application. The second option could, in theory, be implemented at the level of the database management system, through the use of views. In practice, it is rarely possible, because relational database management systems support only views that are themselves tables, rather than complex objects, while the theory of views on object-oriented database management systems is still at an early stage of development. This means that the program structure usually needs to incorporate a mapping level, separate from the user-interface code, which can be easily accessed and modified independently of the remainder of the application.

The important feature of this type of programming is that it is *static*. The program structure is not a reflection of the processes performed by the system, as it is, e.g. in a transaction-based system or a batch system, but is merely a collection of objects linked by a message-passing mechanism. Where window management software (e.g. *Microsoft Windows, Finder* or *Motif*) is used, this structure is mandatory, and its implementation is part of the skill required to program in this environment. When more traditional software

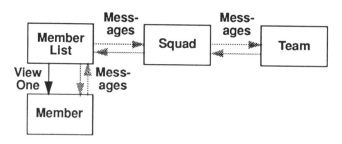

Figure 9.6 Structure of the Club Membership
system.

tools are used, it is the programmer's job to develop such a structure, and to avoid a more process-oriented structure.

Figure 9.6 shows the program structure that might be developed for the Club Membership system. The main difficulty involves the handling of the *Member* object, because there are two representations: the single object, and the list. This can be done in one of two ways:

- Use a single window in which there is a status flag indicating the representation, and allow a display routine to handle the different formats.
- Use separate windows for the two representations.

Since the single-record representation still requires certain list actions (such as *Next* and *Previous* to allow paging), and it is the list representation that represents the overview, *Member List* has been treated as the main object, with *Member* being a child window. Actions specific to the single-record representation, e.g. displaying the record, moving around the display, and altering fields on the display, can be included in the code for this object, but actions common to all representations (e.g. *Next*, *Previous* and *Save*) would be included in *Member List* and executed by passing a message back to it.

There is also a squad window and one or more team windows.

The main messages that need to be passed between the windows concern *Move* actions, e.g. dropping a player can involve a movement between one *Team* window and another. In one window, a player has been selected and dragged across its boundary. If the mouse button is released in another team window or in the squad window, this window must:

- Inform the original window that it has the player, so that the original window will delete them.
- Obtain any required information about that player.

This is done by the receiving window sending a message (which we might call *Received Player*) to the original window, which then responds with a message containing the player's details (called, e.g. *Player Info.*). If the mouse button is released other than in a team or a squad window, the move does not take place.

9.1.3   Security

Most multi-user systems contain security mechanisms which restrict particular users to certain parts of the system, or restrict the actions that they can perform (e.g. they may have read-only access to some data). This is done either directly, by giving the user a *profile* which specifies their access permissions, or indirectly, by assigning them to a *user class*, and giving the class a profile. In either case, the key element is the profile describing the access permissions.

In traditional mainframe systems, the profile consists of a list of transactions which the user can perform. In addition, there may be restrictions on the data that the user can access (e.g. only records from a particular state). These may be included either in the

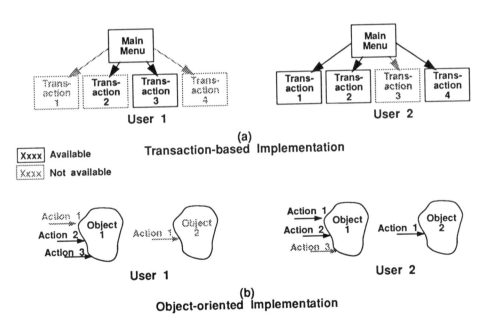

Figure 9.7 Implementation of security restrictions.

profile or in the database definition. The transactions appear on one or more menus. Transactions which the user is not permitted to perform either do not appear at all on the menus, or are unable to be selected.

In its simplest form, a transaction is an action on an object of a particular class. More complex transactions may perform multiple actions on a single object or a number of related objects.

To impose an equivalent level of security within an object/action dialogue, we need to do two things:

- Specify which objects the user may access.
- Specify the actions that they may perform on those objects.

The information will be contained in the profile. Permissions and restrictions may be at the object class level, but they may also refer to individual objects within that class. If a user cannot access the object class at all, there will be no indication of it in the system, while if the restriction is on objects within the class, they will only be able to retrieve those to which they have access. Once an object is on display, only those actions which the user can perform will appear as normal on the menu, with the others being either greyed out or not shown. If an unavailable action is not available on any object, it is best not to show it at all, but if it is still available on other objects, it should be greyed out. Figure 9.7 compares these two approaches to security.

In the club membership system, there are two types of users: the office staff, who handle membership records; and the team selectors, who look at squads and teams for a particular sport, and are required to look at, but not update, membership data. The office staff would be given access to the *Member* and *Member List* objects, and to all actions on those objects. The selectors would be given access to *Member* and *Member List*, but with the *New*, *Save* and *Delete* actions removed, and to all actions on the *Squad* and *Team* objects.

Office staff require access to all objects within the *Member* class, but it can be argued that the selectors should be able to access only those that have a value for the *Interests* attribute of the relevant sport, i.e. cricket selectors can only see instances for which one of the interests is CRICKET. There are two ways of doing this:

- Define a *view* at the database level so that only the relevant records are available.
- Automatically include an additional criterion in any search, at the software level, to impose this restriction.

Operationally, the two are equivalent, but if the database view option is available it is to be preferred, because it is both easier to implement and conceptually cleaner.

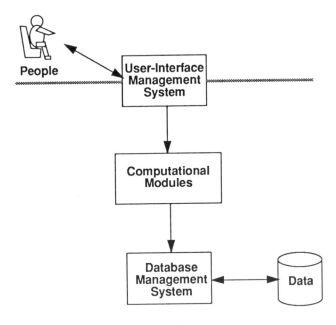

Figure 9.8 A user-interface management
system (UIMS).

Since the squads and teams are named files, the security of these can be left to the operating system. Each sport is regarded as a separate user, and is given a distinct userId, and the files are stored (by default) in that user's private directory, to which other users have no access (unless permission is given).

In the longer term, it is to be hoped that better tools become available. One major line of research at present is into user-interface management systems (Figure 9.8). These are the user-interface equivalents of a database management system, insulating the user-interface component of program code from the computational and database components. Some windowing systems currently perform related functions, but the interfaces are too crude and at too low a level.

It is also possible that object-oriented dialogue specifications, developed into prototype form, may be used as the basis for automatic generation of the implementation of the system. Such an approach has better prospects than those based on data flow diagrams or data models which are incorporated into some of the current generation of CASE tools because the dialogue structure is much more closely related to the final structure of the system than are either of the other two representations.

Figure 9.9 The pitfalls of too much control.

9.2   Project Management

9.2.1   The Development Process

Whenever anyone discusses iterative design with a heavy emphasis on prototyping and incremental development they are always presented with the argument that goes:

"Well this is all very well in theory, but I have to manage my projects and so I need to have proper budgets, proper milestones against which I can be measured, and I cannot afford to be too lax in my control (Figure 9.9)."

We agree with these sentiments. We agree with the idea of close cost control, proper budgets, milestones, and a meeting of targets. We think that the approach adopted in this book will help you meet those budgets and targets rather than hinder them. Using the approach adopted here means you will have a better idea on what you can do, you will know much earlier when budgets are wrong or when the project is in trouble, and you can adjust incrementally rather than let the project collapse. The purpose of control is to know how things are going and to help you take corrective action when things are not as they seem.

To do this you need more achievable, meaningful deliverables and you need to know what it is you are to produce. At the beginning of any project the estimates, no matter how thoroughly prepared, will still be estimates and often be quite wrong. The approach recommended here will give a set of small deliverables; each one we can estimate well, and each one leading into the next set. The project can be adjusted as time goes on, either through removing functionality, reducing documentation, taking other short-cuts, or increasing personnel, but at each stage the next stage is better defined and hence more precise.

Our emphasis on testing ensures that you find problems early. There is clear evidence that finding problems as early as possible is a good way of reducing costs. Correcting design errors once a product is in the field is very expensive. Correcting the same design errors at the sketching stage is a relatively small amount.

If you adopt the approach of "copying" what you can from previous applications, you have an excellent method of estimating. You can say that project XYZ is like project JMK, for which we have good actual costs. However, XYZ will be quicker because we can reuse fifty per cent of the work from JMK.

Our recommended steps for control are:

- Investigate the problem.
- Set the broad scope and goals of your project.
- Make your first estimate from comparison with another project.
- Estimate the total project but divide it into a set of stages, each of which produces a "complete" product.
- Record times and resources used throughout the project.
- Check progress at the end of each stage. Revise all estimates for all remaining stages.
- Revise functionality at each stage. Prune and add functionality as required.

The steps we recommend to control your budgets are on the basis of cost for finished deliverables, rather than cost against some notion of completeness of a final product. Think of your development as building up an onion. You have layers of onion (Figure 9.10) but

Figure 9.10 The onion approach to development.

your first layer is recognisable as an onion. Your next stage is the same thing except it is a bit fatter. At the end of each stage you have a "final" product (or a representation of the final product). You know how many layers you need to have and you know how thick they need to be. As you build one stage so you can estimate the next one. You can at any time remove some functionality, move some functions to the documentation and increase the number of people. You can adjust your onion as it grows in light of the resources available.

People may say you cannot always do this. We maintain you always can. Your "completed" systems might only be sketches on the back of an envelope, but in concept they are complete. The concepts can be tested and tried.

You can always set a definite time and resource limit on investigation. You can allow a certain amount and when the time is finished and the money has been spent you will have a completed investigation. It may not be the best, or truly complete, but it can be finished on time and on budget. You can now start imagining the new product. You will have an idea of an "ideal" package. You will think of many things you think could go into the package and you will make an extensive wish list. If you are writing a payroll package you might think you would like to allow people to get paid, have deductions removed automatically, adjust their tax according to overtime and lumpsum payments, give people a summary of totals for the pay-period and totals for the year etc.

Your first deliverable for the new system might be a set of sketches showing the overall structure of the system and the main inputs and outputs. Before you start this exercise you can make a precise estimate of how long such a quick overview might take, and you can stick to the estimate. What you have at the end may not be the best and you could well spend more time on it, but you can ensure you do complete it. You can test this overview.

You can continue this process throughout development. At each stage you get a more precise measure on the total cost and a good measure on the next cost. The overall cost estimate will be a better estimate at each stage. If you believe the overall cost is too high you might decide to scrap the project. However, with this incremental approach you will know much earlier if your project is in trouble, but you may be able to salvage a smaller system from your first attempts.

Not only will you know more about your project, but you will have confidence in it. Continuous usability testing at all stages means it is unlikely you will produce a poor end-product.

Crossword Designer has less functionality than we had in mind when we first started. We wanted on-line thesauri, extensive help, functions to help people find anagrams, extended dictionaries, etc. We started out with a product that put words into a given crossword pattern. We added functionality to assist in the selection of words, to create patterns, to make "crossed words", at each stage. We wanted Help, an on-line tutorial and a demonstration. We compromised by deferring on-line Help, putting a small tutorial into the user manual, and made a cut-down version of the program as a demonstration.

However, at each stage we had a "complete" working product and at each stage we could get good feedback from users and make good estimates for the next stage.

Some organisations embark on massive development projects involving hundreds or even thousands of staff, and having an organisation-wide impact. In many cases, a total redesign of the operating procedures of the entire organisation is attempted at one go. Most of these projects are fairly disastrous from a management point of view, involving huge overruns in cost and time, significantly reduced functionality, and a very negative impact on staff morale.

These are the projects at which the highly formalised systems analysis and design methodologies, such as structured analysis, are most specifically directed, since it is felt that the development of formal specifications provides the best means of communication between the many people involved on the project.

The weakness of this approach is that the users (and in this case there are a very large number of them) are no more likely to know what they want, and possibly less likely, than with a smaller system.

To some extent, our onion approach is still applicable. It is necessary to develop an overall concept of the required system, and of how it might work. But, once the initial concept is developed (and this is likely to be very general), it is necessary to break the system down into smaller parts in order to make it tractable. The interfaces between these parts then become a problem, because it is at these points that misunderstanding are likely to occur.

The appropriate approach to this problem is not to tackle it, but to avoid it. Instead of developing a single large system, one develops a number of small systems in crucial areas (Figure 9.11). In the beginning, these communicate using whatever existing mechanisms exist in the organisation. As they grow, they come into contact, and merge, until finally there is one, large system. Thus both the systems themselves, and the interfaces between them, evolve, with the problems being tackled at any one time being within the comprehension of the people attempting to solve them.

This approach is already well developed in the area of computer hardware, under the name of the *Open Systems* approach. Instead of buying one large computer, many organisations buy a large number of smaller machines for particular tasks, and link them together using standardised communications protocols. There is no reason why the approach cannot be applied to systems development as a whole.

9.2.2   Pitfalls and Problems

During the development of the programs, programmers commonly make detailed design decisions. These are often of a procedural nature, in particular the detection and handling of errors, but which also reflect either the underlying structure of the code, or the difficulty of performing a particular action. To some extent, this is inevitable, since many of

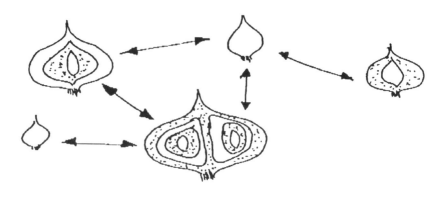

Figure 9.11 An open systems approach to
development of large systems.

the potential error conditions, for example, are only identified during programming. A
problem arises, however, since many programmers are still engrained in a mainframe culture in which the machine, not the user, has control. The result is that, incorporated into
the design, will be rigidities unintended by the designer, e.g.

- A field will be mandatory, or will contain strict edit checks, with the user being
  unable to leave the field until the requirements are satisfied.
- The user will be unable to change a field value, even if it is a genuine
  mistyping.
- The user will be bombarded with error messages, many of them totally
  incomprehensible.

It is also common for process-oriented structures to creep into the dialogue, e.g. the use of
modes and of different representations in different contexts, through "simplifications" of
the dialogue structure in an attempt to save programming time.
  A two-pronged attack on this problem is needed:

- It is essential that the programmers on a project be briefed on the design
  philosophy behind the user-interface, and be given guide-lines (either specific

to the project or organisation, or published material such as this book) on the expected behaviour of the system.

- The designer, or a person with similar knowledge and attitudes, must perform a significant part of the usability testing of the project, in order to identify these problems.

A significant problem in system development is to persuade programmers and project managers to take usability testing of systems seriously. There are two aspects to this:

- The system is never available for testing, because it is always "in pieces" as a "bug" in some routine is being fixed.
- The results of the tests are ignored, because the problems encountered do not cause the system to "crash" or result in wrong answers, so they are not seen as "real" problems or errors in the system.

The solutions in both cases are administrative. Usability tests need to be scheduled as part of the project planning, so that it is up to the programmer to ensure that a testable system is available, even if it does not contain the latest line of code. Problems detected during usability testing can be made into real problems by employing the same administrative mechanisms as are used for the so-called "real" problems. Most organisations maintain fault reporting systems for their systems. If the results of usability tests, and the corrective actions required, are entered into these systems and treated on the same basis as program "bugs", then the same obligations to fix them are generated.

The Program Structure of Crossword Designer

Crossword Designer was first written as a Windows 2 program. The standard form of the Windows dialogue and the software tools to assist the creation of programs in this environment almost mandate the structure of the system. It would be difficult to construct a Windows program with a different structure to Crossword Designer. However, the method fits well with the ideas in this book and facilitates the construction of object/action dialogue applications.

Windows programming is object-oriented. A window is a data object. When an operation occurs that affects the window a message is passed to the window routine associated with the data structure describing the window and the routine processes the message. This approach has many of the ingredients of object-oriented programming. Data and procedures are linked together, messages are passed to data objects (the windows) and the data object processes the message itself. We define a data class for each of the different forms of windows we might invoke and each instance of a win-

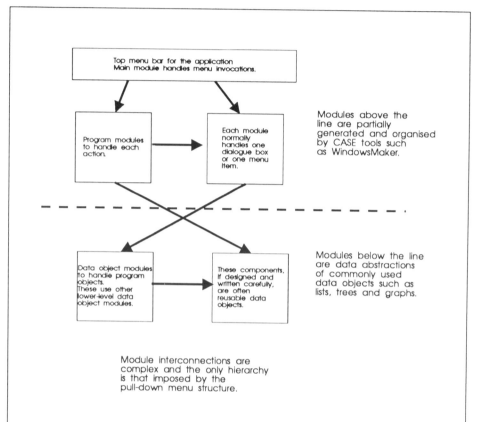

Figure 9.12 Outline of structure.

dow has its own data area and operates independently of the others. Data processed in one window is hidden from other windows and all windows coexist under the control of the windows operating system. Windows themselves can have child windows and the child windows can inherit characteristics from their parent windows. However, the plain windows development environment using C has limited inheritance, no operator overloading, and it is difficult to define new generic data objects.

The Crossword Designer program structure is built around the processing of the main window object. We define and invoke this window object and the top-level structure is defined by the data object messages. If we drew a top-level structure chart for the program we would see it mirrors the actions we can perform on the window. Figure 9.12 shows the overall program invocation structure. The actions are invoked through the pull-down menu or through cursor and keyboard movements. Each of these actions is handled by a separate function and so the main program consists of a set of calls to routines to handle the action selected. Most actions invoked by mouse movement or selecting with the keyboard are mirrored in the pull-down menus, we simply have multiple ways of calling the same routines. Some of these actions pass messages to other windows and each of these windows is processed in a similar way.

Each screen or window requires its own function and we either make a separate C module to handle the window or, if the processing is trivial, we might group several into the one module.

The generic supplied window data object lets us define and handle all the screen data objects in the system. The other major structural determiner for Crossword Designer is the underlying data objects manipulated. The data objects are the word lists, a crossword and a crossword grid. Each of these data objects has a C module with routines to handle the data structure. For historical reasons these objects are handled like normal data abstractions using C. We define a pseudo type via a data structure pointer mechanism and we define instances of the data types and call procedures to act on the object instance. This method gives modular programs and has good data-hiding characteristics. It fits in well with normal C programming and lets us use library routines naturally and easily. However, the limitations of the C language make it difficult to use all the ideas of object-oriented programming. We could have made each data type a window class and used the window operating system to pass messages to the object instances. It would still not give all the facilities of a complete object-oriented environment, but it would be closer than the structure we created. This was not done, chiefly because of our unfamiliarity with the operating system.

Besides the modules built around window data objects, and other data objects, we have modules containing commonly used functions. Most of these routines are provided in standard libraries and contain such things as formatting routines and string routines. Occasionally it is necessary for a programmer to create a set of routines for a common set of operations, but increasingly, in the Windows environment, we find it possible to purchase a set of library routines to carry out the tasks.

The original program was written using the software developer's kit and was written in C. If we were writing the program today we would use a CASE tool, such as WindowsMaker, to help organise the program. Superficially it is attractive to think of using C++ as the programming language because it is an object-oriented language. Unfortunately we know of no good way to integrate C++ objects and Windows objects so using the two together could cause difficulties. WindowsMaker automates and organises the construction of the main window module along the structural lines described above. The main drop-down menu gives the high-level structure, each dialogue entity can be given its own module and the package automates the organisation of all the files necessary to handle the main window.

The tools used to construct Windows programs determine the structure of the programs. We can use other object-oriented language tools to help us construct reusable data objects. It should be noted that software engineering methodologies built around documentation of data flow diagrams, structure charts and data modelling are inappropriate for the design of this type of software. Most of the structural documentation is not needed as it is embedded in the dialogue structure and most of the object documentation can be provided through the definition and explanation of data classes. If we drew a traditional structure chart for Crossword Designer it would be a mass of intersecting lines, we would have cycles in the invocation graph and the chart would be nothing like the well ordered, well structured hierarchy charts favoured by most structured programming methodologies. It would add nothing to our understanding of the system and would only confuse. Descriptions, built around invocation of program elements, are inappropriate for this type of system. Instead, build program descriptions around the data objects manipulated by the system.

It is easy to extend functionality and create reusable modules in this environment by adding new features and facilities to our programming toolbox with dynamic link libraries. These dynamic link libraries give us ways of defining and invoking data objects for different purposes. For example, in another application we use a DLL that handles sound icons, another that generates and displays graphs and another that maintains indexed sequential files on disk.

Summary

In this book, the emphasis has been on user-interfaces based on windows and high-resolution graphics, since these represent, at the time of writing, the best available technology, and hence a suitable objective to aim at. Many systems embody far inferior technology, e.g. full-screen, text-only displays, with or without pop-ups, and often without a mouse. The basic ideas developed in this book, including object/action models and modeless dialogues, are still applicable to these systems. Graphical images may be cruder or absent, and there may need to be minor changes to the dialogue syntax to accommodate the use of function keys and cursor keys, but it is still possible to create user-interfaces that are both usable and imaginative.

An application can be thought of as consisting of a series of objects, each occupying its own window. The program structure of an application reflects this picture, each object being coded separately as a data structure and a set of procedures (methods), one for each action. In addition, there may need to be procedures which map these objects on to the underlying database. The precise details of the coding required depend on the language and development environment used.

Security in systems based on an object/action model is based on assigning each user a profile which gives them access to specific classes or objects, and to specific actions on those objects.

It is often argued that evolutionary design processes are time-consuming and costly, and hard to estimate and to control. The development of a system can, however, be divided into a series of steps, a testable representation of the system being produced at the end of each stage in the design process. This representation can be anything from a few sketches to a completed system. This approach facilitates control, and ensures that effort (and hence cost) is minimised by ensuring that major design decisions are made and tested as early as possible in the design process, when it is possible to make changes quickly and cheaply. It enables estimates for the next stage to be made on a sound basis.

Exercises

1. Design a program structure for the Personal Timetabling system, assuming that the program is to be written in C to run in a windows environment. Specify the data structures required, the main procedures, the parameters passed to them, and describe the tasks that they perform.

2. Obtain a copy of the code for any Macintosh or Microsoft Windows application. Put it through a software tool to find the calling hierarchy for all functions. Now draw the hierarchy. See if it exhibits a fan out and fan in structure. Is the graph of calling sequences a tree, a network, and does it have cycles?

3. One of the design strategies we suggest is to first design the dialogue without too much consideration for implementation details. Of course, in practise we often have to modify our designs to fit what is possible. Make a list of missing or inadequate capabilities that you would like your current machines to have in order to realise some of the ideas you have for your computer applications.

4. Find a project plan from an organisation that produces software products or systems. How close is it to the ideas suggested in this chapter. How much effort is budgeted for usability testing, user-interface design and documentation?

5. Many commercial software development management systems are based on data analysis and modelling. Some of these systems give a methodology for systems design and construction. Investigate such a system and check how many tasks in their systems design and construction methodology involve user-interface issues.

Bibliography

During the preparation of this book we drew upon many sources. Where a particular technique or idea was used directly we have attempted to attribute it to the source with a direct reference. We have included other useful, but not explicitly referenced, items in the bibliography. The bibliography is organised by chapter. Where an item is directly referenced in more than one chapter it is only included in the first chapter bibliography.

Chapter 1 – What Makes a Good Computer System

Laurel, B. (ed.) (1990) *The Art of Human-Computer Interface Design*, Addison-Wesley.

Mackay, W.E. (1990) *Resources in Human-Computer Interaction,* ACM Press: New York.

Perlman, G. (1990) "Teaching user interface development to software engineering and computer science majors", at *ACM CHI'90 Conference on Human Factors in Computing Systems*, Seattle, April 1990.

Norman, D. (1988) *The Design of Everyday Things*, Basic Books: New York.

Perry, T.S. and Voelcker, J. (1989) "Of mice and menus: designing the user-friendly interface", in *IEEE Spectrum September 1989,* pp. 46-51.

Preece, J. and Keller, L. (eds.) (1990) *Human-Computer Interaction,* Prentice-Hall International: Hertfordshire.

Rubinstein, R. and Hersh, H. (1984) *The Human Factor*, Digital Equipment Corporation.

Shneiderman, B. (1987) *Designing the User Interface*, Addison-Wesley.

Chapter 2 – Systems Development

Adams, J.L. (1974) *Conceptual Blockbusting*, W.H.Freeman: San Francisco.

Card, S.K., Moran, T.P. and Newell, A. (1983) *The Psychology of Human-Computer Interaction*, Lawrence Erlbaum Associates: Hillsdale, New Jersey.

Coad, P. and Yourdon, E. (1991) *Object-Oriented Analysis*, 2nd edn, Prentice-Hall: Englewood Cliffs, New Jersey.

Curtis, B. (1985) *Human Factors in Software Development*, IEEE Computer Society: Los Angeles.

De Marco, T. (1980) *Structured Analysis and System Specification*, Yourdon Press: New York.

Gane, C. and Sarson, T. (1979) *Structured Systems Analysis*, Prentice-Hall: Englewood Cliffs, New Jersey.

Hawryszkiewycz, I.T. (1984) *Database Analysis and Design*, SRA.

Jones, J.C. (1970) *Design Methods*, Wiley-Interscience: London.

McKim, R.H. (1987) *Experiences in Visual Thinking*, 2nd edn, PWS Publishers.

Shlaer, S. and Mellor, S.J. (1988) *Object-Oriented Systems Analysis*, Yourdon Press: Englewood Cliffs, New Jersey.

Verplank, B. (1990) "Graphical invention for user interfaces - tutorial", at *CHI'90 Conference on Human Factors in Computing Systems*, Seattle, April 1990.

Walker, D.W. (1989) *Computer Based Information Systems*, 2nd edn, Pergamon.

Yourdon, E., (1989) *Modern Structured Analysis*, Prentice-Hall: Englewood Cliffs, New Jersey.

Chapter 3 – Usability Testing

Bailey, R.W. (1989) *Human Performance Engineering,* 2nd edn, Prentice-Hall: New Jersey.

Boies, S.J., Gould, J.D., Levy, S.E., Richards, J.T. and Schoonard, J.W. (1985) "The 1984 Olympic message system - A case study in system design", *IBM Research Report RC-11138*, T.J. Watson Research Center: Yorktown Heights, New York.

Gould, J.D. and Lewis, C. (1985) "Designing for usability: key principles and what designers think", in *Communications of the ACM,* March 1985, vol. 28, 3, pp. 300-311.

Helander, M. (1988) *Handbook of Human-Computer Interaction*, Elsevier Science Publishing Co.

Molich, R. and Nielson, S. (1990) "Improving a human-computer dialogue", in *Communications of the ACM*, vol. 33, 3, pp.338-347.

Monk, A. (ed.) (1984) *Fundamentals of Human-Computer Interaction,* Academic Press: London.

Nielsen, J. (1989) *The Usability Engineering LifeCycle*, working paper JN-1989-15.2, Technical University of Denmark: Copenhagen.

Pesot, J.F. and O'Neil, D. (1990) "Competitive usability evaluation", at *ACM CHI'90 Conference on Human Factors in Computing Systems*, Seattle, April 1990.

Ravden, S. and Johnson, G. (1989) *Evaluating Usability of Human-Computer Interfaces,* Ellis Horwood: England.

Salvendy, G. (ed.) (1987) *Handbook of Human Factors*, John Wiley and Sons.

Shackel, B. (1990) "Usability: context, framework, definition, design and evaluation", in Shackel, B. and Richardson, S. (eds.) *Human Factors for Informatics Usability*, Cambridge University Press: Cambridge.

Yourdon, E. and Constantine, T. (1979) *Structured Design*, Prentice Hall: Englewood Cliffs, New Jersey.

Wolfe, T. (1981) *From Bauhaus to Our House*, Washington Square Press (Pocket Books): New York.

Wright, P.C. and Monk, A. F. (1991) "A cost-effective evaluation method for use by designers" (in press) , *Int. J. Man-Machine Studies*.

Chapter 4 – Objects and Actions

Goldberg, A. and Robson, D. (1989) *Smalltalk 80: The Language*, Addison Wesley.

Kim, W. (1990) *Introduction to Object-Oriented Databases*, MIT Press: Cambridge, Mass.

Meyer, B. (1988) *Object-Oriented Software Construction*, Prentice-Hall: Englewood Cliffs, New Jersey.

Stroustrup, B. (1987) *The C++ Programming Language*, Addison Wesley.

Chapter 5 – Guide-lines for User-interfaces

Brennan, P. (1991) "Should we or shouldn't we use spoken commands in voice interfaces?", in *Human Factors in Computing Systems* , ACM Press: New York.

Charney, D. Reder, L. and Wells, G. (1988) "No easy answers: investigating computer error messages", in *Effective Documentation*, Doheny-Farina, S. (ed.), The MIT Press.

Dumas, J.S. (1988) *Designing User Interfaces for Software*, Prentice Hall: New Jersey.

Durrett, J. and Trezona, J. (1982) "How to use color displays effectively", *BYTE,* April 1982, pp. 50-53.

Galitz, W.O. (1989) *Handbook of Screen Format Design*, QED Information Sciences: Wellesley, Massachusetts.

Gaver, W.W. and Smith, R.B. (1990) "Auditory icons in large-scale collaborative environments", in *Human-Computer Interaction INTERACT '90,* pp. 735-740.

Grudin, J. (1989) "The case against user interface consistency" in *Communications of the ACM,* October 1989, pp. 1164-1173.

IBM (1989) *SAA Common User Access, Advanced Interface Design Guide* SC26-4582-0, IBM Corporation.

IBM (1989) *SAA Common User Access, Basic Interface Design Guide* SC26-4583-0, IBM Corporation.

Johnson, J., Roberts, T., Verplank, B., Smith, D.C., Irby, C.H., Beard, M. and Mackey, K. (1989) "The Xerox Star: a retrospective", in *IEEE Computer,* September 1989, pp. 11-29.

Marcus, A. (1992) *Graphic Design for Electronic Documents and User Interfaces,* ACM Press: New York.

Microsoft (1987) *Microsoft Windows Software Development Kit, Application style guide (version 2),* Microsoft.

Smith, D.C., Irby, C.H., Kimball, R. and Verplank, B. (1982) "Designing the Star user interface", in *BYTE,* April 1982, pp. 242-282.

Smith, S. L. and Mosier, J. N. (1986) *Guide-lines for Designing User Interface Software,* Electronic Systems Division, AFSC: USAF, Hanscom AFB, MA. Mitre ESD=TR-86-278 MTR 10090.

Tesler L. (1981) "The smalltalk environment", *BYTE,* August 1981, pp. 90-147.

Tufte, E.R. (1991) *Envisioning Information,* Graphics Press: Connecticut.

Whiteside, J., Jones, S., Levy, P. and Wixon D. (1985) "User performance with command, menu, and iconic interfaces", in *Human factors in Computing Systems II. Proceedings of CHI '85,* ACM Press: New York.

Chapter 6 – Designing a Dialogue Mode

Dunfee, W.P., McGehe, J.D., Rauf, R.C. and Shipp, K.O. (1988) "Designing SAA applications and user interfaces", in *IBM Systems Journal,* vol. 27,no. 3, 1988.

Green, M. (1986) "A survey of three dialogue models", in *ACM Transactions on Graphics* 5, pp. 244-75.

Parnas, D.L. (1969) "On the use of transition diagrams in the design of the user interface for an interactive computer system", in *Proceedings 24th National ACM Conference* pp. 379-85.

Wasserman, A.I., Pircher, P.A. and Muller, R.J. (1990) "The object-oriented structured design notation for software design representation", in *IEEE Computer,* March 1990, pp. 50-63.

Chapter 7 – User Documentation

Brockmann, J. (1986) *Writing Better Computer User Documentation,* John Wiley and Sons: USA.

Chapter 8 – Forms of Documentation

Adler, M. (1990) "Adding Hypertext based help to your application using the Microsoft help system", in *Microsoft System Journal,* May 1990, vol. 5 no. 3.

Carroll, J.M. and Rosson, M.B. (1990) "The Nurnberg Funnel: Designing minimalist instruction for practical computer skill", at *ACM CHI'90 Conference on Human Factors in Computing Systems*, Seattle, April 1990.

Cox, K. and Collings, P. (1985) "Training people to use packaged software", *Proceedings of The First Pan Pacific Computer Conference Melbourne 1985,* pp. 1120-1129. Australian Computer Society.

Flower, L., Hayes, J. R., Swarts, H. (1983) "Revising functional documents: The scenario principle", in Anderson P., Brockmann J., Miller C. (eds.) *New Essays in Technical and Scientific Communications: Research, Theory, Practice,* pp. 41-58, Baywood Publishing: Farmingdale, N.Y.

Knuth D. (1989) "The errors of Tex", in *Software Practice and Experience,* vol. 19(7), pp. 607-685 (July 1989).

McKilliam, R. (1985) *How to Produce Successful Computer Documentation,* Rob McKilliam, 8 Greenhood Street, Indooroopilly Queensland.

Strunk, W. and White, E.B. (1959) *The Elements of Style,* Macmillan.

Style Manual (4th edn) (1988)   Australian Government Publishing Service: Canberra ACT.

Van Buren, R., Buehler, M. A. (1980) *The Levels of Edit, 2nd edn,* Jet Propulsion Laboratory: Pasadena, California, 1980, JPL Publication 80-1.

White, J. V. (1988) *Graphic Design for the Electronic Age*, Xerox Press: USA.

Chapter 9 – Implementation

Lewerentz, C. (1989) "Extended programming in the large in a software development environment", in *SIGPLAN Notices* 24, 2, pp.173-182.

Mantei, M.M. and Teorey, T.J., (1988) "Cost/benefit analysis for incorporating human factors in the software lifecycle", in *Commun. ACM* 31, 4, 428-439.

Strelich, T. (1989) "The software life cycle support environment (SLCSE): a computer based framework for developing software systems", *in SIGPLAN Notices* 24, 2, pp.35-44.

Index

4GL
    as prototyping tool 6-232

abstraction
    in design 2-51, 6-218
    timetable example 6-250
action bar
    what to put in it 5-192
actions
    example 4-122
    specifications 4-137
    common 4-145
    in crossword example 6-261
    in timetable system 6-223, 6-251
advertising
    in documentation 7-279
aesthetics
    evaluation 3-107
analogies
    in design 2-52
    use of in modelling 1-13
aphorisms
    as summary 3-112
application
    as object 4-162
attitude
    importance when documenting 7-272
attribute change
    action 4-152
attributes
    data models 2-46
    of objects 4-120
automated
    recording for testing 3-105
automatic teller
    modelling 1-18

bag
    collection 4-156
batch system
    compared to interactive 5-176
benchmarks
    for testing 3-108
black box
    conceptual model 1-16
brainstorming
    in design 2-51
brochure
    use in documentation 8-303

captions
    on screens 5-196
CASE
    use in design 2-37
check-lists
    for usability 3-109
class
    definition 4-122
    formal definition example 4-122
closure
    in dialogues 5-183
collection
    common object 4-156
collections
    moving through them 6-237
colour
    guide-lines 5-199
command language
    for crossword 6-262
    for timetable system 6-255
commands
    universal 5-178
    what to name them 6-235
competitive systems
    for testing 3-108

357

About the Authors

Kevin Cox

Kevin Cox works as a Principal Lecturer at the City Polytechnic in the Department of Computer Science. Previously he lectured in Information Systems at the University of Canberra. He trained as an Engineer and later received an MSc in Computing from the ANU. He has worked in various computing positions in the USA, Indonesia, Australia and Hong Kong since 1963.

David Walker

David Walker works as a Computing Consultant in Canberra. He has lectured in Information Systems at the Canberra College of Advanced Education (now the Univeristy of Canberra) and at the Darwin Institute of Technology. He holds an Engineering Degree and a Ph.D. in Theoretical Physics from Melbourne University. He has been working with computers for thirty years, as a physicist, as a systems analyst, programmer, and as a lecturer.